THE INFLUENCE OF CULTURE ON VISUAL PERCEPTION
An Advanced Study in Psychology and Anthropology

The Influence of Culture
on
Visual Perception

MARSHALL H. SEGALL

DONALD T. CAMPBELL

MELVILLE J. HERSKOVITS

With the *collaboration of* DONALD BENDER, M. BOYE, JILL BUDZIEN, REMI CLIGNET, HAROLD CONKLIN, JAMES FERNANDEZ, JAMES GIMIGLIANO, JULES GOLDEN, JACQUES GOMILA, IGOR KOPYTOFF, NANCY LEIS, PHILIP LEIS, BARBARA LEVINE, ALAN MERRIAM, PHYLLIS MORGAN, DEE NORTON, EVA PERLMAN, H. RUENING, NORMAN SCOTCH, AND SOLVEIG WENAR.

THE BOBBS-MERRILL COMPANY, INC.
PUBLISHERS   *Indianapolis / New York*

ALBERT H. HASTORF,
Consulting Editor

Preface

It may seem surprising that the disciplines of anthropology and psychology do not converge more frequently, particularly when the anthropologist focuses on culture and the psychologist on the learning process in humans. If culture includes the complex of accumulated behavior patterns of a people, and if an individual's habits constitute the residues of his experience, then the study of culture and the study of habit-development are necessarily related.

Yet the approaches of the two disciplines to the phenomena of common interest are different enough to enable each discipline to advance independently of the other. We do not refer here to the casual half-truth that psychology is concerned with the individual, while anthropology is concerned with groups. Rather, we have in mind the psychologist's emphasis on process and the anthropologist's concern for pattern and structure. The journals of both disciplines contain ample evidence that each may prosper in ignorance of the other.

In spite of this difference in emphasis, there have long been psychologists who insist that since human learning does not take place in a cultural vacuum, psychology must include the study of cultural influences on behavior. Similarly, some anthropologists have included in their operational definition of anthropology the study of how human beings learn and manifest their culture. A well-trod meeting ground for those with an interdisciplinary bent has been the area indicated by the rubric "culture and personality." Although the present study departs somewhat from the research model provided by students of culture and personality, it remains in the tradition established by those in both disciplines who maintain that knowledge of human behavior can be advanced by systematic study of the manner in which culture and individual behavior interrelate.

The study reported in this book is one that, by the very nature of the problem under investigation, had to be a joint anthropological-psychological undertaking. The project had its origins in a discussion of the implications of the anthropological doctrine of cultural relativism for the fundamental behavioral processes of perception. A running debate at Northwestern University between Melville Herskovits and Donald Campbell, in which the former stressed that cultural differences might well be of sufficient magnitude to influence perceptual tendencies and the latter argued that the biological homogeneity of culture-learning man would preclude such influence, led to the decision, in 1956, to go into the field with the appropriate psychological instruments and techniques and attack the problem empirically.

As director of the Northwestern University Program of African Studies, Melville Herskovits secured the resources, both financial and human, required to initiate the project. The Program, which from its origins has stressed interdisciplinary cooperation in the study of Africa, expanded its outlook to encompass a project not exclusively concerned with Africa *per se,* although many of the data were collected there. Moreover, many of those who participated in the data-collection phase of the project were at one time or another associated with the Program. It is no exaggeration to state that without the continued support, encouragement, and active participation of the Program and its associates, the project could not have been carried out.

As we have already stated, the question attacked in this research project is a substantive one concerning the role of culturally determined experience in visual perception. The manner in which experience influences perceptual responses has long been of interest to psychologists; indeed, as a research problem it is one of the oldest continuing traditions in experimental psychology. It is thus particularly gratifying that a cross-cultural approach to the issue could attract the participation of so many anthropologists. For the majority of those listed as collaborators on this project are anthropologists who took time from their own fieldwork to administer our materials. We consider them and all others who collected the data presented in this book as co-authors. Accordingly their names are listed on the title page.

There are other institutions and persons whose assistance we gratefully acknowledge:

The Ford Foundation Foreign Areas Training Fellowship Program made possible the participation of Marshall Segall in the data-collection phase of the project. His continued participation in the preparation of this book was facilitated by grants-in-aid from the Columbia University Council for Research in the Social Sciences, the Research Institute for the Study of Man, and the Research Council of the Graduate College, State University of Iowa.

Preliminary data analyses were conducted at Columbia University with assistance from the staff of the Watson Laboratory. Various steps in these analyses were carried out by Daniel Johnson, Michael Silver, and Robert Rogers, all of whom were at the time graduate students in the Department of Psychology in Columbia University.

The final analyses were conducted at the State University of Iowa. Dee W. Norton, Associate Professor of Psychology and Education, provided indispensible guidance in the conduct of these analyses. He contributed time and effort to an extent one would expect only from a member of the project staff. That his name also appears on the title page indicates that we consider him as such. Many hours of communication with the State University of Iowa computer were spent by Clive Davis, graduate student in psychology, and David Lamb, an undergraduate majoring in psychology. Their efforts during two academic years greatly facilitated the publication of this book. Thanks are also due the staff of the University Computer Center, and its director, John Dolch, for the provision of facilities and computer time.

During the several years spent on this study, many other colleagues in anthropology and psychology discussed various aspects of our work with us. Extremely helpful suggestions were received at various stages of the project from Gordon Allport, Leonard Doob, Carl Duncan, Leonard Eron, Frances Herskovits, Julian Hochberg, Igor Kopytoff, Robert McCloud, William McGill, Conrad Mueller, Raoul Naroll, Robert Pollack, Milton Rosenbaum, Paul Rosenblatt, Harry Triandis, John Whiting, and Ronald Wilson. These persons will recognize the impact of their comments at many places in this book.

A preliminary draft of the book was typed and mimeographed at Columbia University by Judith Guthwin and Marjorie Druss, secretaries in the Departments of Psychology and Social Psychology. At the State University of Iowa additional secretarial services were performed by Cynthia Kotok and Linda Yoder, secretaries in the Department of Psychology. At Northwestern University, Irene Nolte performed secretarial duties for Donald Campbell throughout many phases of the project. Selma Segall was responsible for typing the final draft; she also assisted in the many steps intervening between the preparation of the final draft and publication. To all who so cheerfully performed these unrewarding tasks we express our gratitude.

The design and conduct of all research projects depend to some degree on the accumulated research literature in related disciplines. In the present case, our debt to our predecessors is a great one. It is indicated by the extensive list of references cited. In a number of instances, we found it desirable to reproduce parts of previously published works. We gratefully acknowledge permission granted by the publishers to reproduce parts of the following: R. L. Gregory and J. G. Wallace, "Recovery from early blindness," *Experimental Psychology Society Monograph No. 2* (University of Cambridge); A. I. Hallowell, "Cultural factors in the structuralization of perception," in J. H. Rohrer and M. Sherif, eds., *Social Psychology at the Crossroads* (Harper & Row, Publishers, Inc.); A. I. Hallowell, *Culture and Experience* (University of Pennsylvania Press); M. J. Herskovits, "On cultural and psychological reality," in J. H. Rohrer and M. Sherif, eds., *Social Psychology at the Crossroads* (Harper & Row, Publishers, Inc.); Plato, *The Republic*

(Mentor Books: The New American Library); W. H. R. Rivers, "Observations on the senses of the Todas," quoted by permission of the Editor of the *British Journal of Psychology* (British Psychological Society); W. H. R. Rivers, "Primitive color vision," reprinted from *Popular Science Monthly,* May 1901. Complete citations of these works are to be found in the *References* section of the book.

·   ·   ·

In February of 1963, Melville Herskovits died. At the time of his death, he was, characteristically, busily engaged in a number of projects. None of them, however, did he treat with more interest than the present one. One of his last professional activities was to edit an earlier draft and plan the present form of this book. He did not live to see it finished. We are sure he would have derived immense satisfaction from having once again contributed to the literature of the two disciplines he so often served so well—his own, anthropology, and ours, psychology.

MARSHALL H. SEGALL
DONALD T. CAMPBELL

June 1966

Contents

xi

List of Tables

List of Figures

THE INFLUENCE OF CULTURE ON VISUAL PERCEPTION

1

Phenomenal
Absolutism
and
Cultural
Relativism

Is human perception culturally influenced? Can the same stimulus appear differently to different people simply because they are members of different cultures? If culture does in fact influence perception, can unequivocal evidence for such a phenomenon be assembled?

The chapters to come will report in detail research demonstrating cross-cultural differences in the perception of illusory line-drawings. Tentative explanations of these differences will be offered in terms of the differing visual environments of cultural groups and the differing visual inference habits that these environments reinforce. The presentation of these facts and theories and the examination of plausible rival explanations of the data constitute the major justification of this book. Before we go into these often technical details, it seems desirable to provide for the student and general reader some background on the broader issues in anthropology and psychology that led us to undertake the study in the first place and that make the resulting data seem to us exciting and challenging. For it turns out that our data based on responses to optical illusions provide a striking concrete illustration of two seemingly disparate but related social science principles. These involve the anthropological concept of *cultural relativism* and the psychological issue of the *influence of learning on perception.* The latter issue borders on epistemological concerns, and it is with an epistemological comment that we begin.

PHENOMENAL ABSOLUTISM

Phenomenal absolutism as used here refers to one ubiquitous and misleading attribute of naïve conscious experience, namely, that the world is as it appears. But why should we be talking about conscious experience after a period in which psychology's greatest scientific advances have accompanied a behavioristic neglect of conscious experience? Let us pause to explain our attention to it.

Behaviorism successfully established response-oriented psychologies of learning and discrimination and, in so doing, demonstrated important behavioral laws applicable to man along with other vertebrates. To establish these laws, a new formulation of psychology was required that made it possible to neglect the data of conscious experience, unavailable as these data are for lower organisms. We acknowledge this psychology as basic and as having achieved the delineation of fundamental principles of behavior. In applying psychology to social life we want to retain and use the principles so achieved. But the demonstration that a psychology is possible that neglects conscious experience does not at all rule out a behavioristic psychology for humans expanded to encompass any conscious-experience concomitants of the habits or stimulus-response laws that it describes. Such an expanded behaviorism not only seems possible (Campbell, 1963) but also seems particularly valuable as a unifying force in the social sciences, where so much of the evidence of behavioral dispositions is stated in terms

---

This chapter has been written since Professor Herskovits' death. It was a chapter to which he gave great importance and for which he would have written the initial draft had he lived. We had, of course, discussed the form the chapter was to take, and had discussed the general issues in conversations extending over a ten-year period. Upon this background, and borrowing from his several printed presentations of cultural relativism, we have tried to prepare a chapter that would include his views as they related to the study at hand. Undoubtedly the resulting chapter differs at numerous points from the one he would have prepared. It has, for example, many more citations to his own work than he would have allowed, and it probably deals with fewer aspects of the complex problem of cultural relativism than he would have covered. We can only hope that we have conveyed some of the feeling of relevance that moved him so enthusiastically to undertake and forward this study.

of the perceptions, the views of the world, the definitions of the situation, etc., of the social actors under study. Later on in this presentation our more orthodox behavioristic commitments will become more apparent. For the moment, however, we will return without further apology to the discussion of conscious experience and its characteristic phenomenal absolutism.

The normal observer naïvely assumes that the world is exactly as he sees it. He accepts the evidence of perception uncritically. He does not recognize that his visual perception is *mediated* by indirect inference systems. Implicitly, he assumes that the evidence of vision is directly, immediately, unmediatedly given. This attitude we here call phenomenal absolutism; an important aspect of human observing, it has been noted by others under other terms. Sherif (1936) refers to the apparent absolutism of our actually relative cultural norms and to our lack of perspective or awareness of the frames of reference anchoring our judgments. Asch (1952, pp. 45–51) calls it the "objective orientation," and notes that the bases of inference that are in fact relative are not recognized as such. Gibson (1960) expresses a similar idea when he notes that ". . . visual perceiving often enough does not feel like knowing; instead it feels like an immediate acquaintance or a direct contact" (p. 220). "Naïve realism" is a descriptive phrase often employed, although its technical use by philosophers leads to possible confusion when a descriptive psychology is intended.

Socially, one important aspect of phenomenal absolutism is the observer's assumption that all other observers perceive the situation as he does, and that if they respond differently it is because of some perverse willfulness rather than because they act on different perceptual content.

To give an example, normally our perception of fixed and moving objects in our visual field is phenomenally absolute. What is still and what is moving appear to us as directly known, with no empirical assumptions or corrigible inferences involved. However, if we build a room, as did Asch and Witkin (1948; Witkin, 1949), that can be tilted and turned around a person who sits in a stable chair, we can easily demonstrate that perception of the fixity of the room, the perception of up and down, and the perception of one's own stability or movement are fallible inferences based on comparative, not absolute, data. What happens is that when the room tilts, he perceives it to remain stable while he turns (in the opposite direction). What he accurately perceives is the *relative* angular motion between himself and the walls of the room. However, he interprets this by assuming that because walls are normally fixed and upright, therefore it must be he who is tilted. There are so few of these tilting, turning rooms that this assumption usually stands us in good stead, although those who have piloted aircraft in darkness or fog may have experienced how completely and misleadingly the walls of the cabin can dominate one's interpretation of up and down.

Another example comes from an experiment by Duncker (1929; Asch, 1952, p. 58). Consider a darkened room where one can see only the illuminated outline of a large frame and a dot of light within it. When the frame is moved, one perceives instead that the dot has moved, but in the other direction. One perceives the relative movement of the dot and frame quite accurately, but not absolutely; for one unconsciously presupposes that in case of doubt it is the larger bulk of the visual environment that has remained still, the smaller segment that has moved.

The point is that the perception of fixed or moving, of up and down, is phenomenally absolute both when accurate and when illusory. The experiential "objectivity" and certainty of the visual perception not only are fallible guides but, in addition, disguise the comparative inference upon which they are based.

The perceptual mechanisms just illustrated may be innate, may be learned, or may be learned elaborations of quite specific innate possibilities. Whatever the case in these instances, there is no doubt that learning and adaptation do influence visual perception. Indeed, a part of the usual distinction between sensation and perception is that perception contains learned meanings and integrations. Built into the seemingly direct process of perception are learned organizations, delineations, and interpretations. These learned components, too, are phenomenally absolute. In conscious experience we have no awareness of the learned associations that lie behind the vivid givens.

This phenomenal absolutism, or naïve realism, has been the target of philosophical education from the beginning of that discipline. Plato himself, an absolute idealist in other contexts, conveys philosophy's recurrent criticism of naïve phenomenal absolutism in his parable of the cave (Plato, *The Republic,* Book VII, c. 390 B.C.).

"Imagine mankind as dwelling in an underground cave with a long entrance open to the light across the whole width of the cave; in this they have been from childhood, with necks and legs fettered, so they have to stay where they are. They cannot move their heads round because of the fetters, and they can only look forward, but light comes to them from fire burning behind them higher up at a distance. Between the fire and the prisoners is a road above their level, and along it imagine a low wall has been built, as puppet showmen have screens in front of their people over which they work their puppets."

"I see," he said.

"See, then, bearers carrying along this wall all sorts of articles which they hold projecting above the wall, statues of men and other living things, made of stone or wood and all kinds of stuff, some of the bearers speaking and some silent, as you might expect."

"What a remarkable image," he said, "and what remarkable prisoners!"

"Just like ourselves," I said. "For, first of all, tell me this: What do you think such people would have seen of themselves and each other except their shadows, which the fire cast on the opposite wall of the cave?"

"I don't see how they could see anything else," said he, "if they were compelled to keep their heads unmoving all their lives!"

• • •

"Now consider," said I, "what their release would be like, and their cure from these fetters and their folly; let us imagine whether it might naturally be something like this. One might be released, and compelled suddenly to stand up and turn his neck round, and to

nd look towards the firelight; all this would hurt him, and he
be too much dazzled to see distinctly those things whose shadows
seen before. What do you think he would say, if someone told
him that what he saw before was foolery, but now he saw more rightly,
being a bit nearer reality and turned towards what was a little more
real? What if he were shown each of the passing things, and compelled
by questions to answer what each one was? Don't you think he would
be puzzled, and believe what he saw before was more true than what
was shown to him now?"

"Far more," said he.

. . .

"Then we must apply this image, my dear Glaucon," said I, "to all
we have been saying. The world of our sight is like the habitation in
prison."

Modern anatomy and physiology of vision support Plato in this.
In spite of the direct objective certainty with which we seem to see
external objects, we see in fact like the prisoners in the cave, making
inferences from the shadows and reflections of objects.

The critical and skeptical message to the naïve phenomenal
absolutist is conveyed by both Locke and Berkeley with what is
essentially the same illustration. Locke puts it:

. . . the same water, at the same time, may produce the idea of cold by
one hand, and of heat by the other; whereas it is impossible that the
same water, if those ideas were really in it, should at the same time be
both hot and cold [Locke, 1690, Book 2, Ch. 8, Section 21].

Berkeley (1713) has Philonous explain it to Hylas thus:

PHILONOUS: "Is it not an absurdity to think that the same thing
should be at the same time both cold and warm?"
HYLAS: "It is."
PHILONOUS: "Suppose now one of your hands hot, the other cold,
and that they are both at once put into the same vessel of water in an
intermediate state: will not the water seem cold to one hand, and warm
to the other?"
HYLAS: "It will."

PHILONOUS: "Ought we not therefore by your principles to conclude it is really both cold and warm at the same time? That is, according to your own concession, to believe an absurdity?"

HYLAS: "I confess it seems so."

Normally, when we feel hot or cold water, we feel the temperature as residing in the water, as an absolute attribute of the water directly known to the touch. In fact, the sensory base of the perception is a relative one, to which the temperature of the sensing skin contributes half of the resulting contrast.[1] It is phenomenal absolutism that makes it vividly unexpected that hands should thus disagree about the water temperature they report.

In spite of such corrective educational efforts by philosophers and psychologists, each of us slips back into a phenomenal absolutism. Each of us can be surprised by the vivid certainty felt under illusory conditions like those provided by the turning room, the frame and dot, basins of water, or many other illusions not discussed here, such as the distorted room and rotating trapezoidal window of Ames (Kilpatrick, 1961).

ENCULTURATION AND NAÏVE ETHNOCENTRISM

Anthropologists have encountered phenomenal absolutism in man's tendency to perceive and value other cultures in terms unconsciously based upon his own, but phenomenally experienced as absolute and universally applicable (e.g., Boas, 1904b). Widely used to describe this naïve attitude is the term "ethnocentrism" (e.g., Sumner, 1906; Herskovits, 1948, pp. 68–75; Klineberg, 1964). While "ethnocentrism" has many additional meanings, in this setting it can be defined as the view of things in which one's own

[1]This ancient experiment is well worth trying for oneself. Prepare three basins of water: hot, lukewarm, and cold. Rest one hand in the hot, one in the cold, for about three minutes. Then place both simultaneously in the middle warm one, watching your hands as you do. The experience can be surprising even to one primed for the results. Sherif (1936, p. 33) uses this illustration and numerous others to convey this and related messages.

group and its customs are unconsciously used as the standard for all judgments, as the center of everything, with all other peoples and customs scaled and rated accordingly (Sumner, 1906, p. 13).

To understand such ethnocentrism, we must understand the process of enculturation (Herskovits, 1948, pp. 39, 65). All social animals, man included, learn to accommodate their behavior to that of their social fellows. This is a process that involves conflict and cooperation, direct reward and punishment, inhibition of actions, being blocked by others, and the like. Over and above such socialization processes shared by social animals, man undergoes *enculturation,* a process whereby he acquires the culture into which he is born. For example, the quarreling and accommodating between two brothers represents a reward-punishment socialization process such as any two mammalian litter-mates might experience. Beyond this, the objects of their competitive striving, or the choice of insults used to wound each other, represent the products of an enculturative process peculiar to man and largely specific to each particular culture. Deliberate tutelage, punishment of inappropriate behavior, and the rewarding of approved behavior are of course involved in enculturation; but much of enculturation is less direct than this, creating its impact not so much by the choice of alternative that is rewarded or punished as by the limitations of the narrow set of alternatives presented for consideration.

In addition to the active inculcation of the behavioral standards and norms of society, a more subtle, indeed, often unconscious, process of learning by observation occurs among humans. The content of what is available for emulation on the part of the young in each society is itself culturally shaped and limited. A significant feature of the enculturative experience is that the individual typically remains, throughout his lifetime, unaware of how his own habits, which to him appear "only natural," in fact result from a learning process in which he never had an opportunity to attempt alternative responses. Every human being goes through a process of enculturation, and its effects may be detected as easily in the rebel as in the conformist. Many a poorly socialized malcontent proves to be thoroughly enculturated in that he can express his dissent only in the traditional categories of his culture. The dissident worship of the Devil in the Black Mass of the Middle Ages aptly illustrates this. Herskovits (1951) puts it thus:

> The political revolutionary does not refuse to cast his revolutionary songs in the modal structure and scale progressions of the culture he is in process of changing; his formations, if his organized forces are strong enough, will operate in terms of accepted patterns of military procedure. The one who rebels against the religious and moral system of his time will couch his appeals in the linguistic patterns of his people, use established affect symbols, and employ accepted esthetic standards in heightening the responses of his followers [p. 153].

Once the child has acquired language, the bulk of his knowledge of the world is conveyed to him through reports on what others have observed and learned. Even his direct learning in contact with physical objects is usually preceded by expectations based upon second-hand knowledge. For such knowledge the invisible but narrow limitations set by the categories of culture are profoundly important in molding its final form. Just as we are not responsive to the broad bands of qualitatively similar electromagnetic waves that our eyes exclude or neglect in vision, so too are we unaware of the alternative categorizations, evaluations, and behavioral modes that our particular culture excludes or neglects.

More than this, even where enculturation does involve the elimination of alternatives available and expressed in the learning process (as in learning which hand to eat with, for example), once this learning has been thoroughly established, it becomes unconscious. Thus in the end, the most thoroughly enculturated person, isolated from other cultures, is the least aware of his culture and of its role in molding him. Even we in the United States who feel that we live in a culturally heterogeneous country are generally aware only of those aspects of culture about which we and our fellow citizens differ, and fail totally to note the great preponderance of culture that we all share in common. In his classic essay on

"The unconscious patterning of behavior in society," Sapir (1928) provides an especially explicit early statement of this. He points out how the process of language-learning is marked by failures to hear certain sounds in foreign languages until a degree of familiarity is achieved. This lack of recognition of the dominating impact of culture is one of the important lessons of anthropology (e.g., Herskovits, 1948, pp. 21, 27, 40, 44, 63, 67, 68, 626, and *ad passim*).

Initially travelers, missionaries, and anthropologists regarded ethnocentrism as a surprising but recurrent naïveté among isolated peoples who, failing to recognize their "true" position in the world, regarded themselves as the original and optimal type of mankind, centrally located in the world, speaking the language of God, and having the one true morality. Anecdotes illustrating this go back at least to Herodotus (447 B.C.), reporting on his travels as a Greek among the Persians:

> Of nations, they honour most their nearest neighbours, whom they esteem next to themselves; those who live beyond these they honour in the second degree; and so with the remainder, the further they are removed, the less the esteem in which they hold them. The reason is, that they look upon themselves as very greatly superior in all respects to the rest of mankind, regarding others as approaching to excellence in proportion as they dwell nearer to them; whence it comes to pass that those who are the farthest off must be the most degraded of mankind [p. 52].

And in the sixteenth century, for example, awareness of ethnocentrism was cogently expressed by the French essayist Montaigne (1580).

> I think there is nothing barbarous and savage in that nation, from what I have been told, except that each man calls barbarism whatever is not his own practice; for indeed it seems we have no other test of truth and reason than the example and pattern of the opinions and customs of the country we live in [Bk. I, Chap. 31].

Experiences reflecting such ethnocentrism probably have occurred to every anthropologist who has worked among peoples
isolated from contact with outsiders. For example, when Herskovits
did fieldwork among the Bush Negroes of Dutch Guiana in 1929,
he found his hosts incredulous that a man of his apparent wealth
should have only one wife. When this fact was reaffirmed, some
thought he was not telling the truth, others that he was stupid or
foolish. Some thought that it was high time he behaved like a
proper man, and offered him the opportunity to acquire more
wives (Herskovits, 1959b, p. 12). Among the Hopi, the term "Hopi"
is used to refer to moral behavior and the term "Kahopi" to bad
behavior (Brandt, 1954; Eggan, 1956). The nearby Navajos regard
themselves as the true and original "people" (Kluckhohn and
Leighton, 1946). By 1906 Sumner had collected dozens of illustrations of this attitude; for example, he cites the early explorer Fries
to the effect that the Greenland Eskimo thought Europeans had
been sent to Greenland to learn virtue and good manners from the
Eskimo (Sumner, 1906, p. 14).

These illustrations could be extended *ad infinitum*. What should
be emphasized here is the phenomenal absolutism of these judgments, interpretations, and beliefs. They are more like perceptions
than judgments in that the naïve ethnocentric is not aware of
alternatives being compared. He remains unaware of the enculturative learning processes lying behind these automatic, spontaneous,
directly given perceptions of true or false, good or bad, central or
peripheral, etc. They are more like perceptions than inferences
because there is no awareness of an inference process; the ethnocentric evaluations appear as directly given facts, as knowledge
directly known.

The vivid directness of ethnocentrically enculturated moral
judgments is conveyed very emphatically in settings of mutual
revulsion, in which impropriety and disgust are perceived as attributes objectively inhering in the act observed rather than as conditioned preferences of the observer. Were we to see a Hindu peasant

blow the mucus from his nose into the air and onto the street, the act would probably appear to most of us as filthy and revolting. To the Hindu—exposed to a cleanliness training far more exacting, if different, than ours—our habit of wrapping up our nasal discharges in pieces of cloth, which we then carry around with us and with which we will later wipe our faces, appears filthy and disgusting with an equivalent phenomenal absoluteness.

During the action in Algeria in World War II, it happened that United States soldiers and Algerian laborers came into enough contact to be able to observe each other's cleanliness habits. It will surprise no one to learn that the United States soldiers regarded the impoverished, water-and-soap-lacking workmen as filthy. What may be less obvious is that these Algerians perceived the United States soldiers as filthy with a phenomenal absoluteness that, if anything, exceeded the reciprocal view. For the United States soldiers, it turned out, violated one of the most deeply ingrained taboos of the Algerian (and of many African and Arabic peoples) by putting food in their mouth with the same hand used in urinating. Among these people, babies are harshly punished by scandalized parents until they have the habit deeply ingrained of eating with the right hand and toileting with the left. Their revulsion at seeing this taboo broken was comparable to what we would feel at seeing a person employ already used toilet paper.

In such settings we see an act as vividly and obviously unclean, unaware of the culturally conditioned learning sequences that lie behind our automatic evaluative perception. The uncleanliness of the act is there in the act for all to see; it is not a seemingly learned judgment peculiar to a provincial cultural tradition. Boas (1904b) provides many other examples.

As we have seen, travelers and anthropologists initially noticed most clearly the ethnocentrism of the indigenous peoples they studied. Gradually, however, they also became aware that they themselves as Europeans, or even as anthropologists, were guilty of unconsciously ethnocentric judgments. It was, of course, a symp-

tom of their own ethnocentrism that the early explorers found the
ethnocentrism of the native peoples so surprising, amusing, or
remarkable. Boas, the most influential founder of anthropology in
the United States, was among the first to note the problem in this
way:

> It is somewhat difficult for us to recognize that the value which we
> attribute to our own civilization is due to the fact that we participate
> in this civilization, and that it has been controlling our actions since
> the time of our birth; but it is certainly conceivable that there may be
> other civilizations, based perhaps on different traditions and on a
> different equilibrium of emotion and reason, which are of no less
> value than ours, although it may be impossible for us to appreciate
> their values without having grown up under their influence [Boas,
> 1911, p. 208].

A number of training policies developed in anthropology serve
as curbs to the ever-present temptation of ethnocentrism. Whereas
at one time an anthropologist might depend entirely upon reports
of others, today an extended firsthand fieldwork experience is
demanded. This experience is ideally a period of one or more
years spent among a single group, during which time the local
language is learned and an intimate acquaintance with all aspects
of daily life is acquired. While this ideal is justified primarily in
terms of the anthropologist's need to participate in firsthand
research and of his duty to expand the basic pool of ethnographic
evidence, a very valuable aspect of the fieldwork experience is its
role in increasing the anthropologist's objectivity in dealing with
any culture by making him aware of how great his own enculturation has been. Through sustained fieldwork, the anthropologist
acquires a sympathetic inside view of the culture he studies. Customs that initially seemed strange and meaningless come to seem
fitting and proper. In the process the anthropologist comes to
realize how much of what he previously took for granted, how
much he unconsciously presumed, was in fact the end product of
a culturally specific learning process.

Boas in 1904 gave two excellent statements of this goal and method:

> It is given to no one of us to free himself from the constraints which life has placed upon him. We think, feel, and act loyal to the tradition in which we live. The only way of freeing ourselves is submersion in a new life and comprehension of a mode of thinking, feeling, and acting that has not grown from the same roots as our own civilization, but that has its source in another cultural formation [Boas, 1904a].

> The needs of anthropological research have led many investigators to adapt themselves as thoroughly as may be to the ways of thinking of foreign tribes and peoples,—to take part in the joys and sorrows of their life, to penetrate the motives that prompt their actions, and to share the emotions that fill their hearts. The experiences thus gathered have led many of us to think that the gulf does not exist that was once believed to separate the mind of primitive man from that of civilized man. The difference between the type of primitive thought and feeling and that of our own appears to us rather as a product of the diversity of the cultures that furnish the material with which the mind operates than as a result of a fundamental difference in mental organization [Boas, 1904b, p. 243].

Although an anthropologist's initial 25 years of precept and example are not to be overcome by one or even 25 years of new experience as an adult—in this sense the full extent of ethnocentric prejudgment is never overcome—there is no better corrective available for unconscious ethnocentrism and its phenomenal absolutism than extensive total immersion in an initially alien culture. It is noteworthy that every anthropologist in the course of fieldwork finds himself more ethnocentric, more culturally conditioned, than he had realized himself to be. This error of anticipation is a universal one. Even a person who has been attracted to anthropology in part because of resentment of his own culture, who has eagerly studied sympathetic ethnographies of exotic peoples, who has tried to avoid in himself the ethnocentric provincialisms he sees so obvious in his family and fellow countrymen, is surprised in field experience by the magnitude of his residual ethnocentrism. It is always underestimated, never exaggerated. The vividness of this experience leads anthropologists to insist that this be an essential part of professional training in their field.

CULTURAL RELATIVISM

Under the term "cultural relativism" anthropologists, and particularly the students of Boas, have come to summarize the methodological implications of the anthropologist's (or any social scientist's) ethnocentrism. (For an introduction to the literature on cultural relativism, see Herskovits, 1948, pp. 61–78; 1951; 1958; 1963.) Under this principle, the ethnographer attempts to describe the behavior of the people he studies without the evaluation that his own culture would ethnocentrically dictate. He attempts to see the culture in terms of its own evaluative system. He tries to remain aware of the fact that his judgments are based upon his own experience and reflect his own deep-seated enculturation to a limited and specific culture. He reminds himself that his original culture provides no Olympian vantage from which to view objectively any other culture.

Cultural relativism does not at all rule out the eventual discovery of a common human nature. Indeed, it presumes a basic biological homogeneity of culture-learning man. It emphasizes the evidence that culture and biology are independent, that any genetic stock can learn any language and culture. But it warns that in our initial efforts to delineate the culturally learned specifics from the biological and universal, we have a systematic ethnocentric bias in underestimating the cultural contribution. Too readily we assume that what is true for us is true for all mankind. We are unaware of the pervasive influence of our enculturative conditioning, for it is hidden in the phenomenal absolutism, the apparent directness, of our perceptions and cognitions.

Anthropologists have taught, and are teaching, the lesson of cultural relativism to other social scientists. The notion that intelligence tests measured innate ability was based upon the hidden and ethnocentric assumption that everyone's culture provided the same opportunity to learn the numerous verbal and nonverbal skills that the test-makers employed; anthropologists were among those whose criticisms gave us our modern view—for example:

> Environmental background, cultural as well as natural, plays a tremendous part in whatever manifestations of innate intelligence an individual may give us through the results from the application of standardized tests to him. Thus it has been found that the American Indians usually rate somewhat lower in psychological tests than whites, and that this holds true when the tests are of a non-language variety, where the use of words is reduced to a minimum. But the consideration of the fact that the tests ordinarily used have been constructed by persons of a background different from that of the subjects is usually overlooked; and were there to be presented, for consideration as to what is wrong with a given picture, a six-clawed bear rather than a net-less tennis court, one wonders whether the city-dwelling white might not be at a loss rather than the Indians [Herskovits, 1927, p. 3].

Psychologists once assumed that adolescent storm and stress was a universal, biologically based experience; anthropologists (e.g., Mead, 1930) demonstrated that the transition stress of change from childhood to adult status could occur at ages from 5 to 35 in various cultures, or need not occur at all. The anthropological evidence was one of the influences that led psychologists to give up their overelaborated instinct theories in the 1920's. Investigators in the field of language initially expected each language to have equivalents for European kinship terms like "aunt" and "niece," whereas we in fact employ only one of many possible logical ways of classifying kin (e.g., Kroeber, 1909; Goodenough, 1956). Psychologists' descriptions of "universal" stages of mental development have received appropriate criticism (Glenn, 1957; French, 1963). The theory of esthetics and the philosophy of value are other areas that have felt the impact of cultural relativism (e.g., Herskovits, 1959a, 1963).

CULTURAL RELATIVISM AND THE
PSYCHOLOGY OF PERCEPTION

Any field of psychology—or, indeed, of the social sciences—that studies the members of only a single culture and presumes on this basis to generalize to mankind needs to confront the critical message of cultural relativism and the impact of cross-cultural data. One such field in psychology has been the study of visual perception.

As early as 1901 and 1905, Rivers presented striking data showing cross-cultural differences in susceptibility to optical illusions. These studies, although "well known," are never cited in the basic presentation of optical illusions in the textbooks on visual perception and experimental psychology. It is only in texts on social psychology and race differences that the studies get mentioned (e.g., Klineberg, 1935). In the meantime, the Euroamerican results of perceptual research continue to be presented with the implicit assumption that they hold true for all mankind.

Probably because of the phenomenal absolutism of visual perception, experimental psychologists in general have been extremely reluctant to concede that groups or individuals perceive differently. For some, this is related to a strong commitment to the innate determination of perceptual processes—in the intellectual tradition of Hering and the Berlin school of Gestalt psychologists. But even some in the empiricist, environmentalist, associationist tradition, followers of Helmholtz and the behaviorists, while emphasizing the learned components of perception, fail to concede the inevitable concomitant differences in learned perception among those with different environments and past experiences. It is typical of some experimental psychologists to try to explain away evidence of learned differences in perception as merely differences in what the person says he sees—as differences in response to the percept rather than as differences in the percept itself. They assume that learned differences in response and learned differences in perception are logical contraries—that if a learned difference in response has been demonstrated, a learned difference in perception cannot exist and is thus explained away.

When a behaviorist takes such a view, he has implicitly made a commitment to one theory of the psychology of conscious experience. Whereas behaviorism is supposedly silent on the nature of conscious experience, here a choice among competing phenomenological theories has been made, and a naïve choice at that. It results in a view of the process of learning as one in which the learner, after reinforcement, perceives the world just as he always has, but has come to respond differently to it. In the more sophisticated phenomenological theory dominant in social psychology (e.g., Krech and Crutchfield, 1948; Sherif and Sherif, 1948; Asch, 1952), it is recognized that after a series of rewarding events, one perceives the object and the total field differently and correspondingly responds differently. In this light, responding differently and perceiving differently are held to be concomitants rather than mutually exclusive explanations.

While neurological speculation is not characteristic of the phenomenologists in social psychology or philosophy (but see Köhler, 1938), it may help clarify the issue here. The two phenomenological theories described above can be seen as disagreeing about the processes in the central nervous system to which conscious experience corresponds. The anatomy of the nervous system produces a preponderantly one-way transmission of message from the eyes and other sense organs to sensory projection areas in the brain, then through the complex association areas to motor projection areas in the brain, and finally to skeletal musculature in the execution of responses. The naïve phenomenologist implicitly locates conscious experience as a concomitant of central nervous system activity at some site *prior* to the association areas. On the other hand, the more sophisticated phenomenologist implicitly locates conscious experience in the association areas, or subsequent to them, in which case the same learnings that modify responses may well be modifying perceptions.

possible conclus

> . . .we do not really see with our eyes or hear with our ears. If we all saw with our eyes, we should see pretty much alike; we should differ only so far as retinal structure, eyeball structure, etc., differ. We differ much more widely than this because we see not only with our eyes but with our midbrain, our visual and associative centers, and with our systems of incipient behavior, to which almost all visual perceiving leads [Murphy, 1947, p. 333].

A more technical presentation of this analysis is available elsewhere (Campbell, 1963).

Were it not for the biasing effects of the phenomenal absolutism of their own conscious experience, those experimental psychologists emphasizing the learned components of visual perception would correspondingly expect that each person does indeed view the world differently, just as he has different past learning situations and reinforcements. Where substantial differences in learning settings are involved, as in comparisons between different cultures, still larger perceptual divergences should be expected.

We have attempted in this discussion of phenomenal absolutism and cultural relativism to indicate the plausible basis of the expectation, held by many anthropologists and by some psychologists, that human perception is culturally influenced. In the course of this discussion we have also touched upon what we believe is an explanation of the reluctance of some psychologists to admit that perceptual differences are demonstrable. In the following chapter, some of the evidence for culturally mediated differences in perception will be reviewed.

2 Cultural Differences in Perception— The Equivocal Evidence

Plausible as the case is for learned, cultural differences in perception, the actual evidence to date, unfortunately, is for the most part equivocal. This state of affairs reflects, we believe, some difficulties inherent in the phenomena under investigation. Reviewing the culture and perception literature, including some of the classic reports, will therefore be instructive concerning the difficulties that this study has had to face. We will attempt to present both the case for interpreting the existing evidence as indicating differences in perception and the case for its indicating "no difference."

Covering this topic is a difficult task, for an extremely varied literature has accumulated. It may be helpful to the reader to comment on some general features of this complex literature before going on to specific examples. It is important to note first that, however provocative, anecdotal material constitutes equivocal evidence for whatever proposition it is meant to support. Far more weight must be given to the results of systematic research. Indeed, were this a more advanced research area than it is at present, we would urge that only the products of systematic research be considered. However, as will become apparent, some of the most interesting phenomena pointed out by students of culture and perception have not yet come under systematic investigation, in part, perhaps, because of the present unavailability of methods of study appropriate to these phenomena.

Another characteristic of this literature is that its focus ranges broadly. The culture-and-perception literature includes such diverse undertakings as investigations of ethnic differences in sensory acuity (e.g., Rivers, 1905), of variations among societies in color nomenclature (e.g., Ray, 1952), and of the possible influence of the dominant values of two cultures on a perceptual tendency termed "closure" (Michael, 1953). As even this mention of only three papers suggests, the rubric "culture and perception" has come to include a large class of varied phenomena, among which the mutual relevance may sometimes be more apparent than real. In some studies, the term "culture" has specific referents; in others it is pointed to in a general manner as the possible "cause" of observed differences in behavior. In the latter instances, of course, the evidence that culture influences perception is hardly conclusive. To complicate matters further, the term "perception" has been employed to refer to several quite different processes. Moreover, while some writers intend that the term be interpreted quite literally (i.e., as perceiving in the sense of seeing, hearing, or otherwise detecting or discriminating some aspect of the environment), others have employed the term almost metaphorically to designate a world view, an outlook on life, or some other very general cognitive product.

Even when the term "perception" is meant in its literal sense, it may cover differing aspects of behavior. Traditionally, "perception" has been used for a whole class of processes, at one extreme bordering on sensation and, at the other, on concept-formation. When academic psychologists talk of perception, they tend more often to refer to processes that are more nearly sensory; whereas when anthropologists employ the term, they more often refer to processes bordering on cognition. And even within experimental psychology, the term "perception" has been variously employed.

In anthropological research on the influence of cultural variables on perception, a large number of studies have in fact been concerned with cognition. Studies that report differences in classifying, naming, and evaluating and in other ways attaching meaning to discriminable aspects of the environment must be considered as providing equivocal evidence for cultural influence on perception. Such studies might better be classified under the heading "culture and cognition" (see French, 1963; Triandis, 1964). While we would be hard put to specify the boundary between perception and cognition—since both processes can be inferred only from overt behavior—we would argue that the more cognitive the behavior actually studied, the more equivocal the evidence provided for the proposition that culture influences perception.

In the course of this chapter, it will become clear that our own immediate problem area—the influence of the natural and cultural environment on visual perceptual habits, as manifested in susceptibility to geometric illusions—potentially provides less equivocal evidence than is likely in some areas we will review. Working in some of the more equivocal problem areas, investigators have been able to demonstrate that cultural groups classify stimuli differently, with some groups making distinctions that others do not. Such data do not necessarily indicate that the other distinctions are not perceived. On the other hand, it is possible that different classificatory schemes *do* reflect different perceptual habits. These points are best illustrated by the discussion below (pp. 37–48) of the long history of cross-cultural research on the perception of color.

Having made clear that much of the evidence we are about to review is equivocal and less than directly pertinent to the culture and perception question as we framed it in our own research, we turn now to the literature. In preparing this review we have been helped by previous surveys, to which the reader's attention is directed (Klineberg, 1935; Dennis, 1951; Kluckhohn, 1954; French, 1963; Triandis, 1964).

THE PERCEPTION OF PHYSIOGNOMIC SIMILARITIES

One classic report that is often cited (e.g., Klineberg, 1935; Sherif, 1936; Child, 1950; Dennis, 1951) comes from Malinowski's long and intimate experience in the Trobriand Islands. It deals with the perception of resemblance between parents and children, and among children in the same family. It is probably true that in all cultures some persons have a definite, vivid, and spontaneous perception of physical similarity between other persons. That these perceptions are sometimes grounded in objective physical fact, however unmeasurable, we have no doubt. That they are sometimes grounded more in expectation than in fact we also have no doubt. For example, one may "perceive" a child's strong resemblance to a parent, not knowing that the child is adopted. We can thus anticipate that culturally conditioned expectations might contribute to a perceptual end product in ways in which the perceiver is unaware, with the result being a culturally influenced difference in perception of similarity.

Malinowski found a complicated but culturally uniform pattern of such perceptions. Among the Trobriand Islanders, children were perceived to look like their father but not at all like their mother. Furthermore, siblings, children of the same father, did not look like each other. Thus, two brothers might each be said to look just like their father; yet it would be vigorously denied that they looked like each other. Malinowski was very impressed with this surprising perceptual pattern—more surprised than the reader might be, for this was a matrilineal society that regarded the mother and the child as "blood" relatives, but not the father and the child. He reports on it in detail in several places (e.g., Malinowski, 1923–24, 1927, 1929).

This example illustrates a recurrent ambiguity: Did these people really fail to see the occasionally striking similarities between mother and child or between brother and brother that Malinowski could see? Or did they see them but suppress mention of them because of cultural taboos? Malinowski does report strong cultural norms about this. By breaking the rule he discovered that it was very bad manners, embarrassing to the brothers in particular, to mention that two brothers looked alike. A still worse offense was to say a brother looked like his sister. Did such prohibitions lead people to lie in denying similarities that they actually perceived quite clearly? Did the cultural demand that a son look like his father, supported by an elaborate causal theory as to how the father's image became impressed on the foetus, lead people to assert similarities that they actually did not see? Malinowski believed that over and above these restraints on verbal expression, the actual perceptions followed this cultural pattern.

The same interpretive problem exists in our own culture. Does Aunt Emma really see all those parent-grandparent-child similarities that she so effusively points out? Or is she merely lying in an effort to please those involved? How does one decide? The issue borders on the philosophical problems of solipsism and "other minds." In reviewing Malinowski's reports, Arthur Child (1950), a philosopher interested in epistemology and the social sciences, raises the question as to whether we can *ever* demonstrate that people in one culture perceive differently from those in another. On the specific issue dealt with by Malinowski we can never decide with certainty, but Child concludes that in spite of the ambiguities, Malinowski makes a plausible case for perceptual differences.

Malinowski's own conviction was based upon two sorts of evidence. On the one hand, within the culturally approved relationships, his informants and he agreed as to which similarities were most striking. Thus there was enough confirmation of perceptual process to convince him that he and they were communicating successfully about physiognomic similarity. The other line of evidence was Malinowski's estimation of honesty, sincerity, and surprise among well-known informants whom he questioned and challenged. These were people whom on other issues he had found willing to express private dissent from culturally demanded beliefs. When on this issue they persisted, even when talking about specific cases, he found it more plausible that they perceived differently than that they were each systematically lying to him.

HALLOWELL'S OBSERVATIONS

Among anthropologists, Hallowell has perhaps given the greatest attention to the influence of culture on perception (e.g.,
Hallowell, 1951). From his own fieldwork among the Salteaux
Ojibwa he is firmly convinced of the overriding influence of culture upon the individual's perception of his world, and has stated
that ". . . cultural variables are inevitably constituents of human
perception" (1951, p. 166). Much of his early data came from
cultural differences in the interpretation of the ambiguous inkblots
of the Rorschach Test. While this is in a sense a visual perceptual
task, its purposes are tangential to the concerns of this book, and
the relevant literature will not be covered here. (For reviews of
this literature, see Spindler, 1955; Kaplan, 1961a and 1961b;
Lindzey, 1961). Hallowell's subsequent analysis has used perception in a broad sense to include outlook on life, world view, interpretation of events in life, and category systems such as are implied
in language. While Hallowell is concerned most directly with
classificatory behavior, he sees in this persuasive evidence that the
world indeed looks the way a people have learned to talk about it.
A condensed statement of Hallowell's orientation is provided in
the following excerpts:

> What becomes perceptually significant to the *eingestellt* human
> organism cannot be considered apart from a continuum that views
> the human individual as an adjusting organism, motivated, goal-
> directed, and psychologically structured as a functioning unit in a
> socio-cultural system. Culture patterns considered as traditional instru-
> mentalities of human existence function as selective agencies in the
> emergence of the kind of behavioral environment in which a group of
> human beings carry on their activities. Consequently the psychological
> field in which human behavior takes place is always culturally con-
> stituted, in part, and man's responses are never reducible in their
> entirety to stimuli derived from an "objective" or surrounding world,
> in the physical or geographic sense. Inevitably then, personal adjust-
> ment in a behavioral environment with culturally constituted proper-

ties produces variability in the phenomena of set and expectancy so that in any given perceptual situation such factors take on a differential directive importance [Hallowell, 1951, p. 167].

In the vocabulary of the Northern Ojibwa Indians, with whom I have spent considerable time, there is a word—*kinebikominin*—which means "snake berries." Unlike other terms of its class, which usually apply to a single plant species, *kinebikominin* is applied to a number of species. The common feature that is shared by these plants is that their berries are considered inedible by the Indians. Thus the word referred to not only discriminates a special category of berries and provides a verbal symbol that represents them in discourse; at the same time it is a *value* symbol. *Kinebikominin,* as compared with other berries, are no good to eat. I may also say that this evaluation is by no means a simple "adaptive" function to the intrinsic properties of the berries. None of them are poisonous and some other people might place them in the edible category. Thus we can see at once how language provides the Ojibwa with a means of conceptually discriminating one class of berries from another at the cognitive level and at the same time furnishes him with an evaluation of the edible properties of different species of berries. This evaluation, in turn, is integrated with *motivation* in that such berries, once perceptual recognition takes place, are shunned as food. I have seen more than one mother smack the hands of a child who was about to put the berries of the tabued category in his mouth or snatch them away, saying at the same moment—*kinebikominin!* Consequently, the child is not permitted to secure first-hand knowledge of the actual properties of these berries but learns instead to discriminate, evaluate, and avoid objects of this class through the symbolic mediation that language provides. "Snake berries" are not simply objects perceived in the surrounding geographical environment. They are selectively discriminated objects of a special category in a behavioral world conceptualized through language. *Kinebikominin* becomes a word that is emotionally toned for the child. It connotes something forbidden, something to be avoided, something one may be punished for eating; a class of objects with a negative valence. So it is quite easy to see how *both* perceptual discrimination and avoidance of such objects are motivated through the integrating function of language [Hallowell, 1951, pp. 172–173].

In Hallowell's extensive presentation of illustrations supporting his general conclusion, there is little that appeals to an experimental psychologist as evidence of cultural influence upon a perceptual process. The following anecdote comes as close as any. Hallowell points out that *windigo* cannibal monsters were believed by the Ojibwa to be real creatures and that there were sporadic reports of hearing them or seeing them. One old man related the following:

> Once in the spring of the year I was hunting muskrats. The lake was still frozen, only the river was open, but there was lots of ice along the shore. When it began to get dark I put ashore and made a fire close to the water edge to cook my supper. While I was sitting there I heard someone passing across the river. I could hear the branches cracking. I went to my canoe and jumped in. I paddled as hard as I could to get away from the noise. Where the river got a little wider I came to a point that has lots of poplars growing on it. I was paddling quite a distance from the shore when I came opposite to this point. Just then I heard a sound as if something was passing through the air. A big stick had been thrown out at me but it did not strike me. I kept on going and paddled towards the opposite side of the river. Before I got to that side he was across the river already and heading me off. I paddled towards the other side again. But he went back and headed me off in that direction. This was in the spring of the year when the nights were not so long. He kept after me all night. I was scared to go ashore. Towards morning I reached a place where there is a high rock. I camped there and when it was light I went to set a bear trap. Later that day I came back to the river again. I started out again in my canoe. Late in the evening, after the sun had set, there was a place where I had to portage my canoe over to a lake. I left my canoe and went to see whether the lake was open. There were some open places so I went back to get my canoe. Then I heard him again. I carried my canoe over to the lake—it was a big one—and paddled off as fast as I could. When I got to the other end of the lake it was almost daylight. I did not hear him while I was traveling. I went ashore and made a fire. After this I heard something again. I was scared. "How am I going to get away from him," I thought. I decided to make for the other side of an island in the lake. I was sitting by my canoe and I heard him coming closer. I was mad now. He had chased me long enough. I said to myself, "The number of my days has been given me already." So I picked up my axe and my gun and went in the direction of the sounds I had heard. As soon as I got closer to him he made a break for it. I

could hear him crashing through the trees. Between the shore and the island there was a place where the water was not frozen. He was headed in this direction. I kept after him, I could hear him on the weak ice. Then he fell in and I heard a terrific yell. I turned back then and I can't say whether he managed to get out or not. I killed some ducks and went back to my canoe. I was getting pretty weak by this time so I made for a camp I thought was close by. But the people had left. I found out later that they had heard him and were so scared that they moved away [Hallowell, 1955, pp. 257-258].

Hallowell argues convincingly that a genuine perceptual illusion is reported here. The Indians are expert woodsmen, with detailed knowledge of the many sources of sights and sounds. Hallowell reports that they typically gave naturalistic explanations of sounds that had startled him.

It is all the more significant then to discover cases in which the perceptions of individuals have been so thoroughly molded by traditional dogma that the most intense fears are aroused by objectively innocuous stimuli. It is the culturally derived *Einstellung,* rather than the stimuli themselves, that explains their behavior [Hallowell, 1955, p. 257].

Was this a cultural difference in perception? Or a cultural difference in the interpretation of a perception? Where does the border between perception and sensation lie? If one hears a noise, uninterpreted, sensation is involved. If one hears a footstep on the floor, or a cracking twig, perception is involved in that meaningful interpretation is phenomenally immediate, directly given without a conscious experience of interpretation. Hallowell is convinced that there were illusory perceptions of *windigos* at this phenomenally immediate level. He does not believe that they heard noises that were consciously puzzling and ambiguous, nor does he believe that they explained them first as "possibly a *windigo*" and later—as repeated retellings of the event maximized the effect upon the hearers—as "certainly a *windigo.*" Obviously, in this setting we cannot differentiate between postperceptual elaboration (conscious or self-deceived) and the phenomenally immediate auditory perception of objects and acts. Hallowell is convinced that the latter were involved, in this instance at least. The immediate escape actions taken testify to this.

THE PERCEPTION OF PHOTOGRAPHS

Until the last few decades, most anthropologists had the opportunity of being the first to show a photograph of local scenes to members of the group they were studying. While anecdotes on this point have not been systematically reported or collected, reputedly the common finding was a temporary failure of perception that surprised the anthropologist unless he had been primed for this failure through hearing the reports of other anthropologists. For example, Herskovits (1959a) writes:

> I have had an experience of this kind, similar to that reported from many parts of the world by those who have had occasion to show photographs to persons who had never seen a photograph before. To those of us accustomed to the idiom of the realism of the photographic lens, the degree of conventionalization that inheres in even the clearest, most accurate photograph, is something of a shock. For, in truth, even the clearest photograph is a convention; a translation of a three-dimensional subject into two dimensions, with color transmuted into shades of black and white. In the instance to which I refer, a Bush Negro woman turned a photograph of her own son this way and that, in attempting to make sense out of the shadings of greys on the piece of paper she held. It was only when the details of the photograph were pointed out to her that she was able to perceive the subject [Herskovits, 1959a, p. 56; see also Herskovits, 1948, p. 381].

An analysis of the stimulus dimensions of a typical photograph helps explain how it might be perceived by one not familiar with it. Its strongest contours are its rectangular edges, which constitute

its boundaries as a solid thing. Within these edges, the most striking part of the design is the white band around the edge, with its
sharp contour where it meets the black-grey-mottled area. We have
learned to disregard these striking aspects—in part because they
are the same on all photographs, in part because they are irrelevant for the communication purposes of the photograph. Instead,
we pay attention to very weak and fuzzy contours and contrasts,
which are minor stimuli in terms of any physical scoring of stimulus
strength. Doing this has become so familiar to us that we expect
these weak stimuli to be equally obvious to others.

In a limited sense, one can regard the photograph as we use it
as an arbitrary linguistic convention not shared by all peoples. It
may be regarded as conventional to represent something really
large by something very small; this convention is probably very
widely distributed, as dolls and statuettes would testify. It is conventional to attempt to represent three dimensional solid objects by
lines or contours in two dimensions. This convention is much less
widely found; it is so thoroughly ingrained in us, however, that we
would normally not be aware that some people lacked it. A convention based upon the technology of photography and print-
making is that the dominant frame contours be considered irrelevant. It is a convention that colored objects be represented by a
series of greys. Pointing to these as conventions may overstate the
case somewhat. Once the conventions are adopted and understood,
the perception of content in a photograph or a perspective drawing is compelling. However, it is important to note that black-and-
white still photographs have stimulus characteristics, which, if not
ignored, could interfere with content-perception. It is interesting
that the experience of anthropologists shows that motion pictures
are almost universally perceived without trouble and that colored
prints are also—although here the naïveté of the respondents may
be questioned in more recent field experience.

Here is an area in which systematic research should be done to
support anecdote, for naïve respondents on whom to try such

experiments may now or will soon be lacking. The analysis implies that cut-out photographs of persons, done so that paper contour and person contour coincide, would be more easily perceived; and line drawings might be expected to be better perceived than ordinary photographs because of the relevancy of the dominant contours.

LANGUAGE AND AUDITORY PERCEPTION

Still dealing with material that is primarily anecdotal, we move to another illustration concerning phenomena experienced by many anthropologists but not well documented by experimental evidence. These phenomena involve what are probably genuinely perceptual events, viz., hearing the vocal sounds used in a particular language.

In any language, sounds are organized into sets of phonemes used for distinguishing meaningful vocal symbols. In addition to phonemes, each language has many irrelevant, meaningless sound variations, unused potential differentia. The naïve learner of a foreign language expects different *words* to be formed from what he believes are universally employed sound units. When the sounds in these new and foreign words correspond to those of his own language, there is no perceptual problem; on the other hand, his unawareness of the novel phonemic distinctions employed in the foreign language he has set out to learn is often a major obstacle to his progress. It is as if he were deaf to differences in sound that constitute irrelevant differences in his own language (allophones).

The phonemic differences in one's own language have achieved an "acquired distinctiveness of cues" or perceptual accentuation. However, comparable variations in another language, which are quite distinct to a native speaker, may be perceptually indistinguishable to a foreigner. In the course of acquiring a language quite unrelated to one's own, one's perception of the auditory stimuli changes; and by the time one feels really able to hear words in the language, one is—literally?—hearing certain sounds differently than one did initially.

Situations in which people of one culture are actively attempting to learn the language of another would seem ideal settings for controlled psychophysical research on auditory perception. Would such research reveal changes in perceptual threshold (stimulus detectability) for relevant sound distinctions as language-learning proceeds? One laboratory study that bears tangentially on this unresolved issue was performed by Brown and Horowitz (Brown, 1956, pp. 291–299). Native speakers of two languages, English and Navaho, first learned to label eight colored chips, equally spaced along the hue dimension, with one of four sounds read aloud by an experimenter. These sounds varied in two ways: in the vowel employed (*a* vs. *o*) and in vowel length. In one of the languages, Navaho, each of the sounds normally would be distinguished from all the others phonemically; whereas in English the vowel-length difference is normally allophonic, so that the four auditory stimuli normally would be perceived as two random variations of two sounds. When asked to sort the colored objects to which these names had been attached, Navaho respondents classified them into four groups while the English-speaking, non-Navaho respondents dichotomized them. Subsequently, when the English-speaking respondents became motivated to attend more closely to the auditory labels, they did finally detect the originally overlooked variation in vowel length and recognized then the validity of a fourfold classification of the colors.

Whether a real threshold difference was ever present in this study is not clear since procedures for collecting the data required for threshold-determinations were not employed. What is clear, however, is that for members of the two cultural groups the acquired distinctiveness of the auditory cues varied at the outset of the experiment, much in the manner suggested by our speculations in this section concerning language-learning.

THE INFLUENCE OF LANGUAGE ON
COGNITIVE BEHAVIOR

Before leaving the topic of language and perception, it must be noted that anthropological linguists, such as Sapir (1928) and Whorf (1940), argued the proposition that cognitive behavior is influenced by the semantic structure of languages. Implied by many interpreters of what French (1963) has called the Humboldt-Boas-Cassirer-Sapir-Whorf-Lee hypothesis is the view that language first influences cognition, which in turn influences perception. The idea is widely held that because of the semantic characteristics of a particular language, certain discriminations are more readily made than others. However, in most instances in which this latter view is implied, the term "perception" is used more metaphorically than literally. This extensive literature is thus not altogether germane to our present interest in culture and perception, and we will not systematically treat it here. Several excellent reviews are available (e.g., Hoijer, 1954; Kluckhohn, 1954; Brown, 1958; Saporta, 1961). One study, however, serves very well to illustrate how the behavioral phenomena relating to linguistic differences, while of legitimate interest to psychologists, may or may not be perceptual. This recurrent ambiguity is seen in a carefully done study by Brown and Lenneberg (1954).

After first determining the "codability" of a small sample of Munsell colors (codability is defined primarily in terms of the agreement in naming among persons who speak the same language), Brown and Lenneberg found codability to be related to the ability to select the previously viewed sample of colors when they were embedded in a display of 120 color patches. Respondents reported that they could more easily remember what color to search for if it had a definite name or was a good exemplar of a simple color name like red or blue.

Clearly, a linguistic factor here produced a behavioral effect. How the availability of a clear-cut label mediated the color recognition was clarified by a supplementary experiment, in which codability was found to account for *increasing amounts of variance in the recognition task as that task was delayed and complicated.* Presumably the delay and complications taxed the memories of the respondents. The authors therefore interpret their study as demonstrating that lexical aspects of a language relate to the ability to recognize named stimuli, and that the recognition depends mostly on the ability to remember. As Brown and Lenneberg themselves suggest, their data indicate that since a region of experience may be lexically differentiated in one culture but not in another, some stimuli are more codable than others and therefore more easily remembered. The authors of this study do not claim that differential ease of perception is necessarily involved.

THE PERCEPTION OF COLOR

The preceding example illustrates the ambiguous implications for perceptual research of findings dealing with linguistic classification. But since it deals with color-detection, it can serve to introduce the broader topic of color-perception.

When they look at a rainbow or some other solar spectrum, many persons lacking in technical training in the physics and physiology of light and vision tend to see bands of pure colors (possibly red, yellow, green, blue) separated by transition areas of what appear to be mixed colors. If asked which colors seem pure and which seem mixed, they would probably have little difficulty in making this decision or in finding instances of both. Red, yellow, green, and blue might appear pure, while orange, yellow-green, blue-green, etc., might seem mixed. To such a person it would probably come as a surprise to learn that our classification of the spectrum into the colors red, orange, yellow, green, blue, and violet is culturally arbitrary, and that persons in other cultures divide the spectrum quite differently.

This topic, "racial" or cultural differences in color-perception and in color vocabulary, has the longest and most sustained research history in the culture and perception area. Most interesting for our present purposes is the fact that in all phases of the 100 years of study there has been disagreement as to whether genuine differences in perception were ever demonstrated or whether these were merely differences in color vocabulary. The issue is still not resolved.

The argument started in 1858, when W. E. Gladstone, a classics scholar, decided on the basis of his studies of the writings of Homer that the Greeks of that period lacked our modern color concepts. For example, the same color term seemed to be used for blue, grey, and dark colors generally. Gladstone felt that such ambiguous use of words could not have occurred had these colors seemed as distinctly different from one another to the ancient Greeks as they do to us.

The next round of research supported and extended this conclusion. Geiger (1871) studied the Hindu classics, the ancient Biblical Hebrews, the Norse Eddas, ancient Chinese, and ancient Greeks, finding in all of them deficiencies in color vocabulary—universally for blue, sometimes for green, and, in the oldest writings, for yellow. Magnus (1877) followed with a still more thorough examination of ancient writings. He also (1880, 1883) surveyed the ethnological evidence, through the published literature and via a questionnaire with color samples sent to traders and missionaries. He found most non-Europeans to possess a "defective" color vocabulary, similar to that of the ancients, in that words for blue were lacking. A term for green was also frequently lacking. Blue and green were frequently merged, as were blue and black.

Geiger and Magnus concluded that the vocabulary data reflected differences in color-perception, and added a biological evolutionary interpretation to Gladstone's observation. They believed that the human color sense had evolved to its present form in the three thousand or so years since the Homeric Greeks. The issues of race differences and stages in biological evolution persisted in the subsequent literature for another 50 years or more.

Reacting to Gladstone, Geiger, and Magnus, the next wave of research rejected the perceptual interpretation and took the evidence as showing cultural differences in color vocabulary and no more. Virchow (1878, 1879) examined Nubians who had been brought to Germany. These Nubians showed the typical anomalies of color vocabulary, yet were quite able to discriminate colors in all parts of the spectrum, as they demonstrated by sorting and matching colored papers and wools. And Magnus' own later data further supported this independence of vocabulary and discriminatory power.

The most influential critique was contained in chapters on the color sense in man and on the growth of color vocabulary in *The Colour-Sense,* published by Grant Allen in 1879. Allen was a comparative psychologist with a detailed theory in which the evolution of the color sense in vertebrates and insects was related to the evolution of coloration in fruits and flowers. In this he extended Darwin's observations and anticipated the modern view. He saw a symbiotic evolution in which conspicuous flower and fruit colors and attractive flavors evolved jointly with the color sense and taste preferences of the fruit-eating animals and insects that disperse and fertilize the pollen and seeds. Believing that a color sense was very general in the animal world, he could not accept the view that it had been lacking in the ancient Greeks, and correctly saw that the rate of evolution implied in the theory of Geiger and Magnus was much too rapid to be compatible with other biological facts. Spurred by the prominence of their misguided theory (which was supported, at least initially, by A. R. Wallace, codiscoverer with Darwin of the theory of natural selection), he turned from biological arguments to culture history and anthropology in order to discredit the works of Geiger and Magnus on their own grounds.

Allen even preceded Magnus in using a questionnaire to collect systematic data from correspondents all over the world (1879, pp. 204*ff.*). In it, he asked these two types of questions (among others): "Can they distinguish between *x* and *y*?" and "Have they separate names for x and y?" Using "large numbers" of replies from Europe, Asia, Africa, America, and the Pacific Islands, together with many published observations of early explorers, he found no instances of the inability to distinguish colors, in spite of a recurrent lack of color terms. He concluded that his data "bore out *in every case* the supposition that the colour-sense is, as a whole, absolutely identical throughout all branches of the human race" (p. 205). While his data-collection procedures might appear unsophisticated from a contemporary viewpoint, his study was indeed a classic cross-cultural survey.

His scholarship did not stop there. He attacked the philological data of Gladstone, Geiger, and Magnus by showing that the analogous modern English literature of songs, ballads, and odes showed the same strong bias in color-word usage toward the red-yellow region of the spectrum. For this he made tedious word counts of Swinburne and Tennyson and anthologies of Elizabethan and Miltonian poets. He did his own analyses of Homer and the Bible. He looked at the archeological record of painted statuary and in ethnological museums to find the systematic utilization in art of color distinctions lacking in vocabulary. He pointed to defects in the color vocabulary of modern languages such as Welsh and Chinese, for whose speakers no one would claim any perceptual defects.

Beyond all of this he provided a plausible nongenetic theory of sociocultural or linguistic evolution to account for the regularities that Geiger and Magnus had taken to be evidence of biological evolution. According to this theory, color terms develop first where color distinguishes among objects that are otherwise similar. Where color and objects go together uniformly, the object name suffices. The availability of pigments and dyes facilitates the development of abstract color words that are applicable to the color no matter upon what object it is found. Color terms are initially metaphorical extensions of what are originally object names, or else of pigment and dye names.

Extensive analysis of the color vocabulary of English and of classical languages was used to support this view. Other lines of argument were also used, and we have not done justice to his detailed treatment. He was essentially in agreement with present-day students of the problem. Allen, a biologically-oriented comparative psychologist on a social science tangent, has thus provided a neglected classic of the culture and perception literature.

Incidentally, for all his efforts to prove a particular argument on color vision, Allen was not insensitive to the kinds of difficulties inherent in perceptual research that we are stressing in this review.

> By colour-perception, then, we shall understand in the present work the power of discriminating between light-waves having different rates of frequency. If any creature shows by its actions that it is endowed with such a power, we shall say that it possesses a colour-sense. Anything more than this is impossible to prove. Whether the sensation or mental idea *blue,* as perceived or thought by a butterfly or a humming bird, is the same in consciousness with the sensation or mental idea *blue* as perceived or thought by you or me, we can never know [1879, p. 19].

On the other hand, Allen took issue with A. R. Wallace when the latter stated, "The fact that the higher vertebrates, and even some insects, distinguish what are to us diversities of colour, by no means proves that their sensations of colour bear any resemblance whatever to ours" (quoted by Allen, 1879, p. 145). Clearly Allen preferred to adopt the position that the burden of proof is on one who argues for perceptual difference, and his own efforts, as we have seen, were directed oppositely. Still one wonders how much confidence Allen himself felt in concluding that ". . . over the whole known world, among the most civilized and the most savage races alike, the perception of colour now appears to all competent observers exactly identical" (1879, p. 221).

Allen did not settle the issue for long. Rivers' data (1901a, 1901b) provided the next round. Rivers (1901b), in the course of an excellent review of the older literature (which was much more extensive than we have here indicated), was able to say in summary of it: "The idea of the evolution of the color sense in man has been almost universally rejected" (1901b, p. 46). He went on, however, to open the issue again, with a moderate argument in favor of correspondence between color vocabulary and color-perception. He reported on his own studies of the color vocabulary of five peoples of the New Guinea area, plus Eskimos, Australians, Todas of India, etc. For some of these, particularly the Murray Islanders, extensive perceptual tests were also administered by Rivers. It is convenient to summarize his results by a series of quotations:

I tested about 150 natives of this island with Holmgren's wools for color blindness, and failed to find one case in which there was any confusion between red and green. Since red-green blindness exists in about 4 per cent of the male population of Europe, one may conclude that this form of defective color sense was either absent or was much rarer than with us . . . .

As regards other colors, however, the case was different; blue and green were constantly confused, and also blue and violet. Either owing to a lack of interest or to some actual deficiency in color sense, there was a distinct tendency to confuse those colors for which their terminology was deficient. I have also found this tendency to confuse green and blue in several other races.

The behavior of the people in giving names to colors also pointed frequently in the same direction. I have already mentioned that in Mabuiag there was a great tendency to invent names for special colors; on one occasion a man, who seemed to have a special faculty in this direction, gave me as the name for a bright blue wool "idiiridgam-ulnga," which meant the color of the water in which mangrove shoots had been washed to make "biiu," an article of food. In this case there was a deliberate comparison of a bright blue with dirty water, and I frequently came across other instances of the kind, which seemed almost inexplicable, if blue were not to these natives a duller and darker color than it is to us.

This view was confirmed by quantitative observations, made with Lovibond's Tintometer, which had been kindly lent to the expedition by Mr. Lovibond. When the native looked into this apparatus, he saw two square patches of light, either of which could be colored in any intensity of red, yellow, or blue by means of a delicately graded series of glasses of these colors. The "threshold" for each color was then determined by finding the most faintly colored glass which the native could recognize and name correctly. The results showed that the natives recognized a very faint red, a more pronounced yellow, and only recognized blue when of a considerable intensity. Similar observations made on a series of Englishmen showed greatest sensitiveness to yellow and somewhat less to red and blue. The results may be given more definitely in Mr. Lovibond's units of color; in Murray Island, red was perceived on the average at .18 units, yellow at .27 and blue at .60, while the average results from English observers were .31, .20, and .36 respectively. These figures do not show anything approaching blue blindness, but they do show a relative insensitiveness to blue in the Murray Islander, as compared with the European. The former appears also to be relatively more sensitive to red . . . .

These results do not show that these islanders are blue blind, but they do show fairly conclusively that they have a certain degree of insensitiveness to this color, as compared with a European. We have, in fact, a case in which deficiency in color language is associated with a corresponding defect in color sense.

On the question of the cause of this insensitiveness there is room for differences of opinion. It is, of course, possible that the insensitiveness may be apparent only and may be merely due to lack of interest, but there is, I think, little doubt that it depends on physiological conditions of some kind [Rivers, 1901b, pp. 50–52].

Rivers interpreted his results almost entirely in terms of a causal law in which perceptual differences, presumably innate, cause linguistic categories. Although perhaps presaged by Humboldt, it was not until much later with Sapir (1928) and Whorf (1940) that the opposite causal direction, from language and culture to perception, was systematically entertained. Evidence such as Rivers provided, connecting perceptual differences and linguistic differences, equally well supports both these opposing causal hypotheses. They must be distinguished on other grounds.

R. S. Woodworth (1905–1906; 1910a; 1910b), the esteemed experimental psychologist, provided the next round of evidence. At the St. Louis Exposition of 1904, Woodworth and his assistants examined some 1,100 persons assembled from isolated areas all over the world. A few of the many peoples studied were Moros, Igorots, Tinguianes, Bagobos, and Negritos from the Philippines; Patagonians; North American Indians; Eskimos; and African Pygmies. Included among the tests were examinations of color vision. The rates for red-green color blindness were, in general, lower for the more primitive groups and did not exceed European rates (1905–1906). With regard to the relation between color vocabulary and perception, here verbatim is the most extensive of three casual reports on his data:

> As the Filipinos also have no native words for green, blue and violet, the authors tested them as to their power of discriminating these colors. The test employed called for the matching of dark shades of several colors with pale tints of the same. Colored papers were used; the tints were spread out in spectral order, and each dark shade was to be matched with the tint with which it agreed in color. The authors found that the Filipinos, and indeed all other races examined, were inferior to whites in this test; but it was impossible to detect any special deficiency for the greens, blues and violets. These colors were relatively as well matched as the reds, and better than the yellows. Nor was there any tendency, except among the Igorots, to confuse blue, green or violet with neutral gray. The Negritos did better than many more advanced races. The results obtained by the author are thus opposed to the view that the color sense has developed within human history from a more primitive type in which only the red end of the spectrum appeared as colored [1905–1906, pp. 25–26].

Woodworth recognized that his test was too dissimilar from Rivers' to contradict Rivers' findings. He did criticize Rivers' interpretation, however. Perhaps his most plausible suggestion introduces the problem of "response-marginals," a recurrent problem in recent perceptual-threshold research. He suggested that the English respondents, tending to regard clear glass as blue, responded with blue whenever they did not detect one of the other colors. Thus the difference might have been one of response availability, the English responding with blue more frequently no matter what color was being presented. Modern research shows that the availability of responses, in this case familiar color words, does affect computed perceptual thresholds unless the analyses are so done as to obviate this factor (e.g., Goldiamond, 1958; Goldiamond and Hawkins, 1958; Campbell, 1963, pp. 115–117). Rivers' data were not reported in enough detail to make it possible to check on this interpretation. But on the basis of the published evidence, Rivers' results might be judged more adequate than Woodworth's because of the inadequate reporting of the latter.

By titling his most extensive discussion of the problem "The puzzle of color vocabularies," Woodworth (1910a) prefigured the shift of problem away from perception to linguistics that was typical of subsequent studies by anthropologists. In this paper, he explained the cultural differences in color vocabularies by reference to the functional distinctions in everyday life in which color-designations would be helpful—and thus unwittingly repeated the theory more elaborately stated by Grant Allen, whom he failed to cite in this paper although he cited him on color sense in animals in the 1905–1906 paper.

Titchener followed in 1916 with a thorough review of Rivers' work on color vision and on tactile discrimination. While he did no experimentation with non-Europeans, Titchener conducted control studies with his students and colleagues to illustrate his methodological points. On point after point, he plausibly challenged Rivers' interpretation. The problems raised are so subtle and yet fundamental that reading his critique (Titchener, 1916) would seem to be a first requirement for anyone seeking to do further work in this fascinating area.

Regarding the Lovibond Tintometer results, Titchener noted that Rivers was willing to exclude cases from his Murray Islander sample where the performance seemed to show definitely defective vision, but that he left such cases in his English sample; eliminating these English cases removes the Murray Islanders' greater sensitivity to red. Color perception is very difficult to test because of the very rapid adaptation phenomena. Titchener reported that with the faintly colored glass samples for red and blue, there is a flush of color immediately upon exposure that quickly disappears because of adaptation; disregarding this first flush would account for very large differences in threshold. Most serious is Titchener's evidence that the amount of general illumination affects color thresholds and raises the threshold most for blue; from Rivers' report, Titchener assumed that the Murray Islanders were tested in a room in a "disused missionary house" without artificial illumination, whereas the English data were collected in a brightly lit laboratory.

Titchener's detailed analysis extended to Rivers' linguistic data, which Titchener rearranged and reanalyzed. He adopted the theory that naming reflects the functional importance of color-discriminations rather than perceptual ability, citing Woodworth (1910a) but not Allen. He was alert to the possibility that distinctions other than hue are crucial to naming. Retabulating Rivers' data, he challenged the statement that color-naming is more definite for the red-yellow end of the spectrum. He further offered plausible alternative translations of two of the crucial color terms of the Murray Islanders. Whereas Rivers translated *kakekakek* as "white," Titchener suggested "light and inconspicuously colored, —faded." The color name *golegole* comes from the name for cuttle fish. Assuming that the reference is to the inky secretion of the animal, Rivers translated this as "black." Titchener hypothesized that it refers to the animal's color, which, in chameleon-like fashion, changes to suit its background and is variegated and hard to see; using Rivers' extensive reporting of specific interpretations, he made this a plausible alternative.

Such retranslations removed much of the apparent lack of precision in the color terminology. To make this reinterpretation plausible, Titchener did a study at Cornell in which respondents were required to name the color of bits of paper without the use of abstract color names, using instead the names of concrete objects. Analyzing these data in a manner analogous to Rivers, Titchener obtained specious evidence of an insensitivity to blue. Much more detailed analysis was provided than we have cited here, and Titchener in the end found no credible evidence at all that the color perception of the Murray Islanders differs from our own.

Around the turn of the century, then, we have Allen in Great Britain and Woodworth and Titchener in the United States arguing against differences in color-perception, with Rivers in Great Britain arguing in favor of them. This argument has persisted unresolved. Contemporary students of the problem (e.g., Ray, 1952, 1953; Conklin, 1955) substantiate the statement that various cultures divide the spectrum into different segments via the color names employed. In one report (Ray, 1953) on the basic color terms in ten cultures in North America, very little uniformity was found either in the number of terms employed or in the parts of the spectrum to which the various terms apply. This sort of evidence suggests, as Ray says, that "There is no such thing as a 'natural' division of the spectrum."

However, such evidence says nothing conclusive about the extent to which persons in various cultures can detect differences between color samples having either the same or different names. In reviewing the work of Ray, Kluckhohn states, ". . . the central point that perception of color is determined in part by culturally arbitrary standards, and especially by linguistic categories . . . seems unarguable" (Kluckhohn, 1954, p. 936). It is precisely this point, we are here suggesting, that requires some argument, for it is not clear that color-naming is, strictly speaking, a perceptual task. These kinds of data may or may not mean that aspects of the environment bearing different names will be *more readily* discriminated than aspects bearing identical names; clear evidence on this point is not yet available. Certainly the issue of *ability* to discriminate is not apt to be involved since it is estimated that man can discriminate some 7,500,000 colors, with no language having names for more than a few (Triandis, 1964).

Conklin (1960) has reported considerable data dealing with Hanunóo taxonomic behavior, and it is clear from his reports that the plant-classification schemes and color-naming systems of this Philippine society relate systematically to other aspects of the local culture, especially to the ripe-unripe distinction and to linguistic

factors. Again, such data demonstrate that different people orga-
nize the world differently, in accord with cultural forces rather
than in a manner dictated by its intrinsic structure. But we are
probably still dealing here with the more cognitive aspects of what
has been called perceptual behavior.

3 *Cultural Differences in Perception— Some Studies in Visual Perception*

Many papers in the culture-and-perception literature, as we have just seen, deal with the more complex aspects of the way people view the world, with "viewing the world" used metaphorically rather than literally. We now turn to some studies in which reported relations between culture and perception more clearly seem to indicate differences in immediate perception. By "immediate perception" we wish to denote certain steps in the process intervening between the impingement of a stimulus on a receptor organ and an overt response to it, steps that involve relatively simple discriminations. The few studies thus far referred to have indicated that people come to name, classify, and interpret their experiences in accord with pre-existing patterns, often linguistic, that are culturally traditional. What we now ask for is evidence that "the human organism becomes selectively *sensitized* to certain arrays of stimuli rather than others . . . [as] . . . a function of the individual's membership in one cultural group, rather than another, whatever other factors are involved" (Hallowell, 1951, p. 168, our italics).

Is there less equivocal evidence than we have thus far reviewed to indicate that culturally shaped experiences predispose people to attend easily to some features of the environment and, conversely, to have difficulty detecting others? Do persons in some cultures actually have difficulty identifying—not merely in the sense of naming—some kinds of stimulus arrays? Can a particular stimulus array appear to be two quite different entities to persons from two different cultures? Impressions like these seem easily created by various pronouncements on the relation between culture and perception, but thus far the kinds of studies we have discussed do not necessitate acceptance of such a strong and literal interpretation of the culture-influences-perception hypothesis.

We shall now examine a number of perceptual tasks, all involving vision, on which members of different cultural groups have been found to respond in systematically different ways. As we shall see, the nature of these tasks is such that the data strongly suggest differential tendencies to perceive, not merely to classify, certain stimulus complexes.

PERCEPTUAL DOMINANCE AND FAMILIARITY

The first of these perceptual tasks simply requires the identification of the content of photographs presented in pairs via a stereoscopic device. When a person is stereoscopically shown a pair of photographic slides of disparate content, in a manner such that each eye is presented with only one member of the pair, binocular rivalry and dominance occur. One sees only one of the two pictures at a time. For some observers, a ready alternation from one perception to the other occurs. For others, one picture is seen easily, the other only after considerable viewing time has elapsed. In a study of carefully matched Mexican and American (USA) subjects, all of whom viewed ten stereogram-slide pairs, each composed of Mexican and American scenes, Bagby (1957) found that all the American respondents showed American content dominance on at least five of the ten pairs, while none of the Mexican respondents did so. The difference was significant, as were differences based on alternative methods of scoring perceptual dominance. This led Bagby to conclude that cultural differences appear to be critical in effecting perceptual dominance in a conflict-creating viewing situation. He interpreted his findings as supporting a transactional theory of perception (Ittelson and Cantril, 1954; Ittelson, 1960), which argues that differences in ways of perceiving are a consequence of differences in past experience, in this instance the experiential differences being cultural.

The phenomenon Bagby reported is a striking one because of the all-or-none nature of the perception. It is like the traditional examples of the ambiguous figure, where two views are also possible but only one is perceived at any one time. An ultracautious reader might still wish to ponder the nature of the mechanism underlying Bagby's findings. Did his respondents merely find it easier verbally to identify those scenes that were more familiar to them, and thus reported them more readily; or was there some prior, more "primitive" selective perceptual mechanism at work? How were the less familiar scenes suppressed? Where in the chain of events in the visual response system does such a mechanism come into play? While it is true that one must always be concerned with the difficulties of inferring differences in what is actually seen from differences in verbal reporting (see Pierce [1963] for an excellent review and critique of research on form thresholds and their many possible determinants), Bagby's findings constitute strong support for the proposition that the visual experiences most generally available in a particular environment predispose one to identify most readily material similar to the content of those experiences.

A subsequent study in South Africa involving the stereoscopic presentation of photographs of persons of various ethnic origin found some differences in perceptual dominance among Europeans (both English-speaking and Afrikaners), Indians, "Coloreds," and Africans. (Pettigrew, Allport, and Barnett, 1958). While Colored and Indian slides were dominant for all groups of respondents, Afrikaners gave less dominance to them than did any other group of respondents. The Afrikaners had a tendency to report either European or African, which Pettigrew *et al.* described as a bifurcating tendency possibly reflecting the Afrikaners' heightened concern for racial conflict in South Africa. Their findings led the authors to conclude that ethnic-group membership played some role in determining perceptual dominance. These two studies considered together are exceedingly provocative and should be followed by additional research designed both to replicate their findings and to explore further the nature of the mechanism involved.

"RACIAL" DIFFERENCES IN PERCEPTUAL CAPACITY

The need for careful exploration of the mechanisms underlying cultural differences in the performance of simple perceptual tasks becomes apparent when one examines the results of a recent study by Schwitzgebel (1962). This study, as reported by its author, is misleading. One phase of Schwitzgebel's research, done at the University of Natal in South Africa, revealed significantly greater inaccuracies among the responses of 12 young-adult Zulus, as compared with 11 young-adult Afrikaners, when they were asked to make absolute judgments of the lengths of lines. The lines in question were 14 inches long. On two separate tasks involving these lines, the combined median estimates were 12.5 inches and 13 inches respectively; there was thus a general tendency to underestimate, but the majority of the estimates below these medians were made by the Zulu respondents. On a third length-estimation task, where the objective length was only 5 inches, the combined median estimate was 6.5 inches, with no significant difference found in the proportion of respondents in each group on either side of the median. The Afrikaners, however, tended to overestimate more than the Zulus did. If it is safe to conclude anything at all from these three sets of data, it appears that Zulus tend to make smaller estimates than Afrikaners—a tendency that incidentally results in lesser accuracy when a long line is in question and in greater accuracy when a short one is the stimulus.

If there is such a differential tendency, it is obviously of interest to learn how it came about. It should be obvious that such a tendency might not reflect a difference in perceptual habits, that it might reflect differential expectations or different conceptions of the size of the units used in reporting the judgment. Schwitzgebel ignored these other possibilities, however, and concluded without question that his data revealed a fundamental difference in perceptual capacity:

> Our data suggest that certain aspects of even two-dimensional perception may be a constricted or unlearned process among African tribes. Since both our experimental groups were relatively isolated and uneducated, the question of genetic determinants could be raised. . . . Regardless of the relative contribution of learned and genetic factors, certain visual capacities or potentials of the human being have been suppressed, constricted, lost, or diminished among young adult Zulus [Schwitzgebel, 1962, p. 76].

This is an interpretation that appears not to be demanded by the data. The differences they reveal are ambiguous.

Other phases of Schwitzgebel's study involved the estimation of the passage of time (Zulu respondents underestimated an interval of 1 minute to a greater extent than did Afrikaners), the autokinetic word-association test (more Zulus "saw" a meaningful movement of the light than did Afrikaners), a version of the Gottschaldt embedded-figures test (the Zulus averaged 45 seconds per figure, while the mean time for the Afrikaners was 9 seconds), and a circle size-matching task (no significant difference between the groups). It would belabor the obvious to indicate that the reported differences might indicate phenomena other than perceptual and that it is unsafe to conclude, as did Schwitzgebel, that his study confirms the proposition that "certain perceptual organizations are characteristic of cultural groups."

Another study that is based on a task appearing at first glance to tap a perceptual process but very likely involving other factors was carried out recently in Southern Rhodesia (Shapiro, 1960). The task given to 14 illiterate Africans (migrant workers from

Nyasaland employed as street sweepers in a Southern Rhodesian town and ordered to participate in the study by their overseer) was to reproduce with paper and pencil eight geometric designs selected from the Kohs Blocks Drawing Rotation Test. The performance of this group was compared with that of 17 well-educated African school teachers in Southern Rhodesia, 21 widely assorted English "controls" (e.g., ranging in age from 14 to 50 years), 25 brain-damaged patients in English hospitals, 3 groups of "certified mentally defective" Englishmen, and 32 "imbeciles" in Manor Hospital in England.

The aspect of the reproduction performance focused on in this study was the tendency to "rotate," or to produce an essentially correct drawing in a spatial orientation different from that of the model. The illiterate African group had rotation scores significantly higher than the scores of each of the comparison groups, a fact which led Shapiro to the following hypothesis:

> . . . the culture of the illiterate or unintelligent Africans did not provide the necessary opportunity for learning which enabled them to make an adequate integration of the directional properties of the visual world, at least in the two dimensional situation involved in the drawing task [Shapiro, 1960, pp. 28–29].

Quite correctly, Shapiro considered alternative explanations, noting the fact that more rotation occurred on certain figures than on others (e.g., when the design was in a diamond orientation, a common finding in numerous studies), a fact that might reflect nothing more than the operation of a self-instruction factor or a tendency to put right what is considered to be a disoriented design. Were this the case, the phenomenon observed in this study could not be considered perceptual without a drastic change in the meaning of that term. Shapiro also recognized the possibility that his results reflect, among the illiterate Africans, "gross disorganization of attention in the testing situation as a result of wild fears about the purpose of the experiment and extreme unfamiliarity with many aspects of the task." And, just for the record, he made it clear that neither low intelligence, nor brain damage, nor illiteracy, nor membership in the "African race" is a possible explanation of the higher tendency to rotate among the sample of African illiterates because each of these factors can be found in at least one of the low-rotating control groups.

Thus, no conclusive interpretation is possible on the basis of the data obtained in this study. Instead, we have a large and significant difference in the performance of a task that might reflect either some unknown difference in perceptual tendency or any variety of unknown differences in task-interpretation, drawing habits, or other nonperceptual aspects of behavior.

THE PERCEPTION OF DEPTH IN TWO-DIMENSIONAL PICTURES

An interest in possible relationships between perceptual tendencies and the presence or absence of perspective drawing techniques in the traditional art of various cultures stimulated a few studies by British psychologists a number of years ago. Thouless (1933) attempted to explain what appears to be the nearly complete lack of attention to the laws of perspective characteristic of much Oriental art (Indian painting, in particular) as a result of "a measurable difference in the perception of these [Oriental] races." Thouless argued that Oriental artists produce strikingly flat, perspective-free drawings because "they see objects in a manner much further from the principles of perspective than do the majority of Europeans and . . . they tend not to see shadows" (Thouless, 1933, p. 330). The experimental evidence that served as the basis for this statement was the fact that 20 Indian students had higher scores in "phenomenal regression to the real object" than did a control group of 49 British students. One laboratory task in which this was the case involved the selection, out of a set ranging in axis ratio from .25:1 to .95:1, of the one ellipse that best matched the apparent shape of an inclined circle. The Indian students displayed a very high degree of shape-constancy as measured by this task.

If Indians in general do "regress to the real object" to an unusually great extent, this could mean, as Thouless argued, that they have difficulty seeing things except as they know them really to be, and, as a result, have difficulty drawing them in any other fashion. One can distinguish two parts in Thouless' argument, and they require separate discussion.

To take up, first, the original intent of Thouless' paper—which was to explain Indian and other Oriental art in terms of prior perceptual habit—it should be stressed that the data in this paper do not prove his point. There may be no functional relationship at all between the prevalent art style of India and the tendency of Indians to earn high shape-constancy scores. There is the possibility that much Indian art is produced without perspective and shadowing simply because such technique is in accord with culturally sanctioned esthetic tradition. It is quite conceivable that Indian artists have been encouraged to present a view of the world that is more nearly as they know it to be than as it appears from a particular vantage point under particular conditions of viewing. Surely such a point of view is not unknown even in Occidental esthetic theory today. Alternatively, Indian artists might have been late to discover the so-called laws of perspective, which, after all, were arrived at with considerable difficulty and only relatively recently in the history of Western art. Of these two alternatives, the former seems more likely, but in either case the nature of the painting style can be seen as quite independent of the nature of the prevalent perceptual tendencies.

And second, even if one grants the possibility that Indian perceptual habits are related to Indian art styles, it is equally plausible to argue that the relationship exists in the direction opposite from that argued by Thouless. If one were raised in an environment that provided continual opportunities to view Indian paintings, one might tend to represent three-dimensional surfaces according to the artistic conventions one has come to know in those paintings.

The Indian students in Thouless' study might have displayed high "phenomenal regression" because they had learned something from the art of their culture.

However one prefers to speculate on the relation between perception and art, the fact remains that Thouless did not argue merely on the basis of different art styles that Orientals and Westerners are differentially susceptible to phenomenal regression. Thouless' data collected in the laboratory suggest this to be the case. For our present purposes, whether or not his laboratory findings explain the perspective-free characteristics of Indian painting is relatively unimportant. His discovery of a significant difference in scores on this simple laboratory task is a striking example of a cultural difference in a perceptual tendency, which, if not artifactual, constitutes a phenomenon worthy of attention. Additional efforts clearly are required to understand how such a difference could have come about. Although Thouless entitled his report "A racial difference in perception," he made no attempt in it to assess the relative importance of genetic and cultural determinants of this difference. Nor did he even speculate as to the nature of the possible determinants. Be that as it may, Thouless' data are germane to our present topic, and we would point to them as additional support for the hypothesis that culturally mediated experiences help to shape perceptual tendencies.

In a replication of Thouless' study, this time employing West African college students from what were then the Gold Coast and Togoland, a high degree of shape-constancy (regression to a circle) was found (Beveridge, 1935). In this study, considerable size-constancy was also found to be characteristic of the West African sample. The author, like Thouless before him, felt that "this explains some peculiarities of African drawings."

In a subsequent paper by Beveridge (1939) it was shown that African students displayed *less* phenomenal regression for brightness in a matching task, and *more* phenomenal regression for whiteness, than did British students. However, since earlier it had been shown that phenomenal regression for whiteness, but not for brightness, correlates positively with size- and shape-constancy, Beveridge argued that his new findings supported the view, originally put forth by Thouless, that non-Western peoples are more susceptible to the kinds of phenomenal regression that might relate to the characteristics of non-Western art.

On this point, it is interesting to note the supplementary finding, reported in the same paper, that the sample of West African students strongly preferred Western paintings to Oriental paintings. This finding Beveridge considered surprising in view of the Africans' high phenomenal regression scores. However, as Beveridge correctly pointed out, "these subjects had been used to seeing European pictures from their earliest school-days, whereas Oriental art was new to them." Thus, the Africans might have preferred that with which they were most familiar. That they were also familiar with African art, and that this familiarity might have influenced their performance on the shape-constancy test used in the first study (Beveridge, 1935), is a possibility that should not have gone unmentioned.

The question raised by Thouless and Beveridge concerning the relation between perceptual tendencies and prevalent artistic styles was touched upon indirectly in a recent study of human-figure drawings by illiterate Bedouins living in the Syrian desert (Dennis, 1960). These persons are described as having had minimal exposure to Western paintings, drawings, and photographs. Their own traditional art is completely nonrepresentational and is dominated by simple geometric decorations consisting of surfaces bounded by straight or curved lines. When asked to draw human figures, Dennis' respondents typically produced simple stick figures, lacking in perspective, roundness, and detail. As a result, the mean IQ score that would have been assigned to them on the basis of the Goodenough procedure for assessing intelligence from drawings was about 50. However, Dennis properly concluded that the drawings probably revealed little about their intelligence or personality but merely reflected their cultural traditions in art form and their manual skills. (Most of his respondents had never attempted to draw a man prior to their participation in this study.) While Dennis himself did not explicitly raise this question, it seems most unlikely that the drawing style employed to depict the human form reflected the Bedouins' perception of human beings.

Considering together the studies by Thouless, by Beveridge, and by Dennis, several points are worthy of stress. First, one is impressed with the possibility that the art products of a group of people from a particular society may reveal little or nothing about their perceptual habits. On the other hand, the relationships between art style and performance on perceptual constancy tasks in the laboratory might well be more than coincidental. Finally, these relationships, provocative as they are, have not yet been explored to the extent they deserve, nor has there been enough research even to substantiate Thouless' and Beveridge's empirical findings of heightened perceptual constancy among non-Western peoples.

In a study (Hudson, 1960) that escapes many of the ambiguities of interpretation characteristic of most of the research thus far described, 11 samples, varying in educational background, age, ethnicity, and national origin, were tested for their tendency to employ systematically varied cues for depth perception when viewing a set of 11 outline drawings and one photograph. The available depth cues were relative object-size, object-superimposition, and perspective. The samples, all obtained in South Africa, were either currently attending school (6 samples—of which 3 were "black" and 3 were "white," and of which 5 were composed of pupils and 1 was composed of teachers) or not currently attending school (5 samples—of which 4 were "black" and 1 was "white," all adults). With the exception of two samples of mine laborers, the non-school-attending samples either included some persons who had had some education or consisted solely of educated persons. The test was administered individually, and a standardized scoring system was employed to indicate whether or not a response indicated three-dimensional perception. Each sample was then characterized by the proportion of persons giving a 3-d response to each of the figures in the test set. Hudson provided a résumé of the most striking findings:

White and black school-going samples perceive depth more frequently in pictorial material than do illiterate black samples, and samples, both black and white, which have terminated their school course
and live in isolation from the dominant cultural norm. . . . Outline
drawings making use of perspective depth cues are less frequently seen
three-dimensionally than those using overlap or size depth cues. This
finding holds particularly in the case of white primary school pupils.
School-going samples perceive three dimensions in a photograph more
readily than in an outline drawing, but this finding does not apply to
illiterate samples. (None of the illiterates tested saw the photograph
three-dimensionally.) Intelligence and educational level are factors
which independently influence dimensional pictorial perception, but
they appear to do so only with white school-going samples [pp.
201–202].

In discussing his findings, Hudson convincingly argued that 2-d
responses were not artifactual, but rather that "the whole manifest
content of the picture tended to be perceived two-dimensionally,
and appropriately interpreted." After a careful discussion of possible cultural and genetic factors that might contribute to the performance of the task used in this study, Hudson concluded that
both kinds of factors might play a role; but one is most impressed
by the evidence he presented to indicate that both formal schooling
and immersion in a culture containing pictures, books, and magazines are factors that heavily determine the tendency to employ
depth cues when viewing two-dimensional representations of objects in three-dimensional space. Although Hudson's findings may
be specific to the materials employed and the questions asked,
they do suggest that genuine perceptual differences can result from
culturally mediated experiences.

GESTALT "LAWS" OF PERCEPTUAL
ORGANIZATION

If cultural differences in perceptual constancy and in depth-
perception exist, as the findings discussed above would seem to
indicate, they constitute an important challenge to the Gestalt

psychologist's purportedly universal laws of perceptual organization. In a recent cross-cultural study of another Gestalt law of organization (Michael, 1953), an attempt was made to determine whether "closure" is a general law of innate perceptual organization or is dependent on cultural factors. Closure may be defined as the tendency to see an incomplete figure, particularly one that is a nearly complete familiar geometric design, as if it were intact.

Michael's attempt consisted of a comparison of the response patterns to a simple laboratory task of 20 adult white Americans in New Mexico with responses to the same task by 20 adult Navahos living in a nearby reservation. The task required drawing nine simple designs that were tachistoscopically projected one at a time to groups of respondents varying in number from 3 to 6. The designs were all circles, varying in incompleteness from zero to eight degrees in one-degree steps. Four measures were employed to determine differential capacity to perceive the openings in the designs, but no significant differences were found across groups on any of these measures. Michael had chosen to compare white Americans and Navahos because

> West European culture in general and American culture in particular stress the concept of closure. In the area of aesthetics and design, unbroken continuity (e.g., streamlining) and symmetry are emphasized. And among the ideal behavior patterns favored are those stressing task completion, both materially and temporarily, . . . [while] students of the Navaho have long remarked on the Navaho "fear of completing anything" [Michael, 1953, p. 225].

The results of this study seem to indicate that differences in cultural value systems as indeterminate and abstract as those on which Michael focused might not be sufficient to bring about differences in visual perception on as straightforward a task as that employed in his study. Thus, although his study failed to support the proposition that cultural forces influence perception, it can contribute heavily to an understanding of that proposition by suggesting that one focus on more specific kinds of cultural factors than the "stressed" and "emphasized" cultural values. Of course, his study might also indicate that this is the kind of task on which no amount of differential experience can have a significant effect.

CULTURAL SUSCEPTIBILITY TO OPTICAL ILLUSIONS

Two studies, separated by a half-century, have been concerned with the specific issue that constitutes the focus of our own research. These studies investigated the possibility that persons in different parts of the world might be differentially susceptible to perceptual illusions.

As part of a truly classic cross-cultural and interdisciplinary research project at the turn of the century, W. H. R. Rivers collected a wide variety of perceptual data. We have already reported on his study of color-perception. More important are his quantitative data using two geometric illusions (the Müller-Lyer figure and the horizontal-vertical figure) among several samples in the Torres Straits and in southern India. For purposes of comparison, data were also collected among English adults and children. In two reports (Rivers, 1901a; Rivers, 1905) enough data were presented to permit statistical analysis of the intergroup differences reported by Rivers. This analysis substantiates Rivers' conclusion that his non-Western groups were *more* subject to the horizontal-vertical illusion and *less* subject to the Müller-Lyer illusion than were his English groups.

During the Cambridge Expedition to the Torres Straits, Rivers collected data among the Murray Islanders, a Papuan group in New Guinea. He describes them as "a people who were amenable and with whom communication was easy; but on the other hand, who were not far removed from their primitive past" (Rivers, 1901a, p. 6). He reported that "the islands have been subject for a quarter of a century to missionary influence and teaching, with the result that most of the natives are professed Christians, and for about ten years English has been taught to the children" (Rivers, 1901a, p. 6).

A year after the Torres Straits expedition, Rivers studied the Todas, a community of 800 persons inhabiting the Nilgiri Hills of southern India. The people, predominantly buffalo herdsmen, were, according to Rivers, unable to converse in even a pidgin English.

In the Torres Straits, Rivers presented a standard horizontal line and instructed his respondents to draw vertical lines so that they appeared to be equal to the horizontal. The sample consisted of 20 men and 12 boys. Rivers later collected data with this procedure among 20 Todas, 15 English adults, and 12 English children. Depending upon where the vertical was constructed (so as to form an L-, T-, or +-shaped figure), the potency of the illusion varied for all groups; but clearly, the intergroup differences that exist indicate that the nonliterate peoples were more subject to the horizontal-vertical illusion than were the English adults.

After completing his work in the Torres Straits, Rivers constructed a new apparatus for investigation of the horizontal-vertical illusion, one in which either the horizontal or the vertical segment could be adjusted by a respondent in an attempt to equate the variable with the standard. With this apparatus, Rivers collected data from 40 Todas, 90 English adults, and 50 English children. The Todas were significantly more susceptible to the illusion than either of the English groups. When one combines the data collected via both procedures, there is good reason to place confidence in Rivers' conclusion that the non-Western peoples he sampled were subject to the horizontal-vertical illusion to a greater degree than were the English respondents.

To study the Müller-Lyer illusion in the Torres Straits, Rivers used an instrument that he later abandoned because "the lines forming the figure were too thick, and the junction between the stationary and movable parts was in the middle of the variable line" (Rivers, 1905, p. 356). Nevertheless, he used this instrument with 38 Murray Islanders, 42 English respondents, and 20 Todas, so that cross-cultural comparisons were possible. On the basis of data collected with this apparatus it is clear that the non-Western peoples were significantly less subject to the illusion.

In India, Rivers introduced an "improved apparatus" made of thin xylonite, in which one half of the Müller-Lyer figure was placed on a variable, sliding surface. With this apparatus, Rivers obtained adjustment-responses from 20 Todas and compared their scores with those of English respondents studied subsequently in Great Britain. The major finding with this instrument was that the Todas' mean score was not significantly different from that of the English adults; the Toda mean was not unlike that of the Todas who were studied with the earlier form of the apparatus, but the English adults showed a smaller degree of illusion with the improved instrument. However, Rivers found a significant difference between the Todas' mean score and that of a sample of English children, a difference showing the Todas to be less subject to the illusion. This difference was of sufficient magnitude to produce a significant difference between the Todas' mean and that of the combined English samples. The most reasonable conclusion to be derived from work with this instrument is that the nonliterates were not as subject to the Müller-Lyer illusion as were English children, and certainly no more subject to the illusion than English adults. On combining the results of both Müller-Lyer studies the indication is that the nonliterates were less subject to the illusion than were Englishmen.[1]

The most provocative aspect of Rivers' findings is the fact that differences between the Western and non-Western peoples exist in both directions, i.e., that the non-Western peoples seem to be less subject to one illusion while more subject to another. Obviously, the failure to find differences that are consistent in direction eliminates any simple explanation of the existing differences, including the view, prevalent during the nineteenth century, that since "primitive" peoples are less well endowed intellectually than "civilized" peoples, the former ought to be more easily duped by illusions and therefore consistently more subject to them. The suggestion in Rivers' data that the "primitives" might actually be *less* subject to

---

[1] A sample of 28 Uralis and Sholagas, described as jungle peoples, were also studied with the "improved version" of the Müller-Lyer illusion. Rivers (1905, p. 359) considered their scores unreliable and uninterpretable.

the Müller-Lyer illusion is embarrassing to any such hypothesis. That there are differences in both directions suggests that the two illusions studied by Rivers might be representative of two classes of illusion. Rivers himself pursued this line of speculation:

> The illusion of compared horizontal and vertical lines probably belongs to that class of illusion which depends on physiological conditions, and the effect of experience in civilized life . . . is to diminish the illusion. The Müller-Lyer illusion, on the other hand, is one of those for which the explanation is probably more strictly psychological. The psychological factors upon which the illusion depends are however of a simple nature and affect both savage and civilized man, and the reason why the illusion is rather less marked to the Toda and the Papuan is . . . a difference in the direction of attention, the savage attending more strictly to the two lines which he is desired to make equal, while the civilized man allows the figure to exert its full influence on his mind [Rivers, 1905, p. 363].

The present writers are in accord with Rivers' suggestion that the two illusions he studied are members of separate classes. We are also impressed with his suggestion that certain kinds of experience might modify responses to these figures. We depart from Rivers' explanation, however, when he argues that the cross-cultural difference in response to the Müller-Lyer figure is "a difference in the direction of attention," on the grounds that such a statement does not constitute an explanation. In the next chapter, we shall develop our own hypotheses concerning the ways in which culturally mediated experience might modify responses to the kinds of stimuli employed in Rivers' research.

Titchener, who, as we have seen, severely criticized the Cambridge Expedition studies of color vision, expressed considerable doubt concerning Rivers' illusion data. Titchener commented:

> The test of an optical illusion, for example, may tell us nothing of the relative magnitude of the illusion in the case of the savage and civilized subjects, but may nevertheless bring out the psychologically important fact that savage and civilized approach the particular task set them in different ways, or come to it in different attitudes of mind [Titchener, 1916, p. 235].

Since this idea of Titchener's could constitute an alternative interpretation of our own data, we will return to it in the discussion, in
Chapter 7, of our results.

The second well-known study to show differential susceptibility
to an "optical" illusion focused on the reactions of Zulu children to
the rotating trapezoidal window (Allport and Pettigrew, 1957). To
produce this illusion, a nonrectangular "window-frame," usually
containing carpentered detail, is rotated in a uniform circular
motion (see Ames, 1961, for a description). The viewers' tendency,
found in most laboratory studies, is to perceive it as a typical *rectangular* window, located at a different angle of regard than it is in
fact. To preserve this misrepresentation, it is necessary to perceive
the motion as reversing in direction every half-cycle. With distance
reducing the efficacy of various cues that would normally reinforce
a veridical perception of the stimulus, this can be a powerfully
compelling illusion.

With the figure presented under the conditions that are optimal
for the illusion, Allport and Pettigrew found no cultural differences. All groups seemed to be susceptible to the illusion in the
vast majority of cases. This finding was emphasized in the authors'
conclusions. However, under other viewing conditions (binocular
and from a distance of 10 feet) rural Zulus were found by Allport
and Pettigrew to report the illusion only 14 per cent of the time, as
contrasted with urban Zulus, who reported it 64 per cent of the
time. Urban South Africans of European origin reported the illusion 55 per cent of the time under these viewing conditions.
Whether it is appropriate to emphasize the latter findings, or, following Allport and Pettigrew, the former finding of no differences
under optimal illusion conditions, will be a point raised in our discussion in Chapter 7.

There is a noteworthy feature of the procedure employed in
the Allport and Pettigrew study. After each respondent watched
three revolutions of the trapezoid, he was asked, "How does it
seem to you to be moving?" Often the respondent spontaneously
used his hands to indicate the motion. As Allport and Pettigrew
comment, "the use of hand motion by the [respondent] proved to

be fully convincing, for when he reversed the hand at precisely the right moment for the illusion to occur there could be no question concerning his experience" (1957, p. 107). Furthermore, the employment of both a rectangular and a trapezoidal window, and the obtainment of both verbal and motor report in each case, made it possible to record a clear and unequivocal judgment of the respondent's perception. In view of the recurrent equivocality in many of the data discussed in this chapter, it is gratifying to be able to present the unambiguous findings of Allport and Pettigrew. With respect to these data, at least those based on the minimal illusion-supporting conditions, it appears that there are genuine perceptual differences that are determined by environmental factors rather than by racial factors.

Three recent papers (Heuse, 1957; Morgan, 1959; Bonté, 1962) investigate further the question of cultural differences in illusion susceptibility, but since these papers were based upon our own earlier research, we shall postpone a discussion of them until our research has been described.

SUMMARY OF THE LITERATURE

With the mention of those few studies that are most directly pertinent to our own research, we come to the end of this discussion—here and in Chapter 2—of the literature dealing with cultural influence on perception. We have seen that there is a wide variety of studies supporting the hypothesis that perception varies from person to person in accord with selective forces, both inhibiting and reinforcing, provided by culturally mediated experiences. We have also seen, however, that the data offered in support of this hypothesis are often ambiguous and subject to diverse interpretation.

Considerable confusion remains, much of it reflecting the tendency of many researchers to employ the term "perception" in ways that enlarge its meaning to include processes that might better be thought of as cognitive, conceptual, or evaluative. In an attempt to minimize this confusion, we have left out of this review a number of papers to which other reviewers might have given important notice. They have been left out because in our judgment it would drastically stretch the concept "perception" to include them. For example, we have chosen not to include studies of concepts of time among the Tiv of Nigeria (Bohannan, 1953) or of ways in which the Salteaux Indians conceptualize and measure the spatial attributes of their environment (Hallowell, 1942). The reader cannot have failed to note, however, that some studies *chosen* for review here were no more perceptual in a strict sense than the examples just mentioned. Clearly, the rule for rejecting or accepting a study for review was flexible and reflected our intention to be simultaneously cautious and sympathetic, in recognition of the problems inherent in efforts to substantiate perceptual differences.

The studies to which we attached greatest relevance, given the nature of our own research, are those in which the data were based primarily on responses to relatively simple, laboratory-originated perceptual tasks. Even with such studies, however, we were forced in almost every instance to call attention to the "inability of the investigator to determine what the perceptions he proposes to investigate really are" (Child, 1950, p. 303). We also saw that when cross-cultural differences in perception were found, the particular cultural factors that might plausibly be considered causal were often not specified.

It thus appears that at this point in the history of psychological and anthropological concern for this problem there is little unequivocal evidence of cultural influence on perception. On the other hand, for all its inherent ambiguity, the evidence certainly points in that direction. In sum, the materials reviewed here suggest that while additional methodologies and instrumentations may be required, there is considerable likelihood of documenting authentic perceptual differences across cultures. In addition, the literature seems to us to suggest that if cultural differences in perception are to be found, they are likely to be the result of culturally mediated differences in experience, rather than manifestations of biological differences among cultural groups.

4
Some Psychological Theory and Predictions of Cultural Differences

We have suggested that while the proposition that culture influences perception is highly plausible, there exist very few cross-cultural data that unequivocally support this point of view. On the other hand, we saw a considerable accumulation of studies reporting, almost without exception, cultural differences in behavior that could very well indicate differences in perception. As a result, even without full substantiation, the prevailing view in the cross-cultural literature is that perceptual responses *are* subject to cultural influences. Recognizing both the plausibility of the proposition and the difficulties encountered in attempts to substantiate it, we undertook in 1956 to formulate a theoretical rationale that would predict specific kinds of differences in illusion susceptibility, and we then embarked on a cross-cultural study that found them. The present chapter will be devoted to a discussion of that rationale and of related theoretical issues.

Most generally, our interest in cultural differences in perception relates to the nativist-empiricist controversy that has long existed in perceptual theorizing. As we stated when the study was proposed:

Not only will the findings be of interest to those concerned with the comparative study of culture, they will also contribute to the theory of perception, particularly with respect to the role of experience. Currently there are a number of lines of development in the theory of visual perception which create a new interest in the nativist-empiricist controversy. There is new evidence which emphasizes the role of early visual experience in setting the base for adult perceptual processes. Clearly relevant to this topic would be findings on perceptual illusions among peoples whose visual worlds are quite different from that of the European [Herskovits, Campbell, and Segall, 1956, p. 2].

As this excerpt implies, data from the psychological laboratory that support an empiricistic theory of perception enhance the expectation of finding cross-cultural differences in perception. Conversely, of course, cross-cultural data that demonstrate perceptual differences would provide support for an empiricistic theory and weaken the nativists' case. Allport and Pettigrew referred to the nativist-empiricist issue in their report of research with Zulu children and the rotating trapezoidal illusion:

> To gain light on this dispute psychologists have often asked, "How about primitive peoples?" If we can find a tribe or a culture where relevant past experience can be ruled out, we can then determine whether the perception resembles that of Western peoples. If it does so, then the argument for nativism is presumably stronger.

Then Allport and Pettigrew added a caveat:

> . . . we do not believe that comparative perceptual studies on Western and on primitive peoples can solve this particular riddle [Allport and Pettigrew, 1957, p. 105].

While the caveat is appropriate, we would stress the relevance of data like those collected by Allport and Pettigrew to the central issue of the nativist-empiricist controversy, namely, the manner and extent of experiential influence on visual perception. Although cross-cultural data may not settle the issue, there are classes of such data that could substantially illuminate the problem. In the study manual we prepared for our fieldworkers we summarized our conceptualization of the problem as follows:

> If the cross-cultural differences in extent of illusion are found, the initial explanatory effort would be focused on differences in the usual

visual environment. For this reason, it is very important that details of the visual environment of each group be recorded on the form provided. Such details include the typical form of houses, the maximum distance at which objects are typically viewed, whether or not vistas over land or water occur, typical games, skills, artistic training, and other aspects of culture that might affect habits of inference from line drawings.

Two cultural factors are to be of particular significance for this investigation. In the carpentered western world such a great proportion of artifacts are rectangular that the habit of interpreting obtuse and acute angles as rectangular surfaces extended in space is a very useful one. Such an inference pattern would generate many of the line illusions here tested. In a culture where rectangles did not dominate, this habit might be absent. Similarly, elliptical retinal images are interpreted as circles extended in the third dimension. This inference pattern might be absent where objects are truly elliptical in cross-section.

Another cultural factor which might be related to illusions is two-dimensional representation of three-dimensional objects. Perspective drawing is a most pervasive feature of Euroamerican culture. It is a substantial feature of the visual world from childhood on. Children in this culture from a very early age attempt to make representations of this kind themselves. The technique or conventions involved may be related to the habits of inference which some illusions illustrate [Herskovits, Campbell, and Segall, 1956, pp. 2–3].

It should now be clear that from the start our general theoretical position has been that if cross-cultural differences in responses to perceptual illusions were found, they would reflect learned differences in perceptual habits. Thus the discovery of such differences would lend support to an empiricist theory of visual perception. Let us now spell out this position in detail.

THE NATIVIST-EMPIRICIST CONTROVERSY

Two decades ago, Boring termed the nativist-empiricist controversy "one of the two dreariest topics in experimental psychology" (1942, p. 28). However, his review of the topic indicated that no matter how fruitless the controversy may have appeared at times during its long history—particularly as manifested in the speculative efforts of the eighteenth and nineteenth centuries—many issues involved in theories of space-perception had not yet been fully resolved. Subsequent reviews of the controversy, provided by Gibson (1950), Hilgard (1951), Allport (1955), and Hochberg (1957), among others, make it clear that however dull or fruitless the controversy may have seemed, it is not dead. Moreover, as Hochberg notes,

> the perception of space, depth, and distance is frequently treated in the textbooks as a solved problem. Despite the fact that some restricted areas of precise and applicable knowledge exist, however, the basic problems in this area are completely *unsolved* and we must launch a fresh attack on what is historically one of the oldest of the systematic problems of psychology [1957, p. 83].

In 1950 Gibson introduced his treatment of visual perception by stating that

> ... the perception of what has been called space is the basic problem of all perception. Space perception is ... the first problem to consider, without a solution for which other problems remain unclear. That a solution is lacking, most psychologists would agree.

And in very concise terms Gibson states the problem.

> The physical environment has three dimensions; it is projected by light on a sensitive surface of two dimensions; it is perceived nevertheless in three dimensions. How can the lost third dimension be restored in perception? This is the problem of how we perceive space [Gibson, 1950, p. 2].

Allport points out that the nativist-empiricist controversy, as it applies to space-perception, is not an all-or-none issue.

> Scarcely anyone, now or earlier, would be found on the nativist side with respect to all the phenomena of perception [Allport, 1955, p. 86].

It is also true that scarcely any of the modern-day empiricists would entirely rule out certain perceptual potentials that seem to be part of the human biological endowment. Hilgard, in an advocacy of the role of learning in perception, admits that

> . . . the side of the nativists in the argument has a good deal of support [1951, p. 96].

Our view on this general issue represents essentially a "moderate" empiricist position, one that hypothesizes that the pattern of visual experiences in the lifetime of a person can *modify* his perceptions of objects in space. These modifications might not be drastic, but they are subtly manifested in tendencies to perceive the world in accord with pervasively learned expectations. Such phenomena as size- and shape-constancies and the distorted room phenomena (Ames, 1949; Cantril, 1950; Kilpatrick, 1952; Ittelson, 1960) seem to us, as to their originators, obvious examples of perceptual tendencies shaped largely by experience.

This view seems to us to be shared by most contemporary theorists of perception, even by those, e.g., Gibson (1950, 1960) and Pratt (1950), who perhaps give less weight to experience than most. For example, Gibson, while emphasizing that many perceptual responses do not require prior learning, acknowledges that experience contributes to perception:

> The perceiver who has observed the world from many points of view, as we say, is literally one who has traveled about and used his eyes. That is, he has looked at the furniture of the earth from many station points. The more he has done so, the more likely it is that he has isolated the invariant properties of things—the permanent residue of the changing perspectives [Gibson, 1960, p. 220].

Closest to the view that has shaped the present research is that of Brunswik and the Ames group, for whom perception is "the process of apprehending probable significances." Allport has succinctly summarized this position as follows: In the process of perceiving an object, the past experience of the organism plays an important part. Basic to the perception process ". . . is the fact that the organism has built up certain *assumptions* about the world in which it lives. These assumptions, which are usually *unconscious* [result in] the attaching of significances to cues" (1955, pp. 278–279).

Our general theoretical position can perhaps best be epitomized by Brunswik's phrase "ecological cue validity" (Brunswik and Kamiya, 1953; Brunswik, 1956).[1] It involves some general assumptions that Brunswik summarized as "probabilistic functionalism." It is hypothesized that the visual system is functional in general, although not in every specific utilization. The modes of operation are what they are because they are useful in the statistical average of utilizations.

When this is applied to optical illusions, it is hypothesized that the illusion taps a process that is in general functional, although it is misleading in the particular instance because of "ecological unrepresentativeness"; that is, this type of situation is unlike the general run of situations to which the process is functionally adapted and adaptive. Thus, in the illusion of induced movement, it is ecologically unusual for the great bulk of the visual environment to move while a small segment remains fixed. If one creates such a situation artificially, a compelling illusion, or mistaken judgment, occurs. For some constant errors or illusions, we accept nonfunctional explanations, for example, the attribution of perceptual errors to the coarse grain of the retinal mosaic of rods and cones, the finite speed of neural transmission, etc. But illusions of both types require an hypothesis as to why they should be so, and for complex total processes of the kind under study here, the anatomical-limitation approach is not judged to be plausible.

It might be argued that the term "perceptual illusion" is essentially meaningless since all perception, insofar as it is not strictly stimulus determined, is "illusory." It might be further argued that since the sensing organism functions as a transducer, so that the

---

[1]Note here a difference in our use of the term "ecological" from that common in anthropology. Following Brunswik, and in some consistency with sociological and evolutionary theory, we use the term to refer to the total environment, including both man-made artifacts and the natural environment of flora, fauna, and geological structure. Anthropological usage restricts the term "ecology" to the latter.

attributes of sensations and of external stimuli are never identical, perception is *never* stimulus determined. On the basis of a similar line of thought, Mueller (in press) argues that it is misleading to speak of perceptual illusions as if they constituted a separate class of visual-response phenomena. Boring, too, has argued (1942, p. 245) that when the general laws of perception are known, the illusions also will be understood. Still, we find the concept of "illusion" useful in designating those infrequent cases in which one mode of cognition (e.g., unaided vision) is persistently, and in a constant direction, in disagreement with the collective product of other modes of cognition, such as measurement, superimposition, vision aided by reduction screens, and sighting along tilted surfaces. Although it is little remarked upon, in the great bulk of cases visual estimates of magnitude are useful and nondeceptive. Error of fine degree is, of course, present, but by emphasizing systematic bias, or constant error, the psychologist readily distinguishes between problems of illusion and problems of acuity.

Historically, there has been great concern with various geometric figures and with "illusory," or nonveridical, perceptual responses to them. As Boring pointed out (1942, p. 239), "a knowledge of the principles governing the abnormal perception of extent (as in the case of perceptual illusions) would certainly help with the understanding of the normal cases."

Comprehensive reviews of various theoretical accounts of the best-known illusions are available (e.g., Sanford, 1908; Woodworth, 1938; Boring, 1942; Osgood, 1953; Allport, 1955; and others). Two of the accounts described in these reviews are exceedingly relevant to the present research. Brentano (1892, 1893) thought that a significant feature of the Müller-Lyer figure (Figure 2, facing p. 86) was the fact that the context segments are made up of lines forming acute and obtuse angles with the horizontal comparison segments. He argued that acute angles tend to be overestimated and obtuse angles underestimated and that such misestimates of the angles in the Müller-Lyer figure would result in a compression or expansion of the horizontal segments.

The rationale for including the Müller-Lyer figure in our research, as will be made clear (pp. 84–86), is based upon a theoretical interpretation that bears some similarity to Brentano's
explanation of this figure. Boring (1942) describes another explanation, attributed to Thiery (1895, 1896), which perhaps comes even
closer to the view that will be presented below. According to Boring, Thiery referred the phenomenon to perspective. He saw the
illusion in the third dimension, as a sawhorse. The acute-angled
figure would be a sawhorse with the legs extending away from the
observer and with the back near and hence relatively small,
whereas the obtuse-angled figure would be a sawhorse with the
legs approaching the observer, with the belly far away and therefore relatively large.

The view that optical illusions are products of the same processes that mediate normal visual achievements is, as we have just
seen, not at all peculiar to Brunswik. It is at least implicit in the
bulk of older discussions of optical illusions, including those of
Brentano and Thiery cited above. A modern revival of these older
empiricist perspective theories emphasizes the role of perceptual
constancy and, in particular, constancy scaling as factors contributing to the optical illusions (Tausch, 1954; Holst, 1957; Gregory,
1962, 1963; and Green and Hoyle, 1963). For example, Gregory
(1962, p. 16) argues that the mechanism of constancy scaling
"could produce distortion if it were misplaced, and that all the
known illusions have features which commonly indicate depth by
perspective. It is also clear in every case that the illusions go the
right way; those parts of the figures which would normally be
further away in 3-D space appear too large in the illusion figures."

Moreover, the psychologist and physiologist of the visual system
are keenly aware of the inferential, hypothetical, fallible, problematic nature of perception. External objects are in no sense
directly known, and any simple visual system is equivocal in that it
gives identical readings for widely disparate external events. Brunswik, for example, emphasized that actual, functional visual systems, in confronting this problem, use many cues applied in

combination. He emphasized that even cues of only partial, or probabilistic, validity would be useful in reducing equivocality in complex, cue-rich natural settings. Optical-illusion situations, however, typically lack this richness and hence help to isolate a single cue, but under conditions not typical of its normal utilization. In a prototypic study, therefore, Brunswik and Kamiya (1953) attempted to compute—from analyses of photographs of typical scenes of numerous discrete objects—the "ecological cue validity" of various Gestalt principles of visual organization. These cues (proximity, similarity, continuity, and so forth) have been demonstrated by the Gestalt psychologists to contribute to the organization of elements of the visual field. They are interpreted by Brunswik to be cues as to which sense-data segments belong together as cosymptoms of a single object. He finds cue validity correlations on the order of .20, and judges that these low but statistically significant, functionally dependent cue validities are useful, and in fact used, in the visual inference system.

Thus, our theoretical system hypothesizes (1) *that the visual perceptual system uses numerous cues of low and probabilistic (but still positive) validity,* and (2) *that optical illusions demonstrate the function of normally useful cues but provide atypical visual performance settings.* In other words, psychological factors affect the probability that certain inference tendencies rather than others will be acquired and that under certain unusual conditions these tendencies will lead to nonveridical perceptions. So-called geometric illusions provide examples of such unusual conditions.

This orientation obviously calls for specific hypotheses of ecology-function relationships. In the long run the theory must point to the specific ecological cue validities being misexploited in each optical illusion. This task is an unfinished one. Its incompleteness is the major source of weakness in the explanations offered here. However, *afunctional* explanations are regarded as weaker and as implicitly invoking "inexplicability" as an explanation. Chance, coincidence, and so forth are plausible on occasion, but not for learned functions based upon numerous opportunities for differential reinforcement nor even for innate functions involving many complex genetic factors.

The next step in our reasoning is a direct extension of the ecological cue validity theory: (3) *if human groups differ in their visual inference tendencies, it is because their visual environments differ,* that is, the cues in their ecologies have different validities. Accepting this implication leads us to regard our theoretical task as unfinished until we can point to ecological differences that functionally relate to the perceptual inference differences. We assume that neither by learning nor by genetic selection would populations have come to differ on these perceptual processes unless the ecological validities of the processes differed.

It should be noted that owing to modern genetic theory it is no longer possible to explain "inexplicable" group differences, when plausible environmental explanations are lacking, by attributing them to arbitrary genetic differences. Most manifest structural features and their related functional processes are determined by scores of genes. On these genes, each human population is heterozygous and differs from other populations only in relative allele or gene frequencies. These specific gene frequencies are maintained by selection pressures. Populations of the size we are concerned with do not differ from one another unless selection pressures differ. Selection-pressure differences would result where different environments made different structures and processes optimal. In the case of the perceptual processes under study, this would require theories as to how ecological differences made different perceptual functions optimal. Such theories would likewise be useful in explaining learned differences, for the ecology that edits mutation and genetic recombination is usually also the ecology that edits the trial-and-error processes of learning, unless the ecology has been undergoing rapid change.

Thus today, both empiricist theories, based upon a learning process, and hereditary theories, based upon a mutation-recombination selection process, require functional theories relating process to ecology. The "inexplicability" of a group difference is no longer an argument favoring the choice of a hereditary as opposed to an empiricist or learning explanation.

The final step in our preliminary argument is (4) *that given a hereditary and a learning explanation that both fit the data, the learning (empiricist) explanation is the more plausible.* Since the experimental psychology evidence on perception that justifies this position is not generally known, it seems fitting to sample the literature here. Two classes of studies are involved, with both human and animal data for each.

There are, first, the studies of effects of the lack of visual experience in infancy. For human beings, these studies come from cases where surgical operations have given sight to those who have lacked it from birth or early infancy (Latta, 1904; Senden, 1932; Hebb, 1949; and London, 1960.) These studies uniformly report that the interpretation of visual data has to be learned; that even for the identification of simple shapes familiar to touch, there is no matching of visual outline with tactual outline until a process of looking-while-touching has taken place; that even when objects can be identified as discrete, the perception of distance is lacking, with most objects being seen as near. Without learning, then, the visual data provide a "blooming, buzzing confusion," to use William James's famous phrase.

As for animals, Riesen's (1947, 1958) studies of chimpanzees show that experimentally induced infantile restrictions of visual input (total absence of light stimulation or absence of form stimuli) produce comparable defects, and defects that are typically overcome more slowly than those in humans. More recent work with animals shows that, over and above the presence or absence of visual stimuli, early experience with *particular* visual objects and forms facilitates the subsequent perceptual discrimination of these forms (e.g., Gibson, Walk, Pick, and Tighe, 1959).

The most recent account of the postoperative behavior of a human adult who was blind, or near-blind, almost from birth was provided by Gregory and Wallace (1963). We cite it at some length, for it is a particularly fascinating case history, with findings of considerable relevance to the present topic. The patient, possessing preoperative vision "not sufficiently good to be of any material use to him for orientation or recognition of objects . . . appears from all accounts to have led the life of a blind person throughout his life" (Gregory and Wallace, 1963, pp. 12–13). At the age of 52, two successful corneal transplants provided him with vision. He was first examined by the authors 48 days after the first operation (the second had also been completed). Subsequently, until the patient's death 19 months later, numerous observations and tests were made. The results of these observations led the authors to conclude that this patient acquired visual perception far more rapidly than did earlier cases reviewed by Senden (1932), and the authors thus reopen the question of just how much *learning to perceive* is a factor in the postoperative adjustment of such patients.

Be that as it may, certain of the authors' observations point to the conclusion that numerous visual inference habits readily detected in normal-sighted persons were not part of the patient's postoperative behavioral repertory. We will sample a few of these.

When he sat down he would not look round or scan the room with his eyes; indeed he would generally pay no attention to visual objects unless his attention were called to them [Gregory and Wallace, 1963, p. 16. This observation was made during the initial interview with the patient, 48 days after his sight was restored].

We were even more surprised when he named correctly a magazine we had with us. It was in fact *Everybody's* (for January 17th, 1959) and had a large picture of two musicians dressed in striped pullovers. *Although he named the magazine correctly, he could make nothing of the picture* [p. 16, our italics].

At the time we first saw him, he did not find faces "easy" objects. He did not look at a speaker's face, and made nothing of facial expressions [p. 17].

As in previous cases (Latta, 1904), he experienced marked scale distortion when looking down from a high window [p. 17].

It is also worth noting that reflections fascinated him and continued to do so for at least a year after the operation [p. 18].

Although the patient showed a striking ability to recognize

objects already familiar to him by touch—and thus displayed considerable, and in certain respects surprising, bimodal transfer—it is clear from several of the authors' observations that certain normal perceptual abilities were very likely not present for some time after the operation. Most notable is the suggestion implicit in these observations that the ability to interpret the two-dimensional representation of objects was not present immediately upon the patient's acquisition of sight. He also apparently was unable to perceive depth in real space accurately, at least under certain conditions.

Of greatest relevance to our present topic are the patient's responses to several tests of illusion susceptibility. On the Hering illusion, the Zollner illusion, the Poggendorf illusion, the Necker cube illusion, and the Müller-Lyer illusion, all administered during the second postoperative month, the patient displayed either no illusion susceptibility at all or a degree of susceptibility considerably less marked than that typical of normal observers. On the other hand, with the Ames distorted room, the only illusion in this set that is literally three dimensional, the patient displayed what appears to be normal illusion susceptibility. The authors' comment on the two-dimensional optical illusions and the patient's responses to them is particularly instructive.

> The illusion figures presented here seem to produce distortion of visual space by evoking constancy which is inappropriate to the flat plane (visible as a textured surface) on which the figures lie. On this view, we might say that the anomalous results obtained for S. B. show that these figures did not serve to evoke constancy scaling for him, and thus the illusions were absent [p. 19].

We are impressed with Gregory's and Wallace's illusion data and their inference that the patient may have lacked the opportunity to learn the perceptual habits that underlie the illusions.

The second line of research pointing to an empiricist explanation for cue-utilization differences involves the experimental disarrangement of normal visual input by distorting lenses. The oldest continuing research on this concerns inverted retinal images (Stratton, 1896; Ewert, 1930; Snyder and Pronko, 1952). In sum, these studies show rapid improvement of performance during prolonged wearing of the inverting lenses, disruption of performance when the lenses are removed, and, for the first and last studies at least, occasional loss of phenomenal awareness of visual image inversion. A similar study with rhesus monkeys (Foley, 1938) showed both the improvement of performance and its disruption after lens removal, although performance improvement with the lenses was perhaps not as marked as for human subjects. Considering the short periods of visual experience involved (8 days, 15 days, and 29 days for the humans; 7 days for the monkeys), these studies show a remarkable degree of plasticity in the visual system.

Other research involves lenses providing less drastic disturbances, for example, the curvature of straight lines; displacement of images right or left, near or far; segmentation of the visual field by split-color lenses; etc. (Gibson, 1933; Kohler, 1951, as reported in Hochberg, 1957; Held and Schlank, 1959; Held and Bossom, 1961). These studies show adaptation occurring within an hour, with the phenomenal visual field returning completely to normal; the subsequent removal of the lenses is accompanied by illusory distortions complementary to those that the lenses originally produced. It is Held's view that the achievement of eye-hand coordination under these conditions requires active eye-hand coordination experience. Held and Bossom (1961) emphasize the similarity between these results and those of the infantile-deprivation literature and the uniform evidence of greater plasticity in humans than in lower animals.

A final relevant line of evidence comes from the Gestalt psychologists themselves, who have tended in general to be advocates of the nativist position. In research on "figural aftereffects," i.e., distortion in the perception of the position and size of lines and dots following prolonged fixation of other figures, aftereffects persisting for months have been found to result from inspection times amounting to less than a few hours (Köhler and Wallach, 1944; Köhler and Fishback, 1950a, 1950b).

The visual perception of objects distributed in space comes to us with such vivid directness and clarity that it is hard to imagine that vision is affected by learning. The evidence provided by the research cited here shows that naïve introspection, or phenomenal absolutism, is wrong; that in fact, the visual "given" is articulated, in general and in detail, by learned inference systems.

SPECIFIC HYPOTHESES BASED ON THE ECOLOGICAL CUE VALIDITY CONCEPT

Thus far, our explanatory efforts have remained at a fairly general level. The basic line of argument has included the following concepts: ecological cue validity; multiple-cue-utilization under probabilistic levels of validity; ecological differences corresponding to cue-utilization differences; and higher plausibility for learning than for hereditary explanations of cue-utilization differences. In what follows we state our specific hypotheses as to how ecological differences might relate to visual-inference differences. At this more specific level we offer three hypotheses on: (1) *the carpentered world*, (2) *the foreshortening of receding horizontals*, and (3) *symbolizing three dimensions in two*. In this context, we can then predict cross-cultural differences in susceptibility to several geometric illusions.

THE CARPENTERED-WORLD HYPOTHESIS

From 1880 to 1910, when visual line illusions were a principal preoccupation of the most active psychologists of Europe and America, the dominant interpretation was that they were by-products of a tendency to see the lines as representing three-dimensional extent. Sanford (1908) is particularly thorough on the subject and may be taken to represent this literature and this interpretation:

> The tendency to see things spatially is so inveterate that a moderate suggestion of perspective is sufficient to introduce differences in apparent distance and so of apparent size. . . . Certain arrangements of

lines tend . . . to take on a three-dimensional interpretation. This may happen with oblique lines in drawings on paper. . . . This tendency to perceive oblique angles as perspective pictures of right angles is perhaps connected with the tendency to overestimate small angles, and underestimate large ones [pp. 215–217].

Our version of this hypothesis can best be described by applying it to the Sander parallelogram, an example of which is shown in Figure 1. For this drawing, the well-established tendency—at least of Western or Westernized respondents—is to judge the diagonal on the respondent's left as longer than it really is. This bias is understandable if one perceives a nonorthogonal parallelogram drawn on a flat surface as the representation of a rectangular surface extended in space. Given such a tendency, it is clear that the represented *distance* covered by the left diagonal is greater than the represented distance covered by the right diagonal.

A tendency such as this constitutes a habit of inference that has great ecological validity—and great functional utility—in highly carpentered environments. Western societies provide environments replete with rectangular objects; these objects, when projected on the retina, are represented by nonrectangular images. For people living in carpentered worlds, the tendency to interpret obtuse and acute angles in retinal images as deriving from rectangular objects is likely to be so pervasively reinforced that it becomes automatic and unconscious relatively early in life. For those living where man-made structures are a small portion of the visual environment and where such structures are constructed without benefit of carpenters' tools (saw, plane, straight edge, tape measure, carpenter's square, spirit level, plumb bob, chalk line, surveyor's sight, etc.), straight lines and precise right angles are a rarity. As a result, the inference habit of interpreting acute and obtuse angles as right angles extended in space would not be learned, at least not as well.

The application of this line of reasoning to the Müller-Lyer illusion is somewhat more complicated. We again assume, however, that among persons raised in a carpentered world there

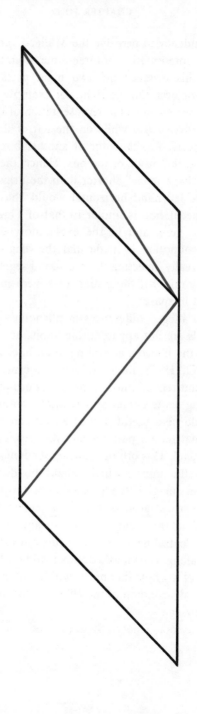

Figure 1   The Sander parallelogram illusion

would be a tendency to perceive the Müller-Lyer figure, shown in Figure 2, as a representation of three-dimensional objects extended in space. In this instance the two main parts of the drawing represent two objects. On the right, for example, if the horizontal segment were perceived as the representation of the edge of a box, it would be a *front edge;* while on the left, if the horizontal segment were perceived as the edge of another box, it would be the *back edge* along the inside of the box. Hence, the right-hand horizontal would "have to be" shorter than the drawing makes it out to be, and the left-hand horizontal would "have to be" longer. This line of speculation is similar to that of Thiery (1895). In the example given here, and in the explanatory device offered by Thiery, the assumption is made that the diagonal segments are perceived as "really" meeting the horizontal segments at 90-degree angles, as they might if those diagonals were meant to represent lines extended in space.

Even if the alleged differences in phenomenal distance of the two horizontals are not apparent, the habits of inference involved may generate the illusion, according to an interpretation given by Brentano (1892, 1893). Brentano saw the central process in the Müller-Lyer and related illusions as one of orthogonalizing angles, of exaggerating acute angles and reducing obtuse angles. Such a tendency would be a useful part of an inference system in which two-dimensional retinal patterns and pictures were interpreted as three dimensional. This orthogonalizing tendency would introduce distortions in the figure, which would be distributed over all parts. One can imagine the process as a turning of the diagonals into the vertical around their own centers, thus compressing the horizontal in this figure $\longleftrightarrow$ and stretching it in this $\succ\!\!-\!\!-\!\!-\!\!-\!\!\prec$. Central nervous system processes in which the extension of a line along its own axis occurs readily, while the horizontal displacement of a whole line meets with resistance, would provide a basis for this distribution of the effects of the distortional process of orthogonalizing.

While Brentano, Thiery, Sanford, and the others were not

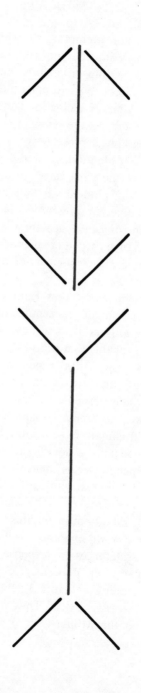

Figure 2 The Müller-Lyer illusion

aware of and were not attempting to explain group differences, their mode of interpreting the "normal case" provides a specific basis for anticipating group differences under the general theory of ecological cue validity. We can make this theory more explicit by stating the ideal kinds of ecological data for testing the hypothesis. One could photograph the views of regard of children to get a sample of photographs representative of all waking hours, seasons, and age levels. Identifying all the junctures of lines, one would then compute the percentages of acute and obtuse angles on the surface of the photograph that had been generated by right angles in the objects represented (some of the angles would, of course, represent objective acuteness and obtuseness). Crude estimates of the relative carpenteredness or relative rectangularity could be made for the environments of different cultural groups (see below, Chapter 5).

We can in general assert that European and American city dwellers have a much higher percentage of rectangularity in their environments than any residents of non-Europeanized cultures. It also seems highly probable that within the United States, or within Europe, or within Africa, rural residents live in less carpentered visual environments than urban ones (even if their houses and furnishings are equally carpentered) because they are out of doors more of the time. On similar grounds, it seems probable that residents of a cold climate have a more carpentered visual environment than residents of a hot climate if their climate leads the former group to spend more of their time indoors. And within the non-Europeanized cultures studied in this research, we would expect square-house cultures to be more rectangular in visual environment than round-house cultures.

This carpentered-world hypothesis is the basis of our predictions of cross-cultural differences in response to the Sander parallelogram and Müller-Lyer illusions. For a perspective drawing included in our materials (Figure 3), the same line of reasoning would hold, but to a lesser extent. Thus, for two figures, the Sander parallelogram and the Müller-Lyer figure, and in part for the perspective drawing, we would predict on the basis of the carpentered-world hypothesis that people who live in non-Western environments would be *less* susceptible than Western peoples to the illusions typically noted with these figures.[2]

THE FORESHORTENING OF RECEDING HORIZONTALS

By this awkward title we designate the relatively greater foreshortening of those lines in the horizontal plane that extend away from the observer more or less *parallel* to his line of regard (in comparison, equally long lines in the horizontal plane that are more or less *transverse* to his line of regard appear as much less shortened). Consider the view of a sidewalk one yard wide and marked off in squares one yard long. Look first at the square at your feet. Now look at a square 50 yards away. In terms of retinal image (or extent on the surface of a photograph), while all dimensions of the square are reduced in the 50-yard case, the edges parallel to the line of regard are foreshortened, that is, they are proportionately shorter, in relation to their actual length, than the transverse edges.

Woodworth (1938, p. 645) states the theory concisely: ". . . a short vertical line in a drawing may represent a relatively long horizontal line extending away from the observer. The horizontal-vertical illusion can be explained by supposing the vertical to represent such a foreshortened horizontal line." Sanford (1908, p. 238) cites Hering (1861–64, p. 355) and Lipps (1891, p. 221) as

---

[2]Ames, in his explanation of the illusory oscillation of the rotating trapezoidal window, employs an hypothesis that also places emphasis on the carperteredness of the environment.

In his past experience the observer, in carrying out his purposes, has on innumerable occasions had to take into account and act with respect to rectangular forms, e.g., going through doors, locating windows, etc. On almost all such occasions, except in the rare case when his line of sight was normal to the door or window, the image of the rectangular configuration formed on his retina was trapezoidal. He learned to interpret the particularly characterized retinal images that exist when he looks at doors, windows, etc., as rectangular forms. Moreover, he learned to interpret the particular degree of trapezoidal distortion of his retinal images in terms of the positioning of the rectangular form to his particular viewing point [Ames, 1951, p. 14].

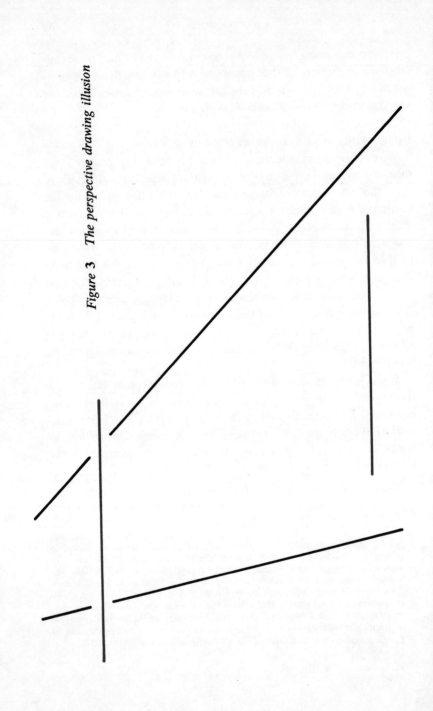

Figure 3   The perspective drawing illusion

hypothesizing "an unconscious allowance for foreshortening, acquired through preponderating experience with squares lying in planes inclined with regard to the plane of vision."

To this theory we add the observation that such an inference habit would have varying cue validities in varying ecologies. Let us consider the most valid extreme—a man living without a house on a flat plain devoid of trees, posts, or poles. Into this plain, furrows have been plowed. For this man the only source of verticals on the retinal image are furrows in the horizontal plane extending away from him. These receding horizontals parallel to his line of regard are much more foreshortened than the transverse horizontals. For such a person there would be great ecological validity in the inference habit of interpreting vertical retinal extensions as greatly foreshortened lines in the horizontal plane extending along the line of regard. This person should be maximally subject to the horizontal-vertical illusions (Figures 4 and 5).

Such an inference habit would have much less utility for the dweller in a rain forest or jungle, away from vistas over water or land, in which the largest real surfaces in the visual regard are, in fact, vertical, with tree trunks and hanging vines the commonest source of retinal verticals. Dwellers in canyon bottoms are in a similar ecology—as would be one who grew up in a courtyard surrounded by the towering walls of apartments if the tendency of apartment-house areas to have long straight streets did not keep them from this extreme. For most regions, rural residents should have a greater degree of susceptibility to the horizontal-vertical illusion than urban residents. In comparable out-of-doors environments with predominantly open fields, warm-climate residents should be more susceptible than cold-climate residents. (Quantitative scorings from photographs would again be required for determinate statements.)

Most important, the cross-cultural differences to be expected for the horizontal-vertical illusion are not identical to those expected for the three other illusions discussed above.

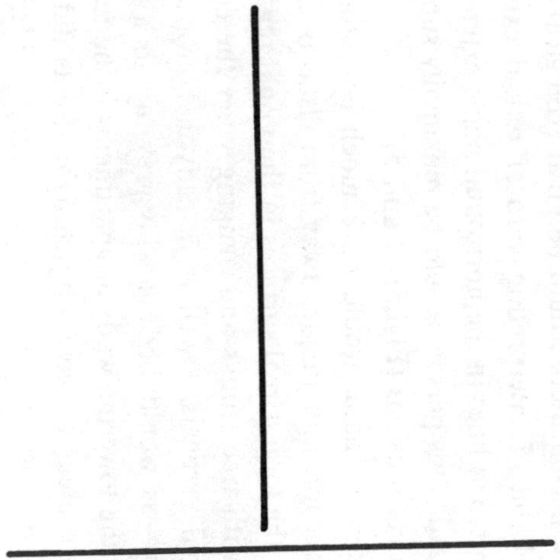

Figure 4 The horizontal-vertical illusion (⊥)

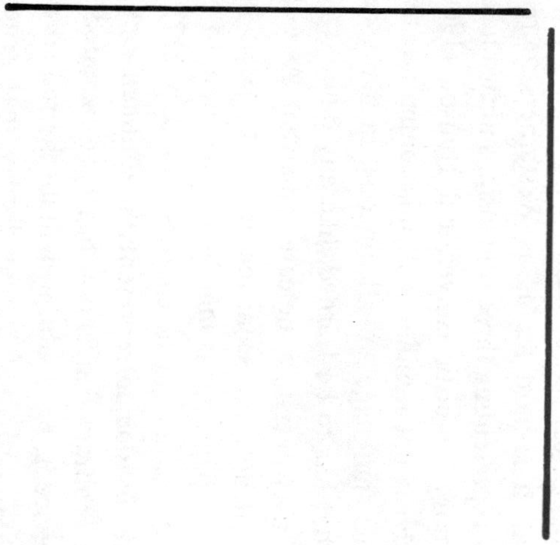

Figure 5 The horizontal-vertical illusion (⌐)

SYMBOLIZING THREE DIMENSIONS IN TWO

Another dominant ecological factor relevant to the line illusions relates to the pervasive use of symbols on paper in many societies. While most of this symbolization is connected with the representation of language, from the very beginning much of it has been employed for a more iconic representation of space, as in maps and figures of persons, animals, and other objects. Within such representational drawing, an increasingly dominant portion over the last thousand years has involved the deliberate effort to represent three-dimensional spatial arrays on the two-dimensional surface of paper, canvas, or wall.

To repeat, it is hard for us as Westerners to realize that the tradition of representing three dimensions in two has the character of an arbitrary linguistic convention. Hudson (1960) has shown that one who is not familiar with this communicative intent does not find this "language" at all obvious. In many respects, it is a language that has to be learned, like any other.

But this may overstate the case somewhat. As Gibson correctly notes, ". . . it does not seem reasonable to assert that the use of perspective in paintings is merely a convention, to be used or discarded by the painter as he chooses" (1960, p. 227). What *is* arbitrary is the *decision* to represent three dimensions in two. Once this useful arbitrary convention has been invented, the optimally efficient device is, no doubt, to imitate the retinal display, to produce a two-dimensional frontal display that generates a retinal display most comparable to that generated by the three-dimensional display that is the topic of the message. Leonardo da Vinci's success in anticipating the photograph indicates how nonarbitrary his principles were. The arbitrariness equally present in painting and photography lies in the decision to represent three dimensions in two.

In the course of distinguishing between the visual field and the visual world, Gibson (1952, p. 149) has pointed to the influence of this cultural tradition:

The visual field . . . is simply the pictorial mode of visual perception, and it depends . . . not on conditions of stimulation but on conditions of attitude. The visual field is a product of the chronic habit of civilized men of seeing the world as a picture [1952, p. 149].

In a similar vein, Hochberg (1961) has emphasized the role of artists, from Leonardo da Vinci to Adelbert Ames, in developing our inventory of cues of depth perception.

This cultural convention relates to the present problem because of the way in which one learns to receive and to send such messages. Frequent exposure to pictures and picture books in childhood and the resultant learning to interpret perspective drawings and photographs are conditions that would contribute to the tendency to interpret acute and obtuse angles as right angles, and hence increase susceptibility to the Müller-Lyer illusion and the Sander parallelogram. (Depending upon the contents, picture experience might also affect the horizontal-vertical illusions, but we are not prepared to say how.) Traditions of nonrepresentational decoration on two-dimensional surfaces, on the other hand, can lead to inference habits of taking two-dimensional drawings "literally," of taking the surface lines in themselves as the "objects" of perceptual inference rather than as mere communicative indicators of three-dimensional objects not actually present. In cultures with such traditions, susceptibility to the Müller-Lyer illusion and the Sander parallelogram should be low.

Learning to communicate by this means, learning to draw good perspective drawings of boxes, tables, houses, etc., is an ecological condition of presumably *opposite* effect. The child's first efforts to draw the box in front of him are impeded by his compulsion to draw all of the angles as right angles. It is only by effort and training that he learns to note "what is in front of his eyes," that is, that several of the rectangular sides of the box are represented in the field of vision by obtuse and acute angles. The artist's devices, (for example, sighting across a pencil or brush held at arm's length to get the appropriate retinal-angle size) are techniques employed to overcome the distracting tendency to draw things as "we know they are" rather than "as they appear." As a result, artists are less subject to the constancy effects, or "phenomenal regression to the real object" (Thouless, 1932). Our inference is that they should also be less susceptible to the Müller-Lyer and Sander illusions, although as far as we know, this has not been tested.

Incidentally, it is on this ground of learning how to represent three dimensions in two that we would explain the universally noted lesser susceptibility to these two illusions of adults as compared with children (Wohlwill, 1960). This "superiority" of adults is, of course, supported by their quite general superiority in ability tasks of all kinds, their greater analytic skill, their greater compensation for known distortions, etc.

SUMMARY OF OUR ATTEMPTS TO EXPLAIN GEOMETRIC OPTICAL ILLUSIONS

1. The so-called optical illusions result, at least in part, from learned habits of inference that possess ecological cue validity.

2. In different physical and cultural environments, different habits of inference are likely to be acquired, reflecting the differing ecological validities.

3. For figures constructed of lines meeting in nonrectangular junctions, there will be a learned tendency among persons dwelling in carpentered environments to rectangularize those junctures, to perceive the figures in perspective, and to interpret them as two-dimensional representations of three-dimensional objects. Such a tendency produces, or at least enhances, the Müller-Lyer illusion and the Sander parallelogram illusion. Since the tendency is assumed to have more ecological validity for peoples in Western, or carpentered, environments, it is predicted that Western peoples

will be more susceptible to these illusions than peoples dwelling in uncarpentered environments.

4. The horizontal-vertical illusion results from a tendency to counteract the foreshortening of lines extending into space away from a viewer, so that the vertical in the drawing that is the stimulus for the illusion is interpreted as representing a longer line. Since the tendency has more ecological validity for peoples living mostly outdoors in open, spacious environments, it is predicted that such peoples will be *more* susceptible than Western peoples in urban environments. On the other hand, some non-Western groups should be *less* susceptible to the illusions, e.g., rain forest or canyon dwellers.

5. Learning to interpret drawings and photographs should enhance some of these illusions, whereas learning to produce drawings representing three dimensions should reduce the illusions.

5
Cross-Cultural Susceptibility to Visual Illusions: The Study Design

In contrast to most studies in the literature (see Chapters 2 and 3), the present one was designed to collect data in several localities with stimulus materials especially constructed to test a specific set of hypotheses (see Chapter 4). After the stimulus materials were prepared, they were distributed to some 20 colleagues, most of them ethnographers engaged in fieldwork for purposes other than those of this study, who in turn collected the data and returned them to us for analysis. These materials were administered between 1956 and 1961 to 13 samples of non-Western peoples, with total sample sizes ranging from 46 to 344, in 12 locations in Africa and one in the Philippines. In addition, responses to the same materials were collected from three samples of Western peoples—208 residents of a suburban community in the American Midwest, 44 South Africans of European descent living in Johannesburg, and 30 undergraduates in an American University.[1] In all, 1,878 respondent protocols were procured.

In order to provide a fair test of our predictions and the hypotheses from which they were derived, we sought samples of groups living under as broad a range of ecological conditions as possible. There were, however, obvious practical limitations to our data-collection efforts. Since we lacked the funds that would have been required to send research

[1]Following the six-year period 1956–61, several additional sets of data from non-Western societies were made available to us; these are described separately (pp. 200–204). Also, our materials have been employed from time to time in the laboratory; here, too, the most relevant data are reported (pp. 179–180, 181–183).

associates to selected areas of the world especially to administer our materials, we had to rely on the gracious cooperation of persons already scheduled to go into the field under other auspices. Partly because the center of our communications network was the Northwestern University Program of African Studies and partly because Africa was, at the time the study was conducted, an exceedingly popular site for anthropological fieldwork, the great bulk of our data comes from Africa. While we would have preferred to sample peoples from a more diverse set of regions, the environmental conditions represented in the samples available to us are sufficiently varied to permit an evaluation of the hypotheses.

A DESCRIPTION OF THE SAMPLES

Among the materials provided each of our colleagues in the field was a questionnaire designed to provide an inventory of the visual environment. Although it was an imperfect substitute for a systematically recorded motion picture record of typical indoor and outdoor scenes, this inventory nonetheless permitted the reporting of various details we believed were the most significant aspects of the natural and man-made environments. The questionnaire is reproduced in Appendix A.

Appendix A also contains a description of each group from whom data were collected. These descriptions, based on the completed questionnaires, contain the tribal designation, a convenient label for each sample, its geographic location, the name of the research associate responsible for collecting the data, and the total sample size. While the reader will wish to consult Appendix A for a detailed description of the samples, a few generalizations derived from this material are presented here.

1. Five samples (Fang, Bété, Ijaw, Dahomean children, and Hanunóo) live in rather dense, compressed environments that do not provide extended vistas; some of these groups, for example,

inhabit areas best described as tropical forests. Six samples (Senegal, Ankole, Toro, Suku, Songe, and Zulu) live in open savanna, where they enjoy broad, though somewhat irregular vistas. Three samples (Evanston, Northwestern University students, and South African Europeans) live in highly carpentered urban environments lacking the extended vistas of the savannas, but with frequent long, flat streets. One sample (Bushmen) inhabits a desert. Finally, one sample (mineboys) cannot be classified because we lack the requisite information.

2. Two samples (Zulu and Bushmen) live in circular houses; the Zulu live predominantly in round houses, although today as many as 25 per cent live in rectangular houses, and the Bushmen live in semicircular windbreaks of a temporary nature. All other non-Western samples live predominantly in rectangular houses of various degrees of carpenteredness. The three samples of Western peoples, of course, live in highly carpentered rectangular buildings.

3. Artwork representing three dimensions on a two-dimensional surface (murals, paintings, drawings) is produced by only three non-Western samples (Fang, Ijaw school children, Dahomean children). In the case of the Fang, it is reported that perspective techniques are *not* employed in two-dimensional drawings; and in the case of the two samples of school children, one can assume that they have had drawing experience in the classroom. Four samples (Ankole, Toro, Songe, and Bété) do not produce indigenous two-dimensional art, but here one can assume that examples of nonindigenous pictures are available to them. Among all other non-Western samples, not only is indigenous two-dimensional art lacking, but there is reason to believe that examples of nonindigenous drawings are relatively rare. For all the non-Western samples, however, it seems reasonable to assume that children, if schooled in a Western-influenced school system, have been exposed to two-dimensional pictures.

4. A considerable degree of rectangularity was noted in the furniture and other artifacts of all but four of the non-Western

samples (Zulu, Bushmen, Senegalese, and Hanunóo). Of these four, the Bushmen live in an environment in which rectangular objects are virtually nonexistent. In all cases, however, one can assume that the degree of rectangularity in the environment of these non-Western peoples falls far short of what it is in urban Western environments.

MATERIALS AND PROCEDURES

The stimulus materials were assembled in a compact 5" × 7" booklet printed on heavy washable paper to ensure their durability under tropical and other taxing conditions. Fifty of the 71 pages in the booklet were devoted to the stimulus materials themselves; the balance contained a discussion of the research for which the booklet had been designed, a detailed set of instructions for administration, and four preliminary stimuli to permit a check on each respondent's comprehension of the task.[2] To complete the package provided each research associate, printed record sheets were enclosed, as well as the questionnaire described above for establishing guidelines for a descriptive inventory of the environment.

The stimulus materials proper consisted of 50 drawings, each one an example of one of five figures constructed of straight lines, generally referred to as geometric illusions. The five figures are the Müller-Lyer illusion (12 exemplars), the Sander parallelogram (7 exemplars), two forms of the horizontal-vertical illusion (9 ⌐ -shaped drawings and 11 ⊥ -shaped drawings), and a simple perspective drawing (11 exemplars); one example of each illusion is shown in Figures 1 through 5 (pp. 85, 87, 90, 92 and 93). The booklet also contained six drawings of the Poggendorf illusion; this is reported on in Appendix B.

[2]The original 100 copies of the field manual (Herskovits, Campbell, and Segall, 1956) have been exhausted. A revised edition of the manual is in preparation at the Bobbs-Merrill Company, Inc.

A variation on the psychophysical method of constant stimuli —the use of color—was employed throughout this research. For each illusion set, the discrepancy in the lengths of the segments to be compared varied from drawing to drawing; and as each drawing was shown to a respondent, his task was simply to indicate which of the comparison segments was the longer. In order to minimize communication difficulties, the comparison segments in each drawing were printed in a color different from that of the context segments, or, where the figure consisted solely of two comparison segments (as in the two horizontal-vertical figures), they were printed in colors different from each other. Red and black were the colors used throughout. As a result of this arrangement, respondents could indicate their choice on each of the horizontal-vertical drawings by saying either *Red* or *Black*. For the other figures, choices were indicated by a response of either *Right* or *Left* (for the Müller-Lyer illusion and the Sander parallelogram) or *Top* or *Bottom* (for the perspective figure) in reply to the standard question, "Which of the two red lines is longer?"

An additional device was adopted in an effort to maximize communication with respondents in non-Western societies. Whereas in the traditionally used form of each illusion the segments of the drawings are all connected, each segment in the drawings used in the present study—except in the case of the Sander parallelogram items—was terminated about a millimeter short of a junction. This procedure, combined with the use of different colors for different segments, was adopted to ensure that when a questioner specified a line, the respondent would interpret that term as intended. It was felt necessary to take this precaution in order that respondents not compare more of the figure than was requested. For example, when the Müller-Lyer figure is usually presented, the "arrow-head" and "feather" segments are joined to the comparison segments; but if in any of the societies sampled in this research the term "line" implies anything more than a *straight line,* crucial misinterpretation of the task could occur. By

Table 1 Item Characteristics

Illusion	Page number	Longer segment	Illusion-supported response	Per cent discrepancy [a]
Müller-Lyer	5	Right	Left	27
	6	Left	Left	−2
	7	Left	Right	20
	8	Right	Left	25
	9	Right	Left	3
	10	Right	Left	38
	11	Left	Right	45
	12	Left	Right	10
	13	Right	Left	48
	14	Left	Right	14
	15	Left	Right	33
	16	Right	Right	−8
Horizontal-vertical (⌐)	17	Equal	Red	0
	18	Black	Red	35
	19	Black	Black	−11
	20	Black	Red	7
	21	Black	Black	28
	22	Red	Black	18
	23	Black	Red	9
	24	Black	Black	−6
	25	Red	Red	−8
Horizontal-vertical (⊥)	26	Red	Black	3
	27	Red	Red	−8
	28	Red	Black	11
	29	Red	Black	66
	30	Black	Red	46
	31	Black	Red	17
	32	Red	Black	53
	33	Black	Black	−4
	34	Equal	Black	0
	35	Black	Red	32
	36	Black	Red	21

Table **1** *(cont.)*

Illusion	Page number	Longer segment	Illusion-supported response	Per cent discrepancy[a]
Sander parallelogram	37	Right	Left	48
	38	Right	Left	75
	39	Right	Left	16
	40	Left	Left	−14
	41	Right	Left	32
	42	Right	Left	2
	43	Right	Left	21
Perspective Drawing	44	Top	Top	−10
	45	Bottom	Top	19
	46	Bottom	Top	40
	47	Equal	Top	0
	48	Bottom	Top	10
	49	Top	Top	−15
	50	Bottom	Top	29
	51	Bottom	Top	5
	52	Top	Top	−5
	53	Bottom	Top	49
	54	Bottom	Top	14

[a] The per cent discrepancy values shown here differ somewhat from those published in the manual. The printing technique resulted in inexact copy-matching, but the *intended* per cent discrepancy value of each item was published unmodified. The values shown here are correct.

separating the comparison segments from the context segments and by printing the comparison segments in a different color, correct interpretation of the task was made more likely.[3]

The discrepancies in length between the comparison segments, which varied from drawing to drawing, covered a broad range for each of the five illusions. This is evident in Table 1, where

[3]These modifications, of course, weakened the illusions somewhat. In a preliminary study done in 1956 with a sample of 20 American college students, the effect of the use of colors in the drawings was determined. This study is reported in Appendix C.

the per cent discrepancy for each drawing is shown, along with other characteristics.

"Per cent discrepancy" is defined as the percentage by which the segment that is usually underestimated (by Western subjects responding under typical laboratory conditions) is actually longer than the other segment. It was computed as the difference between the two segments, divided by the length of the usually overestimated segment. For example, in the Müller-Lyer drawing shown in Figure 2 (facing p. 86), where the horizontal segment to the right (65mm) is 5mm longer than the one on the left (60mm), the per cent discrepancy is +8. The range of discrepancies within each set of illusions was such that the typically underestimated segment was sometimes actually the shorter of the two (resulting in negative per cent discrepancies) and sometimes so much longer that the illusion would have to be more "potent" than ever reported in the literature if a respondent were to be induced into "seeing" it as shorter. For example, in the case of the Müller-Lyer drawings, the range of per cent discrepancy was from −8 to +48.

Table 1 shows, in addition to the per cent discrepancy for each drawing, its page number, the truly longer segment, and the usually overestimated segment (such responses are termed, for convenience, "illusion-supported responses," even in those instances in which the overestimated segment is actually longer). For each illusion set, the order of presentation of the drawings was determined by consulting a table of random numbers and then fixed. Thus the size of the discrepancy of the critical segments was not related to the order of presentation. Moreover, for the Müller-Lyer drawings, the position of the critical segments was varied in haphazard fashion from drawing to drawing so that response sets based on these irrelevant features—order and position—would not introduce an undetectable bias in the protocols.

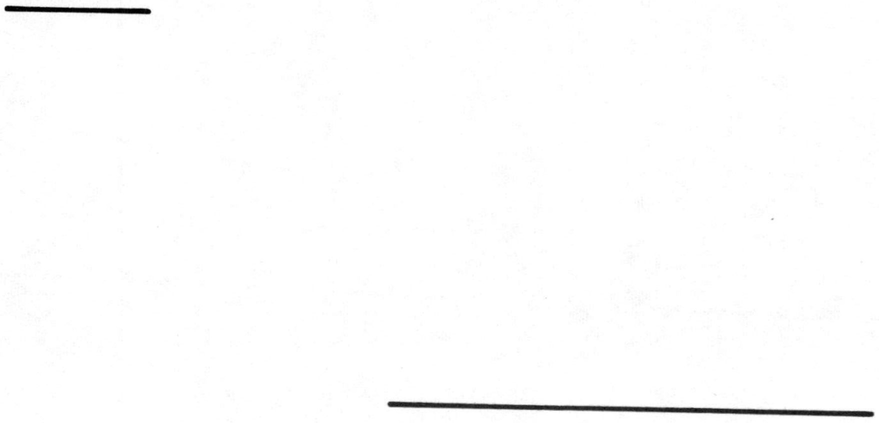

Figure 6   Comprehension check item 1

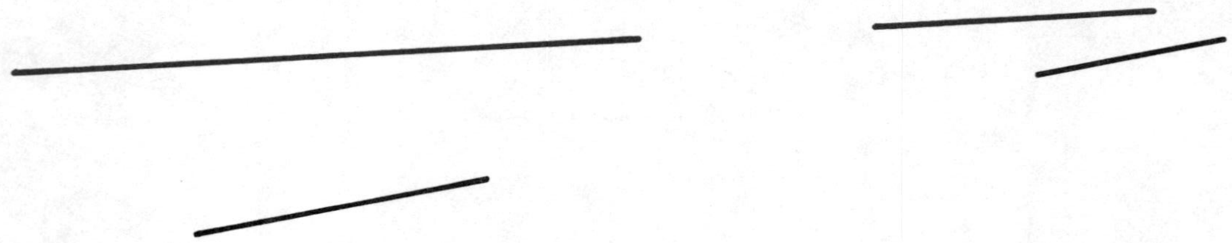

Figure 7 Comprehension check item 2

Figure **8** Comprehension check item 3

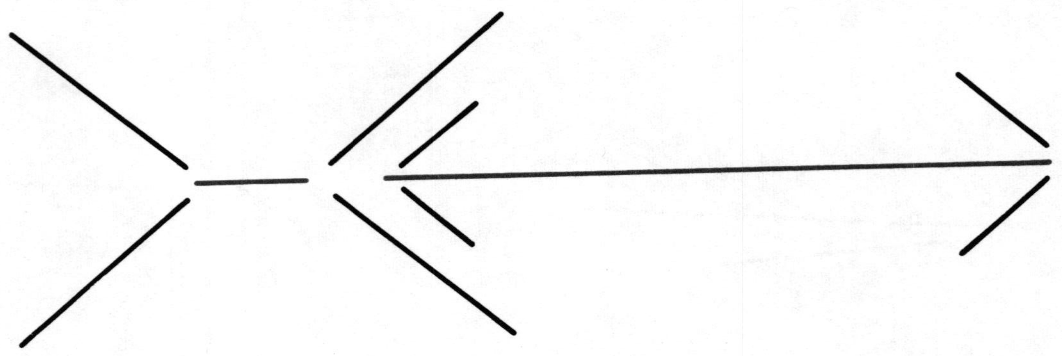

Figure 9 Comprehension check item 4

INSTRUCTIONS FOR THE ADMINISTRATION
OF THE MATERIALS

The following instructions were provided each research asso-ciate (Herskovits, Campbell, and Segall, 1956, pp. 4-6):

It is essential that the data be collected under as standardized conditions as possible, and that all deviations from these procedures be recorded. The location and dimensions of the working area should permit display of the figures at a distance of four feet from the re-spondent, at his eye level, and in a plane perpendicular to his line of vision. Lighting conditions should permit comfortable viewing of the drawings.

Since age and sex differences for the illusions are known to exist, sampling should be carefully controlled on these points. The goal should be to obtain a random sample of 25 males and 25 females ranging in age from 5 years to 11 years, and 25 males and 25 females ranging in age from 18 to 45 years. The sex and age of each respond-ent should be recorded, if possible.

The booklet and record sheets are arranged to enable display of the drawings in prescribed order, and immediate recording of each respondent's choice with each drawing.

Once rapport has been established, the experimenter should, insofar as cultural and semantic factors permit, conform to the following procedure:

Have respondent sit in appropriate position. Instruct him as fol-lows: *I am going to show you some drawings and ask you some ques-tions about them.* Show page 1 [see Figure 6]. *What is the color of this line?* Point to red line. *What is the color of this line?* Point to black line. *Which line is longer, the red or the black one?* Record. Note: In all of the comparisons, the respondent, if possible, is to be forced to choose one line as longer, equal judgments not being allowed, unless rapport is seriously threatened. If equal judgments have to be accepted, modify the record sheets accordingly. Show page 2 [see Figure 7]. *Which of these two red lines is longer?* Record. Repeat p. 2 procedure with pages 3 and 4 [see Figures 8 and 9]. Note: Pages 1 through 4 are intended as comprehension checks. If the responses to these drawings are not correct, further efforts with that respondent may be considered a waste. If he demonstrates compre-hension, the session should be continued.

Record Sheet

PAGE_____

NAME _____

AGE _____

SEX _____

GROUP _____ LOCATION _____ DATE _____ EXPERIMENTER _____

A Cross-Cultural Study of Perception

Melville J. Herskovits, Donald T. Campbell, and Marshall H. Segall

#											#
1	R B	R B	R B	R B	R B	R B	R B	R B	R B	R B	1
2	R L	R L	R L	R L	R L	R L	R L	R L	R L	R L	2
3	R L	R L	R L	R L	R L	R L	R L	R L	R L	R L	3
4	R L	R L	R L	R L	R L	R L	R L	R L	R L	R L	4
5	R L	R L	R L	R L	R L	R L	R L	R L	R L	R L	5
6	R L	R L	R L	R L	R L	R L	R L	R L	R L	R L	6
7	R L	R L	R L	R L	R L	R L	R L	R L	R L	R L	7
8	R L	R L	R L	R L	R L	R L	R L	R L	R L	R L	8
9	R L	R L	R L	R L	R L	R L	R L	R L	R L	R L	9
10	R L	R L	R L	R L	R L	R L	R L	R L	R L	R L	10
11	R L	R L	R L	R L	R L	R L	R L	R L	R L	R L	11
12	R L	R L	R L	R L	R L	R L	R L	R L	R L	R L	12
13	R L	R L	R L	R L	R L	R L	R L	R L	R L	R L	13
14	R L	R L	R L	R L	R L	R L	R L	R L	R L	R L	14
15	R L	R L	R L	R L	R L	R L	R L	R L	R L	R L	15
16	R L	R L	R L	R L	R L	R L	R L	R L	R L	R L	16
17	R B	R B	R B	R B	R B	R B	R B	R B	R B	R B	17
18	R B	R B	R B	R B	R B	R B	R B	R B	R B	R B	18
19	R B	R B	R B	R B	R B	R B	R B	R B	R B	R B	19
20	R B	R B	R B	R B	R B	R B	R B	R B	R B	R B	20
21	R B	R B	R B	R B	R B	R B	R B	R B	R B	R B	21
22	R B	R B	R B	R B	R B	R B	R B	R B	R B	R B	22
23	R B	R B	R B	R B	R B	R B	R B	R B	R B	R B	23
24	R B	R B	R B	R B	R B	R B	R B	R B	R B	R B	24
25	R B	R B	R B	R B	R B	R B	R B	R B	R B	R B	25
26	R B	R B	R B	R B	R B	R B	R B	R B	R B	R B	26
27	R B	R B	R B	R B	R B	R B	R B	R B	R B	R B	27
28	R B	R B	R B	R B	R B	R B	R B	R B	R B	R B	28
29	R B	R B	R B	R B	R B	R B	R B	R B	R B	R B	29
30	R B	R B	R B	R B	R B	R B	R B	R B	R B	R B	30
31	R B	R B	R B	R B	R B	R B	R B	R B	R B	R B	31
32	R B	R B	R B	R B	R B	R B	R B	R B	R B	R B	32
33	R B	R B	R B	R B	R B	R B	R B	R B	R B	R B	33
34	R B	R B	R B	R B	R B	R B	R B	R B	R B	R B	34
35	R B	R B	R B	R B	R B	R B	R B	R B	R B	R B	35
36	R B	R B	R B	R B	R B	R B	R B	R B	R B	R B	36
37	R L	R L	R L	R L	R L	R L	R L	R L	R L	R L	37
38	R L	R L	R L	R L	R L	R L	R L	R L	R L	R L	38
39	R L	R L	R L	R L	R L	R L	R L	R L	R L	R L	39
40	R L	R L	R L	R L	R L	R L	R L	R L	R L	R L	40
41	R L	R L	R L	R L	R L	R L	R L	R L	R L	R L	41
42	R L	R L	R L	R L	R L	R L	R L	R L	R L	R L	42
43	R L	R L	R L	R L	R L	R L	R L	R L	R L	R L	43
44	T B	T B	T B	T B	T B	T B	T B	T B	T B	T B	44
45	T B	T B	T B	T B	T B	T B	T B	T B	T B	T B	45
46	T B	T B	T B	T B	T B	T B	T B	T B	T B	T B	46
47	T B	T B	T B	T B	T B	T B	T B	T B	T B	T B	47
48	T B	T B	T B	T B	T B	T B	T B	T B	T B	T B	48
49	T B	T B	T B	T B	T B	T B	T B	T B	T B	T B	49
50	T B	T B	T B	T B	T B	T B	T B	T B	T B	T B	50
51	T B	T B	T B	T B	T B	T B	T B	T B	T B	T B	51
52	T B	T B	T B	T B	T B	T B	T B	T B	T B	T B	52
53	T B	T B	T B	T B	T B	T B	T B	T B	T B	T B	53
54	T B	T B	T B	T B	T B	T B	T B	T B	T B	T B	54
55	Y N	Y N	Y N	Y N	Y N	Y N	Y N	Y N	Y N	Y N	55
56	Y N	Y N	Y N	Y N	Y N	Y N	Y N	Y N	Y N	Y N	56
57	Y N	Y N	Y N	Y N	Y N	Y N	Y N	Y N	Y N	Y N	57
58	Y N	Y N	Y N	Y N	Y N	Y N	Y N	Y N	Y N	Y N	58
59	Y N	Y N	Y N	Y N	Y N	Y N	Y N	Y N	Y N	Y N	59
60	Y N	Y N	Y N	Y N	Y N	Y N	Y N	Y N	Y N	Y N	60

Response categories (by row group):
- Rows 1–16: Right or Left
- Rows 17–25: Red or Black
- Rows 26–36: Red or Black
- Rows 37–43: Right or Left
- Rows 44–54: Top or Bottom
- Rows 55–60: Yes or No

Instructions: This record sheet provides for the recording of answers by ten respondents. For each respondent record name, ... to each decision by circling that response. Ex.: Respondent says "Left."

Figure 10 Data record blank

Pages 5 through 16 represent the Müller-Lyer illusion. Proceed as above, showing each drawing, and recording each response. Ask: *Which of the two red lines is longer?* Don't point. Record *R* or *L*.

Pages 17 through 25 represent one form of the Horizontal-vertical illusion. The appropriate question with these drawings is: *Which line is longer, the red one or the black one?* Record *R* or *B*.

Pages 26 through 36 represent a second form of the Horizontal-vertical illusion. Proceed directly as above. Ask: *Which line is longer, the red one or the black one?* Record *R* or *B*.

Before moving on to the next set of drawings, a rest period should be introduced. During this time, discussion of the experiment should be avoided, although general conversation is encouraged, if it contributes to the subject's comfort.

Pages 37 through 43 represent the Sander Parallelogram. Show each drawing. Ask: *Which of the two red lines is longer, the one on this side (the right) or the one on that (the left)?* Record *R* or *L*.

Pages 44 through 54 are designed to investigate an illusion which is related to perspective conventions in two-dimensional representations of three-dimensional space. With each drawing ask: *Which of the two red lines is longer, the one on the top or the one on the bottom?* Record *T* or *B*.

The data record sheet included in the kit and referred to above is reproduced in Figure 10.

6 The data analysis was designed to discover cross-cultural differences, if any, in susceptibility to the various illusions. Given the nature of the problem, our major concern was to ensure that whatever sample differences appeared were not artifactual, but indicative of genuine differences in perception. Accordingly, we shall present here a very detailed account of our analysis.

Data
Analysis
and
Findings

MEAN SCORES

Respondents in the cultural samples described in the previous chapter provided a total of 1,878 protocols. Each of these protocols consisted of the record of a respondent's choice of the longer segment on each item. For any item, a choice of the typically over-estimated segment (e.g., the vertical in any horizontal-vertical item) was considered an illusion-supported response. Each respondent was then assigned a score on each set of illusion figures indicating his total number of illusion-supported responses to that set. With all 1,878 respondents thus assigned a total score on each of the illusions, the samples could then be described in terms of the mean—(and variability)—of these scores. The second column of Tables 4, 5, 6, 7, and 8 (pp. 122–126) reports these means.

GROUP PSE's

Alternatively, the individual protocols in each sample can be combined on an item-by-item basis, with samples described in terms of the proportion of individuals making illusion-supported responses. From graphs based upon such data, a group *point of subjective equality*[1] was determined. These PSE's are shown in the third column of Tables 4, 5, 6, 7, and 8. Details of the psychophysical analysis that yielded the PSE's will be presented below (pp. 134–150).

THE DETECTION AND ELIMINATION OF BIASED PROTOCOLS

The last three columns of Tables 4 through 8 are based upon "purified" samples, which, we are convinced, provide a better basis for interpretation. Since any individual protocol could have been shaped in part by response tendencies irrelevant to the assigned task, in some analyses the sample scores were computed with biased protocols eliminated. Setting aside cases in this manner is rightfully suspect, but on the other hand, to ignore the protocol distortions resulting from respondents' misunderstandings or response-sets, particularly when obvious, would result in avoidable, erroneous conclusions about intersample differences.

Erroneous conclusions are particularly likely when the proportion of distorted protocols varies from sample to sample. For example, if several respondents in a sample consistently responded to some irrelevant feature of an illusion (e.g., chose the red segment in the horizontal-vertical drawings), a spurious enhancement of the total score could result, particularly with a sample that was,

[1]The point of subjective equality is that percentage discrepancy at which 50 per cent of a given sample would have perceived the comparison stimuli as equal. PSE's were determined graphically, by dropping a perpendicular from the 50 per cent level on each curve to the abscissa.

in fact, minimally subject to the illusion. Response-sets could also result in the assignment of a spuriously low score. To guard against this kind of error we chose for some analyses to take a path that is common in science, that of discarding obviously erroneous observations—in this instance, eliminating the obvious nonscale, communication-breakdown cases.

How can one tell whether a response pattern provided by a Bushman, which is different from the analogous pattern provided by a schoolboy in Evanston, is the result of a breakdown in communication rather than a different perceptual response tendency from that of the Evanstonian (Campbell, 1964)? Several features were built into our materials to facilitate discrimination between genuine differences in perception and differences due to misunderstanding. These features included (a) the four comprehension-check stimuli administered at the outset of each session and (b) the administration of items in mixed order, with colors, segment positions, and relative magnitudes varied haphazardly insofar as possible. (As was noted above, several other features of the materials were meant to enhance communication between respondent and fieldworker: the use of two colors and the separation of segments within each drawing.)

The use of many items for each illusion set made it possible for orderly, relevant response tendencies not to be confounded with equally orderly but irrelevant tendencies. In the Müller-Lyer figures, for instance, examples of irrelevant tendencies would include choosing the segment on the right, or the segment with the arrowheads, or alternating left and right, and so forth. However, because the order of presentation of items was randomized within each illusion set, a protocol on the raw data sheet is difficult to read. Recall (see Table 1, p. 104) that the item order was random with respect to per cent discrepancy. Thus, for the Müller-Lyer set the order of presentation of items was 27, −2, 20, 25, 3, 38, 45, 10, 48, 14, 33, and −8 per cent. For analysis purposes, the items were reordered by increasing per cent discrepancy to facilitate the detection of systematic irrelevant tendencies. The way such tend-

Table 2 Sample Müller-Lyer Response Protocols, Before and After Item-order Transformation

	Items in order of appearance during administration												Items in order of increasing per cent discrepancy												Treatment
Item number	1	2	3	4	5	6	7	8	9	10	11	12	12	2	5	8	10	3	4	1	11	6	7	9	
Per cent discrepancy	27	-2	20	25	3	38	45	10	48	14	33	-8	-8	-2	3	10	14	20	25	27	33	38	45	48	
Location of ⟩—<	L	L	R	L	L	L	R	R	L	R	R	R	R	L	L	R	R	R	L	L	R	L	L	L	
a No bias, scale type	0	1[a]	1	0	1	0	0	1	0	1	0	1	1	1	1	1	1	1	0	0	0	0	0	0	Score 6
b No bias, scale type	0	1	0	0	0	0	0	0	0	0	0	1	1	1	0	0	0	0	0	0	0	0	0	0	Score 2
c Chose right only	0	0	1	0	0	0	1	1	0	1	1	1	1	0	0	1	1	1	0	0	1	0	1	0	Discard
d Chose left only	1	1	0	1	1	1	0	0	1	0	0	0	0	1	1	0	0	0	1	1	0	1	0	1	Discard
e Alternated r-1	0	1	1	1	0	1	1	0	0	0	1	0	0	1	0	0	0	1	1	0	1	1	1	0	Discard
f Alternated 1-r	1	0	0	0	1	0	0	1	1	1	0	1	1	0	1	1	1	0	0	1	0	0	0	1	Discard
g Chose ⟩—< only	1	1	1	1	1	1	1	1	1	1	1	1	1	1	1	1	1	1	1	1	1	1	1	1	Discard
h Chose <—⟩ only	0	0	0	0	0	0	0	0	0	0	0	0	0	0	0	0	0	0	0	0	0	0	0	0	Discard
j No bias, 1 error	0	1	1	0	1	0	0	1	0	0	0	1	1	1	1	1	0	1	0	0	0	0	0	0	Score 5
k No bias, 1 error	0	1	0	0	1	0	0	0	0	1	0	1	1	1	1	0	1	0	0	0	0	0	0	0	Score 4

[a] 1 indicates an illusion-supported response.

encies would appear is demonstrated in Table 2, where each illusion-supported response is indicated by a *1*.

In the left half of Table 2 are shown ten sample Müller-Lyer
protocols with items in the order in which they would have been
administered. In the right half of Table 2 the same ten protocols
are shown with the items arranged in order of increasing per cent
discrepancy.

Rows *a* and *b* are examples of protocols in which no response
biases are present. When such protocols are transformed, they generate a pattern which has the characteristics of a perfect Guttman
scale (Guttman, 1947): the respondent makes an illusion-supported
response to all items of lower per cent discrepancy than the item
of highest per cent discrepancy to which he made such a response.

Rows *c*, *d*, *e*, and *f* are examples of protocols containing position biases. Note that when transformed, the protocols generate
patterns containing many "errors" in the Guttman sense so that
biases are strikingly obvious.

Rows *g* and *h* demonstrate what would have happened had a
respondent consistently, in all items, made the illusion-supported
response, or, alternatively, always chosen the usually underestimated segment. Since such protocols would have been orderly,
whether or not transformed, our interpretation might have been
less than perfectly decisive. However, since the per cent discrepancy in two items was zero or less and in several items was very
great, we expected everybody to make the illusion-supported
response to some items (-8 and -2 per cent discrepancy) and,
conversely, *not* to make the illusion-supported response to other
items (e.g., 45 and 48 per cent discrepancy). Thus, protocols such
as those shown in rows *g* and *h* would have been interpreted as
evidence of misunderstanding, deliberate attempts to mislead, or a
response bias.

Rows *j* and *k* show protocols that, when transformed, fall short
of perfect scales, in the Guttman sense. They each show a single
threshold reversal, or Guttman error. Such protocols, however,
were not excluded. Somewhat arbitrarily, we considered as "con-

Table 3 Proportion of Cases Eliminated[a]

	Total N	Müller-Lyer	Sander parallelo-gram	Horizontal-vertical ($\perp$)	Horizontal-vertical ($\sqsupset$)	Perspective drawing
Ankole adults	180	.27	.27	.20	.12	.31
Ankole children	164	.43	.21	.29	.19	.36
Toro adults	56	.13	.02	.04	.07	.11
Toro children	53	.30	.06	.04	.13	.21
Suku adults	53	.27	.06	.09	.09	.06
Suku children	23	.09	.09	.09	.09	.09
Songe adults	47	.04	.02	.02	.02	.00
Songe children	51	.14	.00	.12	.04	.06
Fang adults	49	.14	.12	.08	.04	.14
Fang children	61	.30	.13	.13	.05	.30
Bété adults	52	.27	.12	.17	.08	.06
Bété children	43	.14	.07	.16	.07	.16
Ijaw adults	51	.08	.00	.00	.00	.04
Ijaw children	50	.26	.06	.30	.08	.20
Ijaw school children	61	.11	.13	.25	.07	.13
Zulu adults	51	.59	.35	.65	.24	.33
Zulu children	49	.71	.31	.65	.29	.18
Bushman adults	46	.22	—[b]	.11	.15	.04
S. A. European adults	44	.18	.05	.05	.05	.05
Mineboy adults	72	.17	.01	.04	.04	.04
Senegal adults	137	.46	.20	.42	.28	.35
Senegal children	125	.59	.29	.59	.45	.45
Dahomey children	65	.38	.11	.12	.03	.40
Hanunóo adults	43	.14	.09	.09	.05	.12
Hanunóo children	14	.14	.07	.07	.14	.14
Evanston adults	119	.07	.03	.04	.01	.05
Evanston children	89	.13	.09	.06	.04	.08
Northwestern adults	30	.10	.07	.03	.00	.05

[a] Protocols excluded from "pure" samples analysis if more than one threshold reversal occurred.

[b] The Sander parallelogram was not administered to the Bushmen.

sistent" all cases with only a single reversal (as in *j* and *k*)—and, of course, perfect cases (as in *a* and *b*).

By these strict standards, varying proportions of cases in each sample were eliminated. Table 3 shows the resultant proportions of cases temporarily set aside in each cultural group for each of the five illusions. While there are group differences in the proportions of "lost" cases—suggesting that communication of the task was achieved more easily in some societies than in others—within all samples there is an almost perfectly consistent decrease in the percentage of illusion-supported responses as per cent discrepancy increases (see below, pp. 134–135). This recurrence of a common pattern provides assurance that, in general, there has been communication of the task, and that the discarded cases constitute exceptions to general tendencies, exceptions that in most instances can confidently be attributed to detectable response biases.

Finally, to assuage any remaining doubts generated by the elimination of errorful protocols, parallel analyses were performed with groups made up of *all* the 1,878 respondents. Thus, in the presentation of results that follows, it is possible to report and compare results based both on consistent cases only and on all cases.

ANALYSIS OF SAMPLE MEANS AND PSE's— INTERCORRELATIONS

Tables 4 through 8 show, for each of the five illusions, the mean number of illusion-supported responses made by each sample, with separate means shown for children and adults.[2] These tables also contain the PSE scores assigned to each sample. (A sample-by-sample compilation of all scores, including measures of variability within samples, appears in Appendix D.)

In Tables 4 through 8, each sample has four scores assigned to it, two of them based on the performances of all respondents in

[2]Henceforth, children and adults will be treated separately. Thus, the 17 groups described in Chapter 5 and Appendix A, some of which contain both children and adults, now constitute 28 samples.

Table 4   Mean Number of Illusion-Supported Responses
and PSE's: Müller-Lyer Illusion

	ALL CASES			CONSISTENT CASES		
	N	$\overline{X}$	PSE	N	$\overline{X}$	PSE
Ankole adults	180	3.54	7	131	3.34	8
Ankole children	164	4.35	10	93	3.61	10
Toro adults	56	3.16	6	49	3.02	6
Toro children	53	4.40	14	37	4.27	15
Suku adults	53	2.96	4	40	3.03	6
Suku children	23	2.04	0	21	2.05	0
Songe adults	47	2.91	5	45	2.98	5
Songe children	51	3.31	7	44	3.16	7
Fang adults	49	3.41	5	42	2.98	5
Fang children	61	3.84	7	43	3.58	9
Bété adults	52	3.19	4	38	2.74	4
Bété children	43	2.74	3	37	2.70	3
Ijaw adults	51	2.78	3	47	2.89	4
Ijaw children	50	3.84	10	37	3.49	10
Ijaw school children	61	4.10	11	54	3.74	11
Zulu adults	51	4.63	8	21	3.33	6
Zulu children	49	4.57	10	14	4.14	11
Bushman adults	46	2.37	1	36	2.28	1
S. A. European adults	44	4.48	13	36	4.33	13
Mineboy adults	72	2.19	1	60	2.23	1
Senegal adults	137	4.42	10	74	3.88	11
Senegal children	125	5.36	17	51	4.61	14
Dahomey children	65	4.55	12	40	4.22	12
Hanunóo adults	43	3.12	8	37	2.97	8
Hanunóo children	14	3.43	8	12	3.08	7
Evanston adults	119	5.19	19	111	5.21	19
Evanston children	89	5.64	22	77	5.57	21
Northwestern adults	30	4.93	16	27	5.00	16

Table 5   *Mean Number of Illusion-Supported Responses and PSE's: Sander Parallelogram*

	ALL CASES			CONSISTENT CASES		
	N	$\overline{X}$	PSE	N	$\overline{X}$	PSE
Ankole adults	180	2.52	14	132	2.63	17
Ankole children	164	2.71	17	130	2.75	17
Toro adults	56	2.32	12	55	2.31	12
Toro children	53	2.64	17	50	2.68	17
Suku adults	53	2.19	10	50	2.28	11
Suku children	23	1.83	5	21	1.81	6
Songe adults	47	2.21	11	46	2.22	11
Songe children	51	2.59	17	51	2.59	17
Fang adults	49	2.78	17	43	2.72	17
Fang children	61	2.95	18	53	2.98	19
Bété adults	52	2.19	9	46	2.24	10
Bété children	43	2.53	16	40	2.53	16
Ijaw adults	51	2.94	18	51	2.94	18
Ijaw children	50	2.52	13	47	2.53	13
Ijaw school children	61	3.20	19	53	3.15	19
Zulu adults	51	2.71	16	33	2.70	18
Zulu children	49	3.04	20	34	3.24	22
Bushman adults	—	—	—	—	—	—
S. A. European adults	44	2.95	17	42	2.98	17
Mineboy adults	72	2.03	9	71	2.06	9
Senegal adults	137	2.58	11	109	2.59	12
Senegal children	125	2.85	15	89	3.29	18
Dahomey children	65	2.45	14	58	2.55	16
Hanunóo adults	43	2.47	13	39	2.41	13
Hanunóo children	14	2.93	16	13	2.85	15
Evanston adults	119	3.25	19	115	3.23	19
Evanston children	89	3.38	20	81	3.33	20
Northwestern adults	30	3.57	20	28	3.54	20

Table **6**   *Mean Number of Illusion-Supported Responses and PSE's: Horizontal-Vertical Illusion (⊥)*

	ALL CASES			CONSISTENT CASES		
	N	$\overline{X}$	PSE	N	$\overline{X}$	PSE
Ankole adults	180	6.48	22	144	6.56	21
Ankole children	164	6.40	23	117	6.53	23
Toro adults	56	6.50	20	54	6.56	20
Toro children	53	6.30	19	51	6.31	19
Suku adults	53	6.38	21	48	6.65	22
Suku children	23	6.35	20	21	6.33	20
Songe adults	47	5.47	16	46	5.46	16
Songe children	51	5.92	20	45	6.16	20
Fang adults	49	6.31	21	45	6.31	21
Fang children	61	6.08	18	53	6.08	19
Bété adults	52	4.44	8	43	4.37	9
Bété children	43	5.05	11	36	4.92	11
Ijaw adults	51	6.08	20	51	6.08	20
Ijaw children	50	6.12	19	35	6.03	18
Ijaw school children	61	6.33	20	46	6.28	20
Zulu adults	51	4.88	8	18	4.67	8
Zulu children	49	5.65	10	17	4.94	12
Bushman adults	46	5.76	20	41	5.93	20
S. A. European adults	44	5.30	14	42	5.33	15
Mineboy adults	72	6.32	19	69	6.28	19
Senegal adults	137	6.03	24	79	6.48	24
Senegal children	125	5.23	15	51	5.55	17
Dahomey children	65	6.42	22	57	6.49	22
Hanunóo adults	43	5.23	15	39	5.26	15
Hanunóo children	14	6.00	19	13	6.08	19
Evanston adults	119	5.94	20	114	5.93	20
Evanston children	89	5.61	18	84	5.64	18
Northwestern adults	30	5.70	19	29	5.72	19

Table 7   *Mean Number of Illusion-Supported Responses and PSE's: Horizontal-Vertical Illusion (⌐)*

	ALL CASES			CONSISTENT CASES		
	N	$\overline{X}$	PSE	N	$\overline{X}$	PSE
Ankole adults	180	5.94	18	158	6.16	17
Ankole children	164	5.95	14	133	6.15	16
Toro adults	56	6.30	19	52	6.38	19
Toro children	53	6.13	18	46	6.37	21
Suku adults	53	5.38	9	48	5.67	9
Suku children	23	5.91	12	21	5.90	12
Songe adults	47	5.53	10	46	5.54	10
Songe children	51	5.67	9	49	5.65	9
Fang adults	49	5.43	8	47	5.45	8
Fang children	61	5.52	11	58	5.52	11
Bété adults	52	3.75	2	48	3.71	2
Bété children	43	4.05	2	40	3.93	1
Ijaw adults	51	5.24	8	51	5.24	8
Ijaw children	50	5.80	14	46	5.89	14
Ijaw school children	61	5.85	18	57	6.02	18
Zulu adults	51	4.69	7	39	4.77	7
Zulu children	49	5.24	8	35	5.31	8
Bushman adults	46	5.11	9	39	5.15	9
S. A. European adults	44	4.68	5	42	4.67	5
Mineboy adults	72	5.72	12	69	5.71	12
Senegal adults	137	4.39	6	99	4.46	7
Senegal children	125	4.04	5	69	4.42	6
Dahomey children	65	6.51	19	63	6.52	19
Hanunóo adults	43	4.40	5	41	4.44	5
Hanunóo children	14	5.64	13	12	5.58	13
Evanston adults	119	4.92	7	118	4.92	7
Evanston children	89	4.81	7	85	4.86	8
Northwestern adults	30	4.83	7	30	4.83	7

Table **8** *Mean Number of Illusion-Supported Responses and PSE's: Perspective Drawing Illusion*

	ALL CASES			CONSISTENT CASES		
	N	$\overline{X}$	PSE	N	$\overline{X}$	PSE
Ankole adults	180	4.81	4	125	4.78	5
Ankole children	164	5.24	7	105	5.22	8
Toro adults	56	4.75	6	50	4.74	6
Toro children	53	4.28	5	42	4.40	5
Suku adults	53	4.70	6	50	4.72	7
Suku children	23	4.87	6	21	4.90	6
Songe adults	47	4.26	4	47	4.26	4
Songe children	51	4.27	4	48	4.23	4
Fang adults	49	4.82	5	42	4.83	5
Fang children	61	4.85	6	43	4.95	6
Bété adults	52	3.25	−2	49	3.22	−2
Bété children	43	4.14	5	36	4.36	6
Ijaw adults	51	3.98	2	49	4.00	2
Ijaw children	50	4.24	4	40	4.20	5
Ijaw school children	61	5.15	7	53	5.28	7
Zulu adults	51	4.43	4	34	4.56	4
Zulu children	49	4.78	5	40	4.75	6
Bushman adults	46	4.46	5	44	4.39	4
S. A. European adults	44	4.02	3	42	3.98	3
Mineboy adults	72	4.18	3	69	4.20	3
Senegal adults	137	4.05	1	89	4.04	4
Senegal children	125	3.75	1	69	3.99	3
Dahomey children	65	3.83	3	39	4.36	5
Hanunóo adults	43	5.07	7	38	5.03	7
Hanunóo children	14	5.57	8	12	5.50	8
Evanston adults	119	5.59	5	113	4.60	6
Evanston children	89	5.02	7	82	5.00	7
Northwestern adults	30	4.90	7	29	4.90	7

the sample and two based on consistent cases only. In order to
indicate the effect on the scores produced by eliminating noncon-
sistent cases, the correlations among each set of four scores were
computed. These are shown in Table 9. It is apparent from the
correlation matrices shown in Table 9 that all four scores correlate
very highly, but that the one score that deviates most from the
other three is the mean based on all cases. The average of all correlations involving all-cases means is .915, whereas the average of
all correlations involving the other scores is .94. A reasonable conclusion is that the all-cases mean is subject to some distortion as a
result of the performances of those respondents who displayed
irrelevant response tendencies, whereas the all-cases PSE is not. On
the other hand, since the mean based on consistent cases only
correlates highly enough with the two PSE estimates, we have con-

Table **9**   *Correlations Among Sample Scores*

Illusion	ALL CASES $\overline{X}$/ CONSIST-ENT $\overline{X}$	ALL CASES $\overline{X}$/ CONSIST-ENT PSE	ALL CASES $\overline{X}$/ ALL CASES PSE	ALL CASES PSE/ CONSIST-ENT PSE	CONSIST-ENT $\overline{X}$/ CONSIST-ENT PSE	CONSIST-ENT $\overline{X}$/ ALL CASES PSE
Müller-Lyer						
N = 28	.95	.92	.94	.98	.98	.97
Sander parallelogram						
N = 27	.97	.88	.92	.97	.91	.89
Horizontal-vertical ($\perp$)						
N = 28	.96	.88	.89	.99	.95	.95
Horizontal-vertical ($\sqcap$)						
N = 28	.99	.90	.92	.99	.93	.94
Perspective drawing						
N = 28	.91	.84	.87	.95	.92	.93
Av. corr.	.956	.882	.908	.976	.938	.936

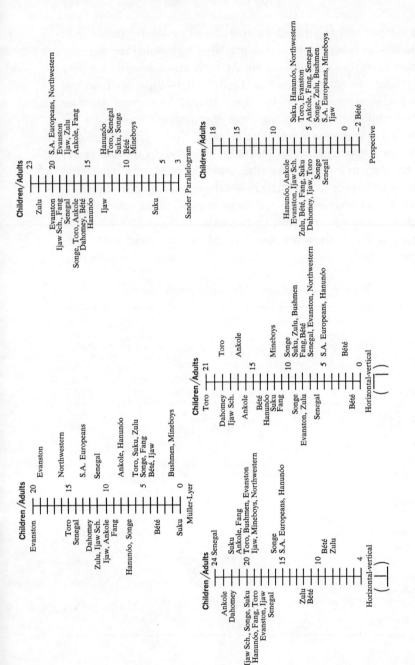

Figure **11** *Percentage discrepancy points of subjective equality for 28 samples on each of five illusions*

fidence in the validity of all three of these scores as estimates of the degree of illusion susceptibility of the 28 samples. Finally, the correlation between the two PSE estimates is so high (the average $r = .976$) that one of them may be ignored simply because it provides no information beyond what the other provides. Accordingly, the two scores that will constitute the primary focus of our analysis will be the mean and the PSE based on consistent cases only. The mean score will be employed in tests of significance of the differences in performance across samples, while the PSE scores will be used primarily to illustrate those differences.

An examination of the scores presented in Tables 4 through 8 reveals that for each illusion both means and PSE scores varied from sample to sample, and further, that these differences among samples varied from illusion to illusion. It should also be noted here that numerous differences between the means are statistically significant, even under stringent criteria of significance (see pp. 153–155). But before attempting to point out in detail the many intersample differences on each of the illusions, we present an over-all view of the complex of differences in Figure 11, which illustrates the manner in which the various samples are arrayed along the percentage discrepancy dimension on each of the five illusions. The position of each of the 28 samples was determined by its PSE based on consistent cases only.

Certain features of the relative illusion susceptibilities of the various samples are obvious. The most striking is that the European samples (Evanston children, Evanston adults, Northwestern students, and South African Europeans) all display extremely high illusion susceptibility on both the Müller-Lyer and Sander parallelogram illusions, whereas those same samples earn scores that place them very near the medians for the two horizontal-vertical illusions. Examination of Figure 11 also suggests positive interillusion correlations for the Müller-Lyer and Sander illusions on the one hand and for the two horizontal-vertical illusions on the other, but not across these two pairs of illusions. *These are the two most important features of our results, and the balance of our analytic*

Table **10**   *Rank Order of Samples on Each of Five Illusions*

	M-L	Sander	H-V (⊥)	H-V (⌐)	Perspective
Ankole adults	14	14	5	5	11
Ankole children	11	11	2	6	2
Toro adults	20	22	7	3	13
Toro children	4	13	14	1	16
Suku adults	19	23	3	13	9
Suku children	28	27	8	9	8
Songe adults	22	24	22	12	20
Songe children	16	15	10	14	21
Fang adults	21	12	6	16	10
Fang children	13	6	16	11	6
Bété adults	24	25	27	27	28
Bété children	25	17	26	28	19
Ijaw adults	23	8	11	18	25
Ijaw children	12	19	19	7	22
Ijaw school children	10	5	9	4	3
Zulu adults	18	9	28	22	15
Zulu children	8	1	25	17	12
Bushman adults	26	a	12	15	18
S. A. European adults	6	10	23	25	27
Mineboy adults	27	26	15	10	23
Senegal adults	9	21	1	23	24
Senegal children	5	7	21	24	26
Dahomey children	7	16	4	2	17
Hanunóo adults	15	20	24	26	4
Hanunóo children	17	18	17	8	1
Evanston adults	2	4	13	20	14
Evanston children	1	3	20	19	5
Northwestern adults	3	2	18	21	7

[a]The Sander parallelogram was not administered to the Bushmen.

efforts will be devoted to substantiating and clarifying these findings.
A third fact made obvious by Figure 11 is the restricted range of
scores on the perspective drawing illusion, with all but one of the
28 samples clustering between PSE's of 2 and 8.

The next step in the analysis was to investigate the correlations
among the various illusions. This could be done in several ways,
and, indeed, we employed two procedures, one based on sample
ranks, the other on individuals' scores.

The rank order of the 28 samples was determined for each
illusion on the basis of their PSE scores, with mean illusion scores
used to break the tie ranks resulting from identical PSE's (27 samples were used for the Sander parallelogram since the Bushmen
were not administered this illusion). The resultant ranks are shown
in Table 10. These five distributions of ranks were then intercor-
related, with the resultant matrix shown in Table 11. The correlations in this matrix confirm the suggestion based on the examination of Figure 11 above, viz., that there is a high positive correlation
between the Müller-Lyer and Sander parallelogram illusions (.69),
a high positive correlation between the two versions of the horizontal-vertical illusion, (.58), and zero or slightly negative correlations between one or another of the horizontal-vertical illusions
and either the Müller-Lyer or the Sander parallelogram illusions.

Table **11**   *Rank-Order Correlations Among Five Illusions* [a]

	Müller-Lyer	*Sander*	*Horizontal-vertical* (⊥)	*Horizontal-vertical* (⌐)	*Perspective*
Müller-Lyer	—	.69	− .01	− .03	.16
Sander		—	− .16	− .13	.24
Horizontal-vertical (⊥)			—	.58	.23
Horizontal-vertical (⌐)				—	.35
Perspective					—

[a] N = 28 groups, except in correlations involving the Sander parallelogram, where
N = 27.

A fourth feature of this correlation matrix, not anticipated by an examination of Figure 11, is the slight-to-moderate positive correlation between the perspective drawing illusion and each of the other four.

Since the correlations presented in Table 11 were based on rankings of samples, the N is an N of samples. To obtain a more stable estimate of the intercorrelations among illusions, product-moment correlations involving individual respondents' illusion scores were also computed. This was done separately for samples of children and samples of adults; in each instance they include all cases. The two resulting matrices are presented in Table 12. The picture that emerges from these matrices is similar to that shown in Table 11. For all adults combined ($N = 1,030$), the correlation between the Müller-Lyer and the Sander parallelogram illusions is

Table **12**   *Product-Moment Correlations Among Illusions Based on All Individuals*

	Müller-Lyer	Sander	Horizontal-vertical ($\perp$)	Horizontal-vertical ($\sqsupset$)	Perspective
Adults (N = 1,030)[a]					
Müller-Lyer	—	.35	.02	−.14	−.03
Sander		—	.06	−.05	.03
Horizontal-vertical ($\perp$)			—	.38	.10
Horizontal-vertical ($\sqsupset$)				—	.03
Perspective					—
Children (N = 848)					
Müller-Lyer	—	.23	−.05	−.16	−.01
Sander		—	−.04	−.07	.04
Horizontal-vertical ($\perp$)			—	.28	.13
Horizontal-vertical ($\sqsupset$)				—	.04
Perspective					—

[a] N reduced by 46 for adults in correlations involving the Sander parallelogram.

.35, and the correlation between the two versions of the horizontal-vertical illusion is .38. These are the only significant positive correlations in the matrix. The correlations involving the perspective drawing illusion are slightly positive or near zero, but in no case are they significantly different from zero. A moderately negative correlation between the Müller-Lyer illusion and the ⌐-shaped horizontal-vertical illusion appears for the first time, but all other correlations between either the Müller-Lyer or the Sander figures and the horizontal-verticals are effectively zero. Essentially the same pattern of intercorrelations is shown in the matrix based on all children (N = 848): The Müller-Lyer and Sander illusions again correlate positively; so do the two versions of the horizontal-vertical; and there is a negative correlation between the Müller-Lyer and the ⌐-shaped horizontal-vertical. No other correlation is significantly different from zero.

Considering the three correlation matrices shown in Tables 11 and 12, it appears that the Müller-Lyer and the Sander parallelogram figures together constitute one set of illusions, sharing some common response-inducing features, and that the two horizontal-vertical figures constitute another set.

Perhaps because of the restricted range of scores on the perspective drawing illusion, this set of figures does not correlate highly with any of the others and does not correlate higher with any one than with any other. Whereas the correlations between the Müller-Lyer and Sander figures and between the two horizontal-vertical figures might well reflect factors unique to each of those pairs, the perspective drawing illusion is more equivocally interpreted. In the interest of parsimony, it seems reasonable to consider that illusion as some joint product of the two independent factors most clearly defined by the other four illusions.

As we shall frequently reiterate, we suspect that the factor shared by the Müller-Lyer and Sander figures is related to the fact that they both contain nonorthogonal junctions, which makes them both subject to a biasing tendency of a particular perceptual habit, while the horizontal-vertical figures are subject to a different bias resulting from a *different* perceptual habit. Furthermore, as we have implied in the statement of the theoretical rationale of the study in Chapter 4, and shall make explicit in the discussion of the results, these perceptual habits are independent of each other.

One more comment is in order before moving on to a more detailed look at the data. That is, our results essentially replicate the half-century-old findings of Rivers and lend support to his notion that the Müller-Lyer and horizontal-vertical figures belong to two different classes of illusion. Also, like Rivers, we find that Western samples display *higher* illusion susceptibility than non-Western peoples on the Müller-Lyer, and that the Western samples are *less* susceptible to the horizontal-vertical illusion than at least some non-Western peoples. This finding of cultural differences in more than one direction we consider one of the most important results of our data.

THE PSYCHOPHYSICAL ANALYSIS

One of the analytic methods employed in this study was to compute the proportion of each sample making the illusion-supported response to each item, and then to construct psychophysical ogives from these proportions in order to determine graphically an estimate of the PSE for each sample. Tables 13 through 17 contain these proportions, based on both total samples and consistent cases only. A notable feature of the data, as displayed in these tables, is that among total samples, with just a few exceptions, there is a consistent decrease in illusion response as percentage discrepancy of items increases. For example, for every adult total sample, on the Sander parallelogram there is an orderly descent in the proportion of illusion responses, while for total samples of children on that illusion there are only six minor departures from this pattern (see Table 14). This consistent orderliness constitutes justification of the faith expressed above (p. 121) that the task was generally understood by respondents in all samples.

Further evidence of the widespread orderliness of the data, within which some isolated instances of possible bias or confusion are easily detected, may be found in the fact that most of the psychophysical functions drawn from the material presented in Tables 13 through 17 are relatively smooth ogives. A few samples are presented in Figures 12 through 15 in order to illustrate some salient aspects of the data graphically.

In Figure 12, ogives based on the Müller-Lyer responses of five adult samples are presented. These ogives are based on both purified cases and all cases. Graph *a* (Evanston) summarizes the behavior of a European sample that is highly susceptible to this illusion, while graph *b* (Senegal) depicts the performance of the most susceptible of the non-European samples and graphs *c* (Ankole) and *d* (Bushmen) respectively represent the performances of two non-European samples of moderate and low susceptibility. Graph *e* (Zulu) is included in this figure to illustrate how the psychophysical function reflects the general nature of the performance of a sample; in this instance, the considerable irrelevancies that must have marked the Zulu responses to the Müller-Lyer figures are obvious, but the PSE's for the purified and the total cases are still remarkably similar. Incidentally, the performance of this sample on this illusion was the most erratic in the entire set of data; the Zulu sample provided relatively disorderly performances on the other illusions, although in not so marked a manner as on the Müller-Lyer.

This last point is illustrated in Figure 13, where, among other things, it may be noted that the ogive constructed from the Zulu responses to the Sander parallelogram is slightly less than smooth and not particularly S-shaped. Also notable in Figure 13 is the relative flatness of all the ogives, in contrast to those shown in Figure 12. Clearly, for people in general, the Sander parallelogram stimuli we employed were not quite as discriminable one from the other as the Müller-Lyer stimuli. In spite of this, intersample differences in response to the Sander items were obtained, as has already been stated, and these differences were similar to those obtained with the Müller-Lyer items.

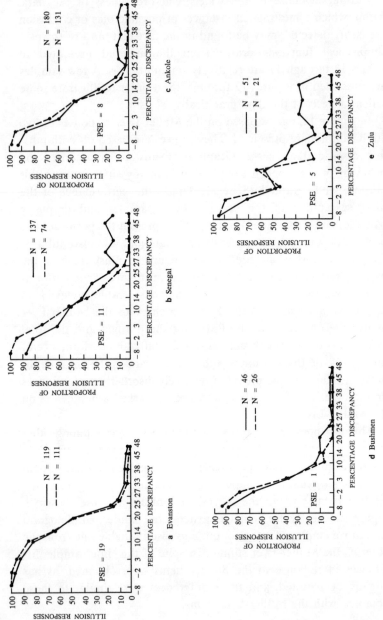

Figure 12   Proportion of illusion-supported responses as a function of percentage discrepancy on the Müller-Lyer illusion

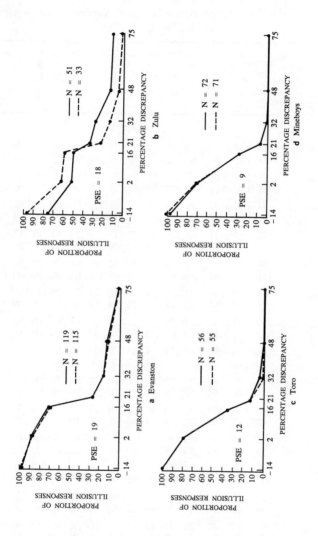

Figure **13** *Proportion of illusion-supported responses as a func-tion of percentage discrepancy on the Sander parallelo-gram illusion*

Table **13** *Proportion of Illusion-Supported Responses to the Müller-Lyer Illusion*[a]

Item number		16	6	9	12	14	7	8	5	15	10	11	13		
Per cent Discrepancy		−8	−2	3	10	14	20	25	27	33	38	45	48		
Sample	N													PSE	Rep
						ADULTS									
Evan	119	1.00	.97	.93	.82	.64	.47	.17	.11	.03	.03	.02	.01	19	.974
	111	1.00	.99	.95	.86	.66	.46	.15	.10	.02	.02	.01	.00	19	
N. U.	30	1.00	1.00	.97	.83	.57	.33	.13	.10	.00	.00	.00	.00	16	.981
	27	1.00	1.00	1.00	.89	.59	.33	.11	.07	.00	.00	.00	.00	16	
Euro	44	1.00	.93	.91	.75	.43	.27	.07	.07	.00	.00	.02	.02	13	.962
	36	1.00	.97	.94	.69	.47	.25	.00	.00	.00	.00	.00	.00	13	
Sene	137	.87	.81	.61	.50	.39	.32	.17	.11	.20	.13	.19	.13	10	.886
	74	.99	.95	.73	.53	.35	.20	.09	.04	.00	.00	.00	.00	11	
Anko	180	.92	.86	.59	.43	.27	.10	.02	.07	.08	.06	.08	.06	7	.938
	131	.98	.95	.66	.45	.21	.06	.02	.01	.01	.00	.00	.00	8	
Zulu	51	.94	.73	.47	.57	.39	.33	.14	.16	.27	.25	.27	.10	5	.840
	21	.95	.90	.43	.62	.14	.19	.05	.05	.00	.00	.00	.00	5	
Suku	53	.89	.81	.53	.26	.17	.11	.06	.04	.08	.00	.00	.02	4	.961
	40	.95	.90	.65	.25	.13	.08	.08	.00	.00	.00	.00	.00	6	
Toro	56	1.00	.93	.61	.34	.14	.13	.00	.00	.00	.00	.00	.02	6	.979
	49	1.00	.92	.59	.35	.14	.02	.00	.00	.00	.00	.00	.00	6	
Songe	47	.96	.94	.55	.28	.09	.04	.02	.02	.00	.02	.00	.00	5	.986
	45	1.00	.96	.58	.29	.09	.04	.02	.00	.00	.00	.00	.00	5	
Fang	49	.94	.90	.57	.29	.20	.20	.06	.08	.06	.04	.06	.00	5	.961
	42	.98	.93	.57	.26	.14	.10	.00	.00	.00	.00	.00	.00	5	
Hanu	43	.93	.88	.72	.35	.02	.12	.02	.02	.02	.00	.00	.02	8	.971
	37	.92	.89	.73	.38	.00	.05	.00	.00	.00	.00	.00	.00	8	
Ijaw	51	.96	.90	.51	.27	.12	.02	.00	.00	.00	.00	.00	.00	3	.995
	47	1.00	.96	.55	.28	.09	.02	.00	.00	.00	.00	.00	.00	4	
Bété	52	.92	.88	.52	.25	.12	.13	.06	.06	.10	.04	.06	.06	4	.958
	38	.95	.97	.53	.18	.05	.05	.00	.00	.00	.00	.00	.00	4	
Bush	46	.87	.67	.37	.15	.11	.11	.02	.00	.02	.02	.02	.00	1	.966
	36	.94	.78	.39	.08	.08	.00	.00	.00	.00	.00	.00	.00	1	
Mine	72	.88	.68	.33	.17	.04	.06	.01	.00	.01	.00	.01	.00	1	.980
	60	.97	.77	.38	.12	.00	.00	.00	.00	.00	.00	.00	.00	1	

Table **13**   (*cont.*)

Item number	16	6	9	12	14	7	8	5	15	10	11	13		
Per cent Discrepancy	−8	−2	3	10	14	20	25	27	33	38	45	48		
Sample N													PSE	Rep
CHILDREN														
Evan 89	.99	.97	.90	.88	.65	.61	.30	.21	.06	.03	.03	.01	22	.958
77	1.00	.97	.95	.91	.69	.57	.30	.17	.01	.00	.00	.00	21	
Sene 125	.86	.78	.66	.68	.55	.47	.29	.14	.34	.18	.29	.11	17	.853
51	.96	.94	.84	.73	.47	.35	.14	.10	.06	.02	.00	.00	14	
Toro 53	.94	.91	.70	.66	.49	.34	.08	.04	.11	.04	.06	.04	14	.932
37	.97	1.00	.73	.73	.54	.24	.05	.00	.00	.00	.00	.00	15	
Daho 65	.97	.89	.88	.60	.43	.23	.12	.22	.09	.06	.03	.03	12	.927
40	.98	.98	1.00	.55	.43	.18	.08	.05	.00	.00	.00	.00	12	
Zulu 49	.88	.82	.57	.51	.33	.31	.24	.04	.16	.12	.39	.20	10	.859
14	1.00	1.00	.71	.57	.36	.29	.21	.00	.00	.00	.00	.00	11	
Ijaw Sch. 61	.97	.98	.80	.54	.25	.18	.10	.07	.05	.07	.08	.02	11	.959
54	.98	.98	.83	.54	.22	.13	.04	.00	.02	.00	.00	.00	11	
Anko 164	.91	.90	.65	.49	.38	.24	.13	.05	.18	.13	.13	.14	10	.909
93	.96	.97	.74	.52	.28	.12	.03	.00	.00	.00	.00	.00	10	
Fang 61	.95	.95	.66	.39	.36	.15	.13	.08	.07	.05	.03	.02	7	.943
43	.98	1.00	.67	.47	.26	.12	.05	.05	.00	.00	.00	.00	9	
Ijaw 50	.94	.96	.70	.52	.26	.16	.08	.12	.06	.00	.02	.02	10	.950
37	.97	1.00	.70	.49	.24	.05	.03	.00	.00	.00	.00	.00	10	
Songe 51	1.00	.98	.69	.35	.14	.08	.04	.00	.00	.02	.00	.02	7	.979
44	1.00	1.00	.70	.36	.09	.00	.00	.00	.00	.00	.00	.00	7	
Hanu 14	1.00	.86	.79	.43	.14	.07	.00	.07	.00	.00	.00	.07	8	.970
12	1.00	.83	.75	.33	.08	.08	.00	.00	.00	.00	.00	.07	7	
Bété 43	.88	.86	.47	.16	.07	.07	.07	.09	.02	.02	.02	.00	3	.973
37	.97	.92	.49	.16	.08	.03	.03	.03	.00	.00	.00	.00	3	
Suku 23	.87	.83	.13	.13	.04	.00	.04	.00	.00	.00	.00	.00	0	.982
21	.90	.86	.10	.14	.05	.00	.00	.00	.00	.00	.00	.00	0	

[a] The proportions in the first row for each sample were computed over all cases, while the proportions in the second row are based on internally consistent protocols only.

Table **14** *Proportion of Illusion-Supported Responses
to the Sander Parallelogram illusion*[a]

Item number		40	42	39	43	41	37	38		
Per cent Discrepancy		−14	2	16	21	32	48	75		
Sample									PSE	Rep
				ADULTS						
N. U.	30	1.00	.93	.90	.37	.17	.20	.00	20	.967
	28	1.00	.93	.89	.39	.18	.14	.00	20	
Evan	119	.99	.91	.72	.29	.17	.14	.03	19	.975
	115	1.00	.90	.71	.29	.17	.12	.03	19	
Euro	44	1.00	.82	.57	.23	.20	.09	.05	17	.968
	42	1.00	.83	.60	.24	.19	.10	.02	17	
Ijaw	51	1.00	.94	.71	.24	.06	.00	.00	18	.992
	51	1.00	.94	.71	.24	.06	.00	.00	18	
Fang	49	.98	.82	.53	.27	.06	.06	.06	17	.965
	43	1.00	.84	.56	.26	.07	.00	.00	17	
Zulu	51	.76	.53	.51	.35	.29	.14	.12	16	.905
	33	.97	.64	.61	.24	.15	.06	.03	18	
Anko	180	.88	.69	.47	.16	.16	.06	.09	14	.944
	132	.98	.80	.55	.18	.08	.02	.02	17	
Sene	137	.81	.69	.41	.24	.23	.10	.09	11	.938
	109	.96	.80	.39	.21	.16	.04	.04	12	
Hanu	43	.98	.91	.37	.09	.00	.07	.05	13	.980
	39	1.00	.95	.38	.08	.00	.00	.00	13	
Toro	56	1.00	.80	.36	.13	.04	.00	.00	12	.992
	55	1.00	.80	.36	.13	.02	.00	.00	12	
Suku	53	.96	.79	.30	.09	.02	.02	.00	10	.992
	50	1.00	.84	.32	.10	.02	.00	.00	11	
Bété	52	.92	.65	.33	.12	.06	.06	.06	9	.975
	46	1.00	.70	.35	.11	.04	.04	.00	10	
Songe	47	1.00	.70	.38	.09	.02	.02	.00	11	.988
	46	1.00	.72	.39	.09	.02	.00	.00	11	
Mine	72	.97	.69	.28	.07	.01	.00	.00	9	.986
	71	.99	.70	.28	.07	.01	.00	.00	9	

Table 14 (cont.)

Item number		40	42	39	43	41	37	38		
Per cent Discrepancy		−14	2	16	21	32	48	75		
Sample									PSE	Rep

CHILDREN

Sample		40	42	39	43	41	37	38	PSE	Rep
Evan	89	.97	.87	.78	.47	.15	.12	.03	20	.952
	81	.99	.90	.80	.44	.14	.06	.00	20	
Sene	125	.77	.65	.49	.37	.33	.11	.14	15	.935
	89	.97	.84	.58	.40	.31	.09	.09	18	
Zulu	49	.76	.69	.59	.47	.37	.08	.08	20	.898
	34	.94	.79	.62	.53	.26	.06	.03	22	
Ijaw Sch.	61	.95	.84	.69	.31	.13	.18	.10	19	.951
	53	1.00	.89	.68	.32	.15	.08	.04	19	
Fang	61	.90	.84	.57	.30	.21	.08	.05	18	.946
	53	.96	.89	.64	.28	.17	.04	.00	19	
Hanu	14	.93	.93	.50	.36	.14	.07	.00	16	.969
	13	1.00	1.00	.46	.31	.08	.00	.00	15	
Anko	164	.86	.74	.60	.20	.20	.04	.07	17	.923
	130	.95	.83	.63	.19	.10	.02	.02	17	
Toro	53	.96	.75	.53	.30	.08	.00	.02	17	.968
	50	.98	.78	.56	.30	.06	.00	.00	17	
Songe	51	.98	.90	.55	.13	.04	.00	.00	17	.986
	51	.98	.90	.55	.13	.04	.00	.00	17	
Daho	65	.92	.77	.46	.14	.05	.06	.05	14	.969
	58	.98	.84	.50	.14	.03	.03	.02	16	
Ijaw	50	.94	.82	.40	.22	.10	.04	.00	13	.969
	47	.98	.87	.40	.19	.04	.04	.00	13	
Bété	43	1.00	.74	.51	.16	.07	.02	.02	16	.977
	40	1.00	.80	.53	.15	.05	.00	.00	16	
Suku	23	.96	.57	.26	.00	.00	.04	.00	5	.969
	21	1.00	.62	.19	.00	.00	.00	.00	6	

[a]The proportions in the first row for each sample were computed over all cases, while the proportions in the second row are based on internally consistent protocols only.

Table **15** *Proportion of Illusion-Supported Responses
to the Horizontal-Vertical (⊥) Illusion* [a]

Item number		27	33	34	26	28	31	36	35	30	32	29		
Per cent Discrepancy		−8	−4	0	3	11	17	21	32	46	53	66		
Sample	N												PSE	Rep
						ADULTS								
Suku	53	.96	.96	.94	.96	.83	.87	.49	.21	.09	.04	.02	21	.981
	48	1.00	1.00	.98	1.00	.88	.92	.52	.23	.08	.02	.02	22	
Anko	180	.94	.94	.94	.97	.86	.71	.52	.26	.11	.14	.09	22	.949
	144	.99	.99	.98	1.00	.90	.76	.51	.23	.08	.08	.03	21	
Toro	56	1.00	1.00	.98	1.00	.96	.70	.48	.23	.04	.11	.00	20	.976
	54	1.00	1.00	.98	1.00	1.00	.72	.46	.24	.04	.11	.00	20	
Sene	137	.90	.79	.81	.81	.70	.60	.57	.28	.25	.20	.13	24	.891
	79	1.00	.99	.96	.99	.86	.62	.61	.23	.14	.06	.03	24	
Fang	49	1.00	1.00	1.00	1.00	.88	.61	.49	.22	.02	.06	.02	21	.978
	45	1.00	1.00	1.00	1.00	.91	.64	.51	.18	.02	.04	.00	21	
Mine	72	1.00	1.00	1.00	.99	.94	.71	.33	.17	.07	.08	.03	19	.985
	69	1.00	1.00	1.00	.99	.94	.70	.35	.16	.06	.06	.03	19	
Ijaw	51	1.00	1.00	.98	1.00	.90	.73	.39	.06	.02	.00	.00	20	.993
	51	1.00	1.00	.98	1.00	.90	.73	.39	.06	.02	.00	.00	20	
Evan	119	.99	1.00	.99	.97	.73	.69	.46	.06	.03	.02	.01	20	.980
	114	.99	1.00	.99	.97	.74	.70	.44	.06	.03	.01	.00	20	
Bush	46	.98	.98	.89	.93	.74	.74	.37	.09	.02	.02	.00	20	.966
	41	1.00	1.00	.93	.98	.78	.78	.34	.10	.02	.00	.00	20	
N. U.	30	1.00	1.00	1.00	1.00	.67	.57	.40	.03	.03	.00	.00	19	.991
	29	1.00	1.00	1.00	1.00	.69	.59	.38	.03	.03	.00	.00	19	
Songe	47	1.00	1.00	.94	.96	.81	.47	.26	.02	.02	.00	.00	16	.985
	46	1.00	1.00	.93	.98	.83	.46	.24	.02	.00	.00	.00	16	
Euro	44	.98	1.00	.98	.95	.59	.43	.30	.05	.00	.00	.02	14	.977
	42	1.00	1.00	.98	.98	.60	.45	.31	.02	.00	.00	.00	15	
Hanu	43	1.00	1.00	.93	.98	.72	.33	.23	.05	.00	.00	.00	15	.979
	39	1.00	1.00	.97	1.00	.74	.33	.21	.00	.00	.00	.00	15	
Zulu	51	.84	.63	.90	.86	.22	.27	.22	.08	.18	.49	.20	8	.834
	18	.94	1.00	.89	.94	.28	.28	.17	.06	.06	.06	.00	8	
Bété	52	.98	.92	.85	.79	.35	.25	.17	.04	.02	.06	.02	8	.956
	43	1.00	.95	.88	.84	.35	.21	.12	.02	.00	.00	.00	9	

Table **15**   *(cont.)*

Item number		27	33	34	26	28	31	36	35	30	32	29		
Per cent Discrepancy		−8	−4	0	3	11	17	21	32	46	53	66		
Sample	N												PSE	Rep
						CHILDREN								
Anko	164	.96	.87	.90	.93	.83	.71	.56	.29	.10	.20	.05	23	.921
	117	1.00	.97	.95	.99	.89	.75	.57	.26	.05	.08	.02	23	
Daho	65	1.00	.95	.97	.98	.83	.68	.52	.29	.12	.05	.02	22	.964
	57	1.00	.98	.98	1.00	.89	.70	.53	.25	.12	.02	.02	22	
Suku	23	1.00	1.00	1.00	1.00	.91	.74	.39	.22	.09	.00	.00	20	.984
	21	1.00	1.00	1.00	1.00	.90	.76	.43	.19	.05	.00	.00	20	
Toro	53	1.00	.98	.94	.96	.91	.70	.36	.21	.09	.09	.06	19	.979
	51	1.00	1.00	.96	.98	.90	.71	.37	.20	.08	.08	.04	19	
Ijaw Sch.	61	.95	.95	.98	.95	.80	.67	.44	.23	.16	.13	.05	20	.936
	46	1.00	1.00	.98	1.00	.87	.70	.48	.17	.07	.02	.00	20	
Songe	51	.98	.98	.88	.96	.86	.63	.43	.10	.04	.04	.02	20	.975
	45	1.00	1.00	.98	.98	.93	.64	.47	.07	.04	.02	.02	20	
Fang	61	1.00	1.00	.97	1.00	.85	.62	.30	.23	.08	.03	.00	18	.969
	53	1.00	1.00	.96	1.00	.89	.64	.32	.21	.02	.04	.00	19	
Ijaw	50	.96	.90	.90	1.00	.76	.58	.40	.30	.10	.18	.04	19	.935
	35	1.00	.97	.97	1.00	.86	.57	.37	.20	.06	.03	.00	18	
Hanu	14	1.00	.93	.86	1.00	.79	.64	.36	.14	.07	.14	.07	19	.968
	13	1.00	1.00	.92	1.00	.77	.62	.38	.15	.08	.08	.08	19	
Evan	89	1.00	.99	.98	.96	.62	.57	.35	.10	.01	.03	.00	18	.969
	84	1.00	.99	.99	.96	.64	.60	.33	.10	.01	.02	.00	18	
Sene	125	.81	.67	.68	.76	.56	.46	.46	.33	.24	.17	.10	15	.863
	51	.96	.84	.86	.92	.73	.49	.45	.18	.06	.04	.02	17	
Zulu	49	.86	.82	.84	.84	.45	.41	.20	.12	.29	.45	.39	10	.833
	17	.88	.88	1.00	.88	.53	.35	.06	.12	.12	.12	.00	12	
Bété	43	1.00	.98	.91	.93	.49	.33	.23	.05	.05	.07	.02	11	.960
	36	1.00	.97	.94	.94	.50	.33	.19	.03	.00	.00	.00	11	

[a]The proportions in the first row for each sample were computed over all cases, while the proportions in the second row are based on internally consistent protocols only.

Table **16**   *Proportion of Illusion-Supported Responses to the Horizontal-Vertical (⌐) Illusion* [a]

Item number		19	25	24	17	20	23	22	21	18		
Per cent Discrepancy		−11	−8	−6	0	7	9	18	28	35		
Sample	N										PSE	Rep
					ADULTS							
Toro	56	1.00	1.00	1.00	.96	.88	.73	.55	.14	.04	19	.978
	52	1.00	1.00	1.00	1.00	.88	.79	.54	.13	.04	19	
Anko	180	.94	.95	.90	.97	.83	.61	.49	.22	.04	18	.954
	158	.97	.97	.98	.97	.87	.68	.48	.19	.04	17	
Mine	72	.99	1.00	1.00	.97	.74	.58	.31	.10	.04	12	.980
	69	1.00	1.00	1.00	.97	.75	.57	.32	.09	.01	12	
Suku	53	.96	.92	.94	.91	.74	.45	.32	.09	.04	9	.975
	48	1.00	.98	.98	.96	.81	.48	.31	.10	.04	9	
Songe	47	1.00	1.00	1.00	.98	.87	.55	.11	.02	.00	10	.991
	46	1.00	1.00	1.00	.98	.89	.57	.11	.00	.00	10	
Fang	49	1.00	.98	1.00	.96	.78	.39	.27	.04	.02	8	.975
	47	1.00	.98	1.00	.98	.79	.40	.23	.04	.02	8	
Ijaw	51	1.00	1.00	1.00	.98	.75	.37	.14	.00	.00	8	.996
	51	1.00	1.00	1.00	.98	.75	.37	.14	.00	.00	8	
Bush	46	.96	.96	.91	.96	.63	.48	.13	.09	.00	9	.947
	39	1.00	.97	.95	.97	.69	.44	.13	.00	.00	9	
Evan	119	.99	.99	1.00	.97	.51	.32	.13	.01	.00	7	.987
	118	.99	.99	1.00	.97	.52	.32	.12	.01	.00	7	
N. U.	30	1.00	1.00	1.00	.97	.53	.20	.13	.00	.00	7	.996
	30	1.00	1.00	1.00	.97	.53	.20	.13	.00	.00	7	
Zulu	51	.92	.92	.88	.84	.57	.18	.22	.14	.02	7	.932
	39	.92	1.00	1.00	.92	.59	.18	.08	.08	.00	7	
Euro	44	1.00	.95	.98	.89	.34	.32	.20	.00	.00	5	.967
	42	1.00	.95	.98	.88	.36	.33	.17	.00	.00	5	
Sene	137	.84	.84	.75	.74	.51	.34	.10	.10	.16	6	.923
	99	.98	.94	.91	.74	.46	.26	.06	.06	.05	7	
Hanu	43	.98	1.00	.98	.79	.37	.16	.12	.00	.00	5	.990
	41	1.00	1.00	1.00	.78	.39	.17	.10	.00	.00	5	
Bété	52	.98	1.00	.79	.67	.13	.10	.06	.02	.00	2	.976
	48	1.00	1.00	.81	.65	.13	.08	.04	.00	.00	2	

Table **16** (*cont.*)

Item number		19	25	24	17	20	23	22	21	18		
Per cent Discrepancy		−11	−8	−6	0	7	9	18	28	35		
Sample	N										PSE	Rep
				CHILDREN								
Daho	65	1.00	.98	.98	.98	.94	.77	.54	.23	.08	19	.973
	63	1.00	1.00	1.00	.98	.94	.78	.54	.22	.06	19	
Toro	53	.98	.94	.92	.96	.83	.64	.51	.26	.08	18	.954
	46	1.00	.98	.98	.96	.87	.70	.59	.24	.07	21	
Anko	164	.93	.94	.88	.93	.92	.55	.46	.26	.07	14	.937
	133	.98	.98	.97	.95	.95	.59	.47	.20	.04	16	
Ijaw Sch.	61	.97	.97	.95	.93	.80	.54	.51	.18	.00	18	.964
	57	.98	1.00	1.00	.98	.82	.56	.51	.16	.00	18	
Suku	23	1.00	1.00	1.00	.96	.96	.57	.39	.00	.04	12	.976
	21	1.00	1.00	1.00	.95	1.00	.57	.38	.00	.00	12	
Ijaw	50	.94	.96	.96	.92	.74	.60	.42	.18	.08	14	.951
	46	.98	.98	.98	.96	.76	.61	.39	.17	.07	14	
Songe	51	1.00	.98	1.00	1.00	.84	.41	.31	.10	.02	9	.974
	49	1.00	.98	1.00	1.00	.84	.43	.33	.06	.02	9	
Hanu	14	.93	1.00	1.00	.79	.71	.57	.43	.14	.07	13	.929
	12	1.00	1.00	1.00	.83	.75	.50	.42	.08	.00	9	
Fang	61	1.00	.97	.98	.98	.72	.56	.28	.02	.02	11	.976
	58	1.00	.98	.98	.98	.72	.59	.24	.02	.00	11	
Zulu	49	.98	.86	.96	.82	.55	.37	.39	.27	.06	8	.932
	35	1.00	.94	.97	.86	.63	.40	.31	.14	.06	8	
Evan	89	.99	.97	.94	.89	.54	.28	.19	.01	.00	7	.972
	85	.99	.99	.95	.89	.56	.29	.16	.01	.00	8	
Sene	125	.76	.73	.62	.70	.41	.38	.18	.12	.16	5	.892
	69	.94	.86	.84	.74	.45	.32	.13	.10	.04	6	
Bété	43	1.00	.95	.91	.56	.30	.14	.12	.02	.05	2	.979
	40	1.00	.98	.90	.55	.28	.15	.08	.00	.00	1	

[a]The proportions in the first row for each sample were computed over all cases, while the proportions in the second row are based on internally consistent protocols only.

Table 17 Proportion of Illusion-Supported Responses to the Perspective Drawing Illusion[a]

Item number		49	44	52	47	51	48	54	45	50	46	53		
Per cent Discrepancy		−15	−10	−5	0	5	10	14	19	29	40	49		
Sample	N												PSE	Rep
ADULTS														
Hanu	43	1.00	.98	.91	.93	.65	.19	.30	.05	.05	.05	.02	7	.966
	38	1.00	.97	.97	.92	.66	.21	.24	.03	.03	.03	.03	7	
Fang	49	.98	.90	.92	.82	.47	.24	.20	.12	.10	.06	.08	5	.970
	42	1.00	.98	.95	.83	.50	.24	.17	.10	.07	.05	.05	5	
N. U.	30	1.00	.90	1.00	.87	.67	.20	.17	.10	.00	.00	.00	7	.973
	29	1.00	.90	1.00	.86	.69	.21	.17	.07	.00	.00	.00	7	
Anko	180	.89	.95	.86	.79	.45	.23	.32	.08	.08	.07	.09	4	.921
	125	.99	.98	.94	.89	.51	.21	.24	.02	.01	.00	.00	5	
Suku	53	.98	.96	.89	.74	.58	.28	.13	.09	.02	.00	.04	6	.981
	50	1.00	.96	.90	.74	.62	.30	.12	.06	.02	.00	.02	7	
Toro	56	1.00	.98	.95	.82	.54	.20	.16	.05	.04	.00	.02	6	.972
	50	1.00	1.00	1.00	.84	.52	.18	.14	.04	.02	.00	.00	6	
Evan	119	.99	.95	.95	.84	.50	.17	.18	.01	.00	.00	.00	5	.981
	113	.99	.96	.96	.84	.53	.17	.14	.01	.00	.00	.00	6	
Zulu	51	.90	.96	.76	.78	.41	.25	.18	.08	.06	.04	.00	4	.936
	34	1.00	1.00	.94	.94	.41	.18	.06	.03	.00	.00	.00	4	
Bush	46	.96	.96	.89	.65	.50	.17	.15	.09	.07	.02	.04	5	.968
	44	.95	.98	.89	.64	.48	.18	.14	.09	.05	.02	.02	4	
Songe	47	1.00	1.00	.98	.79	.40	.04	.04	.00	.00	.00	.00	4	.996
	47	1.00	1.00	.98	.79	.40	.04	.04	.00	.00	.00	.00	4	
Mine	72	1.00	.99	.90	.72	.32	.08	.10	.06	.01	.00	.00	3	.981
	69	1.00	.99	.91	.75	.33	.09	.09	.03	.01	.00	.00	3	
Sene	137	.77	.82	.66	.54	.36	.20	.14	.14	.20	.14	.12	1	.916
	89	.96	.96	.83	.62	.35	.13	.07	.04	.04	.06	.04	2	
Ijaw	51	.98	.96	.92	.65	.29	.10	.06	.00	.02	.00	.00	2	.980
	49	1.00	.98	.92	.65	.29	.08	.06	.00	.02	.00	.00	2	
Euro	44	1.00	.93	.86	.61	.41	.02	.16	.02	.00	.00	.00	3	.969
	42	1.00	.93	.86	.60	.43	.02	.12	.02	.00	.00	.00	3	
Bété	52	.92	.79	.73	.40	.19	.08	.08	.04	.00	.02	.00	−2	.979
	49	.94	.80	.73	.39	.20	.08	.08	.00	.00	.00	.00	−2	

Table 17 (cont.)

Item number		49	44	52	47	51	48	54	45	50	46	53		
Per cent Discrepancy		−15	−10	−5	0	5	10	14	19	29	40	49		
Sample	N												PSE	Rep
CHILDREN														
Hanu	14	.93	1.00	1.00	.93	.79	.21	.36	.07	.14	.14	.07	8	.948
	12	1.00	1.00	1.00	1.00	.83	.17	.33	.08	.08	.08	.00	8	
Ijaw Sch.	61	.97	.95	.85	.90	.70	.20	.38	.08	.07	.03	.03	7	.960
	53	.98	1.00	.94	.92	.75	.23	.34	.06	.04	.02	.02	7	
Anko	164	.88	.95	.77	.84	.66	.30	.43	.11	.15	.05	.11	7	.905
	105	.98	.97	.92	.92	.72	.31	.31	.07	.00	.00	.00	8	
Evan	89	.98	.98	.99	.80	.62	.27	.30	.04	.03	.02	.02	7	.971
	82	.98	.98	.99	.80	.65	.27	.27	.04	.04	.02	.01	7	
Fang	61	.95	.89	.82	.79	.59	.25	.31	.11	.07	.03	.07	6	.942
	43	1.00	.93	.93	.86	.60	.26	.26	.05	.07	.02	.00	6	
Suku	23	1.00	.96	.87	.87	.65	.17	.26	.04	.04	.00	.00	6	.964
	21	1.00	1.00	.90	.90	.62	.19	.24	.05	.00	.00	.00	6	
Zulu	49	.92	.92	.80	.88	.51	.33	.33	.06	.04	.00	.00	5	.946
	40	.93	.95	.88	.90	.53	.33	.23	.03	.00	.00	.00	6	
Daho	65	.80	.72	.72	.57	.46	.09	.23	.08	.05	.08	.06	3	.933
	39	.95	.92	.95	.72	.51	.10	.15	.03	.03	.03	.03	5	
Toro	53	.96	.91	.81	.68	.51	.15	.19	.06	.00	.00	.02	5	.949
	42	1.00	.93	.88	.74	.55	.12	.19	.00	.00	.00	.00	5	
Songe	51	1.00	.96	.82	.75	.47	.12	.14	.02	.00	.00	.00	4	.970
	48	1.00	.96	.85	.73	.46	.13	.10	.00	.00	.00	.00	4	
Ijaw	50	.98	.90	.76	.70	.48	.08	.24	.04	.04	.02	.00	4	.942
	40	1.00	.93	.83	.73	.50	.05	.15	.03	.00	.00	.00	5	
Bété	43	.93	.84	.79	.70	.49	.19	.19	.02	.00	.00	.00	5	.966
	36	1.00	.86	.86	.75	.56	.19	.14	.00	.00	.00	.00	6	
Sene	125	.62	.75	.59	.54	.39	.19	.17	.15	.18	.10	.10	1	.898
	69	.81	.93	.75	.62	.42	.17	.13	.10	.04	.04	.01	3	

[a]The proportions in the first row for each sample were computed over all cases, while the proportions in the second row are based on internally consistent protocols only.

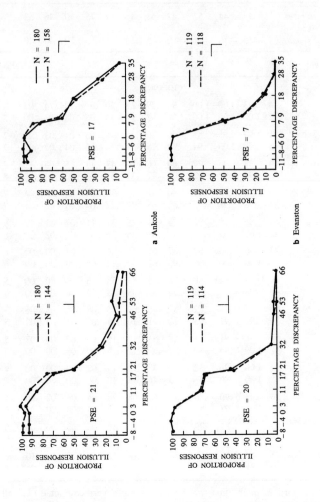

Figure **14**   *Proportion of illusion-supported responses as a function of percentage discrepancy on two versions of the horizontal-vertical illusion*

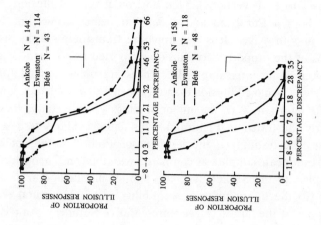

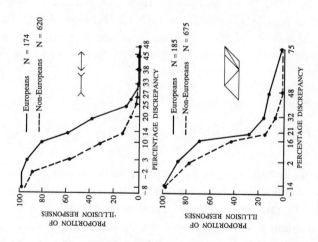

Figure **15**   *Proportion of illusion-supported responses as a function of percentage discrepancy on four illusion-inducing figures by European and non-European adult samples*

Figure 14 presents a small selection of graphs based on responses to both versions of the horizontal-vertical illusion. Here, with both a European and a non-European sample, one again sees smooth ogives. It is also apparent from these graphs that, in terms of the proportion of illusion-supported responses to each of the items, the intersample differences are more marked for the inverted ⌐-shaped illusion than for the inverted ⊤-shaped illusion.

To return now to the major findings of this study, they are clearly illustrated in Figure 15. This figure contains four sets of ogives illustrating: (i) the lesser susceptibility of the combined non-European samples, as compared with the combined European samples, to the Müller-Lyer and Sander parallelogram illusions; and (ii) the intermediate susceptibility to the horizontal-vertical illusions of the largest, most representative European sample. The graphs in Figure 15 are based on internally consistent cases.

Thus, the analysis of proportions of illusion-supported responses item by item, as summarized in Tables 13 through 17 and illustrated in part by Figures 12 through 15, reveals in a detailed way how the various samples differed from one another in their susceptibility to the illusions, yet resembled each other in the orderliness of performance of the task.

GUTTMAN REPRODUCIBILITY COEFFICIENTS

A better indication of this is given by the Guttman reproducibility coefficients (Reps) shown in the right-hand column of Tables 13 through 17. The reproducibility coefficient is an index of the extent to which a sample of individuals responds to a set of items as if these items all represented points along a single dimension. In the present case, if a respondent fails to give an illusion-supported response to a particular item but makes such a response to items below and above it in percentage discrepancy, this failure would constitute an "error." Each such "error" in a sample's protocols diminishes that sample's coefficient of reproducibility. Reps were calculated for each sample, with, of course, all cases included, and constitute the proportion of all responses in each sample that are "errorless" in the Guttman sense. Considering that the present calculations include those individual cases with sufficient "error" in their protocols to justify our eliminating them from our "purified" score calculations, the reproducibility coefficients are very high indeed.

However, it is perhaps more interesting at this point to note that while most Reps are above .95, a few of these coefficients are, by contrast, only moderately high. While in absolute value they are by no means low, they depart sufficiently from the majority of Reps to direct attention to samples that possess these lower Reps. For example, on the Müller-Lyer illusion, the Zulu adults and children both have relatively low Reps (.840, .859), and the Senegalese adults are also lower than most other samples (.886). On the Sander parallelogram, the only samples with a Rep below .92 are the adult and children Zulu groups (.905, .898). The Senegalese and Zulu, both adults and children, are lower than any other samples on the two versions of the horizontal-vertical illusion. On the perspective drawing illusion the Ankole and Dahomeans join the Senegalese and Zulu in lower Rep indices.

That these high Guttman-error rates show the same thing as a high proportion of distorted individual protocols may be seen by noting the proportions of cases eliminated from these samples as shown above in Table 3 (p. 120). Returning to that table, we note once more that our elimination of cases was justifiable since those instances in which a significant number of cases in a sample were eliminated involved, for the most part, those few samples with relatively low reproducibility indices. (With this reiterated, there is a different point to be noted here: Since relative nonscalability is characteristic of two societies [Zulu and Senegalese] over all five illusions, we might wish to question *all* Zulu and Senegalese sample scores, even those based only on cases that meet our requirements of consistency. This point will be recalled later.)

STATISTICAL SIGNIFICANCE OF THE INTERSAMPLE DIFFERENCES

As the results already presented indicate, there are varied, and substantial, cross-cultural differences in susceptibility to the various illusions employed in this study. The picture as it has thus far been drawn from the sample performances is one of greater susceptibility among European groups than among non-European groups to the Müller-Lyer and Sander illusions; of only moderate susceptibility to the horizontal-vertical illusions by European groups, with certain non-European groups displaying high, others low, susceptibility; and of a relatively undifferentiated clustering of scores on the perspective drawing illusion. We have also presented in considerable detail some analytic steps that indicate that the differences are not artifactual. We must now ask with what confidence may it be concluded that these intersample differences in performance are the result of something other than chance.

Table **18**   *Analyses of Variance*

	Adults		Children	
	F	df	F	df
		CONSISTENT CASES		
Müller-Lyer	29.73	14, 779	19.68	12, 547
Sander parallelogram	7.62	13, 846	5.68	12, 707
Horizontal-vertical ($\perp$)	22.25	14, 847	5.32	12, 613
Horizontal-vertical ($\sqsupset$)	23.09	14, 912	18.08	12, 701
Perspective drawing	6.11	14, 855	5.00	12, 617
		ALL CASES		
Müller-Lyer	27.11	14, 1015	20.66	12, 835
Sander parallelogram	25.25	13, 969	4.81	12, 385
Horizontal-vertical ($\perp$)	10.99	14, 1015	6.38	12, 835
Horizontal-vertical ($\sqsupset$)	19.99	14, 1015	21.87	12, 835
Perspective drawing	6.02	14, 1015	8.87	12, 835

Simple analyses of variance were performed on the number of illusion-supported responses of consistent adults and of consistent children on each of the five illusions. In all of these ten analyses, between-groups variance was significant. The values of F are shown in Table 18. The results of these analyses thus indicate that among all the individuals whose protocols satisfied our criterion of consistency, variance in scores on each of the five illusions is confidently attributable to differences in mean performance of the groups sampled. The same conclusion holds for *all* respondents, consistent or not, as shown by the results of similar analyses of variance of scores of all cases, shown in the bottom half of Table 18. The outcome of the analyses of variance justifies a detailed statistical analysis of differences among the mean performances of all samples on all the illusions, and it is to this analysis that we now turn.

To ascertain the pattern of significant differences in mean performances of the various groups on each of the five illusions, a complete set of comparisons of pairs of means was performed separately for samples of children and for samples of adults. Thus, for the Müller-Lyer illusion, all possible pairs of 15 adult means were compared, and all possible pairs of 13 children means were also compared. This procedure was repeated for each of the other four illusions. Were we then to evaluate the resultant t-values in each set as if they were mutually independent, an artifactual enhancement of the number of "significant" t's would have resulted. To cope with this problem inherent in multiple, nonindependent comparisons, we adopted the Scheffé procedure for interpreting t-ratios and will describe as significant only those t's that satisfy the ultra-stringent criteria of the Scheffé test. In the tables that follow, only the t's that fall to the left and below the solid line satisfy those criteria of statistical significance.

The procedure devised by Scheffé (1953) is discussed in some detail by McHugh and Ellis (1955) and by Stanley (1957). It was employed here in an effort to compensate for the fact that our sample mean comparisons are nonindependent and of a "postmortem" nature. We applied this procedure in the following way: A t-ratio was computed for all possible intersample comparisons (separately for adults and for children and on each of the five illusions). Each t was then squared to produce values of F. Then, rather than evaluate the obtained F's by comparing them with the usually appropriate tabled values of F at the .05 level, we modified the tabled values in accord with the formula

$$F_{\text{modified}_{df_1 = 1, df_2 = n_1 + n_2 - 2}} = (K - 1)[F_{.05df_1 = K - 1, df_2 = n_1 + n_2 - 2} - 2],$$

where K is the total number of groups from among which a given pair was drawn.

As Stanley (1957) notes, "Scheffé's procedure is more conservative than necessary for most comparisons of interest to psychologists." In the present case, employment of the Scheffé procedure clearly results in fewer significant differences than would have resulted had alternative procedures been employed. Indeed, although we do not report them in detail here, we did alternative analyses, including between-groups t-tests using an estimate of common within-group variance and a similar set of t-tests using separate error terms. Both of these approaches resulted in many more "significant" t's than we will claim in our report of the Scheffé analysis.

By adopting the stringent criteria, we gain some ease of interpretation of results because we have fewer "significant" differences to explain. And, as it turns out (see below), the differences we have to explain are in essential accord with our major hypotheses. More lenient criteria of significance would have resulted in problems of interpretation because the orderings of mean scores in all cases contain at least some reversals when viewed in the light of our hypotheses. With the Scheffé procedure, many of these details of ordering turn out to be unreliable and can thus be ignored. On the other hand, we very likely are missing some significant differences as a result of using the Scheffé procedure. Moreover, we have some doubts as to the appropriateness of the Scheffé logic as it is applied to our data, particularly in those instances in which all t's involving a particular sample are of a considerable magnitude. The Scheffé test is obviously appropriate where a whole set of t's approximates the population of t's expected if there were no true differences; but in the present study there is a considerable degree of departure from the null model, and we accordingly feel somewhat uneasy about our decision not to interpret certain t-values.

However, in view of the very nature of our findings and of the fact that a considerable body of opinion in contemporary psychology would consider cultural differences in illusion susceptibility an unlikely finding, we choose to base our conclusions on extremely conservative tests of significance. Thus, if the technique of statistical inference-testing employed here has led to any errors in conclusion, such errors can only be failures to reject the null hypothesis when it should have been rejected. We feel, therefore, that confidence in what we describe as significant differences has been maximized.

Finally, for the reader who shares our uneasiness about the possibility of missing significant differences, the following tables contain all t-values that surpass the .05 level of significance (approximately 1.96) usually employed in t-tests. The interested reader should also note that the .01 level of significance normally employed is approximately 2.70 and the .001 level is approximately 3.65.

Table 19 Comparisons of Mean Scores on the Müller-Lyer Illusion: Adults

SAMPLE:	Evan	N. U.	Euro	Sene	Anko	Zulu	Suku	Toro	Song	Fang	Hanu	Ijaw	Bété	Bush	Mine
$\overline{X}$	5.21	5.00	4.33	3.88	3.34	3.33	3.03	3.02	2.98	2.98	2.97	2.89	2.74	2.28	2.23
s.d.	1.54	1.27	1.01	1.65	1.225	1.43	1.405	1.13	1.10	1.32	1.09	1.11	1.06	.94	.85

Significant t's

SAMPLE:	n	Evan	N. U.	Euro	Sene	Anko	Zulu	Suku	Toro	Song	Fang	Hanu	Ijaw	Bété	Bush	Mine
Evan	111	—														
N. U.	27	ns	—													
Euro	36	4.26	2.43	—												
Sene	74	6.99	4.26	2.03	—											
Anko	131	12.28	7.01	5.15	3.05	—										
Zulu	21	6.55	4.92	3.23	ns	ns	—									
Suku	40	9.86	6.89	5.20	3.56	ns	ns	—								
Toro	49	11.39	7.48	5.80	4.03	ns	ns	ns	—							
Song	47	11.40	7.56	5.91	4.17	1.95	ns	ns	ns	—						
Fang	42	10.50	7.23	5.56	3.90	1.78	ns	ns	ns	ns	—					
Hanu	37	10.73	7.32	5.66	3.98	1.84	ns	ns	ns	ns	ns	—				
Ijaw	47	11.96	7.92	6.33	4.60	2.44	ns	ns	ns	ns	ns	ns	—			
Bété	38	12.10	8.27	6.75	5.10	3.11	ns	ns	ns	ns	ns	ns	ns	—		
Bush	36	14.63	10.05	8.81	7.27	5.61	3.44	3.02	3.35	3.11	2.91	2.94	2.76	1.97	—	
Mine	60	17.76	11.18	10.20	8.62	7.19	3.84	3.57	4.08	3.79	3.48	3.54	3.40	2.46	ns	—

Table **20** Comparisons of Mean Scores on the Müller-Lyer Illusion: Children

SAMPLE:		Evan	Sene	Toro	Daho	Zulu	IjSc	Anko	Fang	Ijaw	Song	Hanu	Bété	Suku
	$\overline{X}$	5.57	4.61	4.27	4.22	4.14	3.74	3.61	3.58	3.49	3.16	3.08	2.70	2.05
	s.d.	1.51	1.77	1.28	1.35	1.56	1.275	1.35	1.42	1.04	.88	1.08	1.24	.92

Significant t's

SAMPLE	n	Evan	Sene	Toro	Daho	Zulu	IjSc	Anko	Fang	Ijaw	Song	Hanu	Bété	Suku
Evan	77	—												
Sene	51	4.14	—											
Toro	37	5.59	ns	—										
Daho	40	5.83	ns	ns	—									
Zulu	14	3.94	ns	ns	ns	—								
IjSc	54	9.02	3.85	2.47	2.30	ns	—							
Anko	93	10.60	4.49	2.96	2.79	ns	ns	—						
Fang	43	8.68	3.95	2.65	2.49	ns	ns	ns	—					
Ijaw	37	9.54	4.47	3.13	2.97	ns	ns	ns	ns	—				
Song	44	12.10	6.19	4.74	4.59	2.71	2.39	2.44	ns	ns	—			
Hanu	12	7.51	4.31	3.36	3.24	2.36	ns	ns	ns	ns	ns	—		
Bété	37	12.44	7.29	6.00	5.87	3.78	3.98	4.15	3.40	3.15	1.97	ns	—	
Suku	21	13.99	9.14	7.93	7.82	5.31	6.17	6.48	5.53	5.36	4.39	2.83	2.35	—

1. The Müller-Lyer Illusion

ADULTS   The results of tests of significance of the difference between adult means on the Müller-Lyer are shown in Table 19. From these results it is clear that the Evanstonians ($\overline{X} = 5.21$, PSE = 19) were significantly more susceptible to the Müller-Lyer illusion than any of the non-Western samples. The same is true of the Northwestern University students ($\overline{X} = 5.00$, PSE = 16) and the South African Europeans ($\overline{X} = 4.33$, PSE = 13), except for the fact that the Senegalese ($\overline{X} = 3.88$) and Zulu ($\overline{X} = 3.33$) means were not significantly different from the two Western sample means. (The Senegalese and Zulu performances on this illusion, however, are suspect [see p. 151].) The three Western samples did not differ significantly among themselves, nor, with few exceptions, did the non-Western samples. Only 5 of 66 comparisons among non-Western samples proved significant. Thus, the evidence is strong that among adults, Western peoples are significantly more susceptible than non-Western peoples to the Müller-Lyer illusion.

CHILDREN   The only Western sample that contained children was the Evanston sample. The Evanstonian children, as shown in Table 20, had significantly higher mean scores on the Müller-Lyer illusion than did *all* the non-Western groups of children, except for the Senegalese and Zulu children. Among the non-Western samples, there were 13 significant differences, 8 of which stemmed from comparisons involving the Suku children, a group that obtained an extremely low mean score ($\overline{X} = 2.05$, PSE = 0).

Table **21** *Comparisons of Mean Scores on the Sander Parallelogram Illusion: Adults*

SAMPLE:	N. U.	Evan	Euro	Ijaw	Fang	Zulu	Anko	Sene	Hanu	Toro	Suku	Bété	Song	Mine
$\overline{X}$	3.54	3.23	2.98	2.94	2.72	2.70	2.63	2.59	2.41	2.31	2.28	2.24	2.22	2.06
s.d.	1.07	1.35	1.41	.86	1.03	1.51	1.10	1.34	.715	.94	.83	1.18	.94	.83

Significant *t*'s

	n	N. U.	Evan	Euro	Ijaw	Fang	Zulu	Anko	Sene	Hanu	Toro	Suku	Bété	Song	Mine
N. U.	28	—													
Evan	115	ns	—												
Euro	42	2.09	ns	—											
Ijaw	51	2.53	ns	ns	—										
Fang	43	3.27	2.67	ns	ns	—									
Zulu	33	2.89	2.21	ns	ns	ns	—								
Anko	132	4.20	4.21	ns	1.97	ns	ns	—							
Sene	109	4.22	4.12	ns	2.07	ns	ns	ns	—						
Hanu	39	4.73	4.70	2.49	2.83	ns	ns	ns	ns	—					
Toro	55	5.21	5.40	2.97	3.43	2.03	ns	2.00	ns	ns	—				
Suku	50	5.36	5.61	3.11	3.61	2.19	ns	2.21	ns	ns	ns	—			
Bété	46	5.13	5.11	3.03	3.41	2.16	ns	2.12	ns	ns	ns	ns	—		
Song	46	5.44	5.62	3.27	3.75	2.39	ns	2.42	2.04	ns	ns	ns	ns	—	
Mine	71	6.62	7.65	4.33	5.24	3.52	2.67	4.05	3.43	2.04	ns	ns	ns	ns	—

Table 22 Comparisons of Mean Scores on the Sander Parallelogram Illusion: Children

SAMPLE:	Evan	Sene	Zulu	IjSc	Fang	Hanu	Anko	Toro	Song	Daho	Ijaw	Bété	Suku
$\overline{X}$	3.33	3.29	3.235	3.15	2.98	2.85	2.75	2.68	2.59	2.55	2.53	2.525	1.81
s.d.	.975	1.65	1.35	1.25	1.15	.99	1.04	1.10	.83	1.05	1.08	1.01	.60

Significant t's

	n	Evan	Sene	Zulu	IjSc	Fang	Hanu	Anko	Toro	Song	Daho	Ijaw	Bété	Suku
Evan	81	—												
Sene	89	ns	—											
Zulu	34	ns	ns	—										
IjSc	53	ns	ns	ns	—									
Fang	53	ns	ns	ns	ns	—								
Hanu	13	ns	ns	ns	ns	ns	—							
Anko	130	4.15	3.35	2.24	2.25	ns	ns	—						
Toro	50	3.55	3.04	2.24	2.20	ns	ns	ns	—					
Song	51	4.43	3.77	2.74	2.79	2.20	ns	ns	ns	—				
Daho	58	4.51	3.87	2.85	2.91	2.15	ns	ns	ns	ns	—			
Ijaw	47	4.28	3.73	2.81	2.85	2.12	ns	ns	ns	ns	ns	—		
Bété	40	4.18	3.66	2.79	2.81	2.10	ns	ns	ns	ns	ns	ns	—	
Suku	21	7.56	6.82	5.45	5.79	5.22	3.21	4.89	3.87	3.67	3.44	3.18	3.08	—

2. The Sander Parallelogram Illusion

ADULTS   The results of tests of significance of the difference between adult means on the Sander parallelogram are shown in Table 21. As was the case with the Müller-Lyer illusion, the three Western samples ranked highest and the bulk of the significant differences were found among comparisons involving two of them, the Evanstonians and the Northwestern University students. Five non-Western samples (mineboys, Songe, Bété, Suku, and Toro) had mean scores significantly lower than the means of the Evanstonians and the Northwestern students. These 10 significant t's except for one resulting from the Ijaw–mineboys comparison, were the only significant differences found among 91 possible ones. The South African Europeans had a mean score that was not significantly higher than the non-Western means, but neither was it significantly lower than the other two Western means. Thus, compared to the Müller-Lyer results, there are relatively few significant differences among adult mean scores on the Sander parallelogram, but those that do appear, with only one exception, involve the high-scoring Northwestern and Evanston samples. Again, significantly greater illusion susceptibility is characteristic of the two most Western samples.

CHILDREN   The only significant differences found among children means on the Sander parallelogram were 6 differences, all involving comparisons with the Suku, the lowest ranking sample of children. We would therefore be inclined to conclude that this particular set of data, shown in Table 22, provides virtually no evidence of significant differences in susceptibility.

Table 23 Comparisons of Mean Scores on the Horizontal-Vertical Illusion ($\perp$): Adults

SAMPLE:	Suku	Anko	Toro	Sene	Fang	Mine	Ijaw	Evan	Bush	N. U.	Song	Euro	Hanu	Zulu	Bété
$\overline{X}$	6.65	6.56	6.56	6.48	6.31	6.275	6.08	5.93	5.93	5.72	5.46	5.33	5.26	4.67	4.37
s.d.	1.345	1.48	1.28	1.64	1.31	1.43	1.09	1.27	1.25	1.36	1.15	1.24	1.02	1.645	1.415

	n						Significant t's								
Suku	48	—													
Anko	144	ns	—												
Toro	54	ns	ns	—											
Sene	79	ns	ns	ns	—										
Fang	45	ns	ns	ns	ns	—									
Mine	69	ns	ns	ns	ns	ns	—								
Ijaw	51	2.55	2.68	2.24	1.96	ns	ns	—							
Evan	114	3.62	4.28	3.35	3.09	ns	ns	ns	—						
Bush	41	2.97	3.11	2.70	2.45	ns	ns.	ns	ns	—					
N. U.	29	3.37	3.48	3.13	2.91	2.13	2.12	ns	ns	ns	—				
Song	46	5.17	5.86	4.98	4.79	3.67	3.83	2.89	2.49	2.00	ns	—			
Euro	42	5.47	6.12	5.29	5.11	4.03	4.20	3.30	2.96	4.42	ns	ns	—		
Hanu	39	5.97	6.81	5.82	5.66	4.49	4.71	3.77	3.49	2.82	ns	ns	ns	—	
Zulu	18	5.73	5.92	5.57	5.42	4.74	4.80	4.20	3.95	3.61	2.84	2.32	ns	ns	—
Bété	43	9.21	10.21	9.17	9.10	7.79	8.22	7.32	7.43	6.17	4.79	4.51	3.85	3.64	ns	—

Table 24 Comparisons of Mean Scores on the Horizontal-Vertical Illusion ($\perp$): Children

SAMPLE:		Anko	Daho	Suku	Toro	IjSc	Song	Hanu	Fang	Ijaw	Evan	Sene	Zulu	Bété
	$\overline{X}$	6.53	6.49	6.33	6.31	6.28	6.16	6.08	6.08	6.03	5.64	5.55	4.94	4.92
	s.d.	1.45	1.525	1.20	1.67	1.22	1.30	1.89	1.25	1.60	1.34	1.95	1.89	1.25
	n					Significant t's								
Anko	117	—												
Daho	57	ns	—											
Suku	21	ns	ns	—										
Toro	51	ns	ns	ns	—									
IjSc	46	ns	ns	ns	ns	—								
Song	45	ns	ns	ns	ns	ns	—							
Hanu	13	ns	ns	ns	ns	ns	ns	—						
Fang	53	2.39	ns	ns	ns	ns	ns	ns	—					
Ijaw	35	2.08	ns	ns	ns	ns	ns	ns	ns	—				
Evan	84	5.27	4.10	2.56	3.04	3.36	2.42	ns	2.17	ns	—			
Sene	51	4.36	3.69	2.54	2.87	3.08	2.34	ns	2.12	ns	ns	—		
Zulu	17	4.52	4.18	3.40	3.62	3.76	3.25	2.24	3.09	2.75	1.97	ns	—	
Bété	36	7.43	6.35	4.68	5.38	5.73	4.91	2.73	4.80	3.92	3.22	2.34	ns	—

3. The Horizontal-Vertical Illusion (⊥-shaped)

ADULTS Results here constitute a distinct departure from the pattern of results noted for the Müller-Lyer and Sander parallelogram illusions. The three Western adult samples, which ranked 1st, 2nd, and 3rd on the two acute- and obtuse-angled figures, all fall near the median on this version of the horizontal-vertical illusion. Among 15 adult sample means, the Evanstonians rank 8th, the Northwestern students 10th, and the South African Europeans 12th. However, as shown in Table 23, neither the Evanstonians nor the Northwestern students had a mean score that was significantly lower than the means of any of the non-Western samples. On the other hand, the South African Europeans mean was significantly smaller than the means of four non-Western samples (Suku, Ankole, Toro, and Senegalese). Nine significant *t*'s were found on comparisons involving the lowest ranking sample, the Bété. Other significant *t*'s in the matrix shown in Table 23 were found on comparisons involving the four top-ranked samples (Suku, Ankole, Toro, and Senegalese) *vs.* the non-Western samples (Songe, Hanunóo, and Zulu) that ranked near the bottom along with the South African Europeans and the Bété.

CHILDREN Among the samples of children on this illusion, few significant differences in mean scores appeared, as Table 24 indicates. There were only 7 significant *t*'s, 6 of which involved comparisons between the lowest ranking sample (Bété) and samples ranked 1, 2, 4, 5, 6, and 8. The other significant difference shown in Table 24 was that between the means of the Evanstonians, who ranked 10th out of 13, and the Ankole children, who ranked 1st. That there are so few significant differences in this matrix is a reflection of the small dispersion of mean scores among these 13 samples of children. They range from 6.53 (PSE = 23) for the Ankole children to 4.92 (PSE = 11) for the Bété, but 11 of the 13 means are between 5.55 and 6.53.

Table 25 Comparisons of Mean Scores on the Horizontal-Vertical Illusion (⌐): Adults

SAMPLE:	Toro	Anko	Mine	Suku	Song	Fang	Ijaw	Bush	Evan	N.U.	Zulu	Euro	Sene	Hanu	Bété
X̄	6.385	6.165	5.71	5.67	5.54	5.45	5.235	5.15	4.92	4.83	4.77	4.67	4.465	4.44	3.71
s.d.	1.16	1.33	1.25	1.31	.81	1.14	.97	.93	1.02	1.05	1.135	1.20	1.62	1.18	1.05
n						*Significant t's*									
Toro 52	—														
Anko 158	ns	—													
Mine 69	3.36	2.79	—												
Suku 48	3.23	2.63	ns	—											
Song 46	4.21	3.85	ns	ns	—										
Fang 47	4.35	3.97	ns	ns	ns	—									
Ijaw 51	5.66	5.61	2.46	2.00	ns	ns	—								
Bush 39	5.73	5.62	2.71	2.27	ns	ns	ns	—							
Evan 118	8.31	9.49	4.81	3.92	3.83	2.88	ns	ns	—						
N.U. 30	6.48	6.38	3.80	3.34	3.09	2.52	ns	ns	ns	—					
Zulu 39	7.13	7.20	4.33	3.78	3.58	2.93	2.12	ns	ns	ns	—				
Euro 42	7.61	7.78	4.83	4.23	4.08	3.39	2.60	2.12	ns	ns	ns	—			
Sene 99	9.77	10.80	6.71	5.75	5.86	4.88	4.10	3.43	2.90	ns	ns	ns	—		
Hanu 41	8.60	8.93	5.86	5.13	5.12	4.37	3.64	3.11	2.50	ns	ns	ns	ns	—	
Bété 48	12.74	14.11	10.01	8.83	9.24	8.10	7.55	6.75	6.95	4.71	4.70	4.26	3.87	3.24	—

Table **26** *Comparisons of Mean Scores on the Horizontal-Vertical Illusion* (⌐): *Children*

SAMPLE:	Daho	Toro	Anko	IjSc	Suku	Ijaw	Song	Hanu	Fang	Zulu	Evan	Sene	Bêté
X̄	6.52	6.37	6.14	6.02	5.905	5.89	5.65	5.58	5.52	5.31	4.86	4.42	3.925
s.d.	1.105	1.31	1.30	1.30	.77	1.57	1.03	1.165	1.10	1.745	1.255	1.89	1.37

Significant t's

	n	Daho	Toro	Anko	IjSc	Suku	Ijaw	Song	Hanu	Fang	Zulu	Evan	Sene	Bêté
Daho	63	—												
Toro	46	ns	—											
Anko	133	2.30	ns	—										
IjSc	57	2.34	ns	ns	—									
Suku	21	2.66	ns	ns	ns	—								
Ijaw	46	2.78	ns	ns	ns	ns	—							
Song	49	4.43	3.22	2.79	ns	ns	ns	—						
Hanu	12	2.78	2.22	ns	ns	ns	ns	ns	—					
Fang	58	5.27	3.92	3.69	2.62	ns	ns	ns	ns	—				
Zulu	35	4.66	3.77	3.39	2.74	2.01	1.99	ns	ns	ns	—			
Evan	85	9.26	7.27	8.19	6.15	3.60	4.67	4.20	2.17	3.59	ns	—		
Sene	69	9.92	8.25	8.93	7.28	5.87	5.93	6.27	3.30	5.10	3.22	2.14	—	
Bêté	40	11.43	9.78	10.58	8.91	7.44	7.53	7.35	4.58	6.91	4.79	4.22	2.00	—

4. The Horizontal-Vertical Illusion (⌐-shaped)

ADULTS   As was the case with the other form of the horizontal-vertical illusion, the three Western adult samples ranked
below the median. The Evanstonians ranked 9th, the Northwestern
students 10th, and the South African Europeans 12th. All three of
these samples had mean scores that were significantly smaller than
the means of the two top-ranked samples (Toro and Ankole). The
two top-ranked samples also had mean scores significantly higher
than the means of six other non-Western samples (Ijaw, Bushmen,
Zulu, Senegal, Hanunóo, and Bété). Several other significant differences are shown in Table 25, all of them involving the three
lowest-ranking samples (Senegal, Hanunóo, and Bété).

It is interesting to note that the adult Ankole and Toro samples, both of which account for the majority of significant differences on this version of the horizontal-vertical illusion, also
account for nearly half the significant differences on the other version (Table 23, above). The reader is reminded that these two
samples are drawn from East African tribes who live in adjacent
districts of Uganda. Their environments are nearly identical. That
two samples, so nearly replications of each other, perform so similarly with materials so closely related is further reason for investing
confidence in the validity of our data.

CHILDREN   Of 13 samples of children, the Evanstonians
ranked 11th. The Evanstonian mean was significantly smaller than
the means of the first four ranked groups (Dahomean, Toro,
Ankole, and Ijaw school children). Other significant differences
shown in Table 26 almost all involve the two lowest ranking
groups (Senegal and Bété).

Table **27** Comparisons of Mean Scores on the Perspective Drawing Illusion: Adults

SAMPLE:		Hanu	Fang	N.U.	Anko	Suku	Toro	Evan	Zulu	Bush	Song	Mine	Sene	Ijaw	Euro	Bété
	X̄	5.03	4.93	4.90	4.78	4.74	4.74	4.60	4.56	4.43	4.26	4.20	4.10	4.00	3.98	3.22
	s.d.	1.48	1.98	1.37	1.21	1.69	1.19	1.26	.93	1.87	.94	1.20	1.87	1.19	1.35	1.67
	n							*Significant t's*								
Hanu	38	—														
Fang	42	ns	—													
N.U.	29	ns	ns	—												
Anko	125	ns	ns	ns	—											
Suku	50	ns	ns	ns	ns	—										
Toro	50	ns	ns	ns	ns	ns	—									
Evan	113	2.13	ns	ns	ns	ns	ns	—								
Zulu	34	2.02	ns	ns	ns	ns	ns	ns	—							
Bush	44	2.27	ns	ns	ns	ns	ns	ns	ns	—						
Song	47	3.39	2.60	2.47	3.02	2.09	2.31	1.96	ns	ns	—					
Mine	69	3.70	2.86	2.73	3.49	2.38	2.65	2.36	ns	ns	ns	—				
Sene	89	4.00	3.17	3.04	3.86	2.73	3.02	2.79	ns	ns	ns	ns	—			
Ijaw	49	4.29	3.47	3.35	4.21	3.07	3.37	3.19	2.46	ns	ns	ns	ns	—		
Euro	42	4.14	3.38	3.26	3.91	2.97	3.23	3.00	2.39	ns	ns	ns	ns	ns	—	
Bété	49	6.86	5.98	5.86	7.41	5.81	6.29	6.47	5.38	4.36	4.43	4.31	3.73	2.21	2.92	—

Table **28** Comparisons of Mean Scores on the Perspective Drawing Illusion: Children

SAMPLE:	Hanu	IjSc	Anko	Evan	Fang	Suku	Zulu	Daho	Toro	Bété	Song	Ijaw	Sene
$\overline{X}$	5.58	5.30	5.22	5.04	4.98	4.91	4.75	4.41	4.41	4.36	4.23	4.20	4.04
s.d.	1.62	1.44	1.26	1.59	1.71	1.34	1.60	1.70	1.40	1.50	1.24	1.29	2.22

Significant t's

SAMPLE	n	Hanu	IjSc	Anko	Evan	Fang	Suku	Zulu	Daho	Toro	Bété	Song	Ijaw	Sene
Hanu	12	—												
IjSc	53	ns	—											
Anko	105	ns	ns	—										
Evan	82	ns	ns	ns	—									
Fang	43	ns	ns	ns	ns	—								
Suku	21	ns	ns	ns	ns	ns	—							
Zulu	40	1.99	2.41	2.06	ns	ns	ns	—						
Daho	39	2.78	3.61	3.43	2.50	1.96	ns	ns	—					
Toro	42	2.87	3.92	3.83	2.75	2.12	ns	ns	ns	—				
Bété	36	2.91	3.85	3.71	2.74	2.16	ns	ns	ns	ns	—			
Song	48	3.38	4.93	5.08	3.79	2.92	2.26	2.03	ns	ns	ns	—		
Ijaw	40	3.38	4.79	4.85	3.69	2.90	2.28	2.05	ns	ns	ns	ns	—	
Sene	69	3.77	5.42	5.59	4.37	3.48	2.78	2.63	ns	ns	ns	ns	ns	—

5. The Perspective Drawing Illusion

ADULTS The only adult sample mean that differed significantly from other sample means was that of the Bété, as shown in
Table 27. Since the Bété mean was so low ($\overline{X} = 3.22$, PSE $= -2$)
as to indicate that a number of Bété respondents failed to make
illusion-supported responses even to items in which the per cent
discrepancy was negative, that mean score must be considered
somewhat invalid. Therefore, we would conclude that there are no
genuine significant differences among adult samples on the perspective drawing illusion. No sample exceeded a PSE of 8.

CHILDREN Only 6 significant differences occurred among
the comparisons shown in Table 28, even though the range of
scores was slightly larger than that of the adult scores. The mean
of the Evanstonian children was not significantly different from
any other sample mean.

REVIEW OF THE INTERSAMPLE DIFFERENCES

The matrices of *t*-test results in Tables 19 through 28 provide
considerable evidence that adults in different societies are differentially susceptible to four of the five illusions employed in this
study. Even with extremely cautious standards of statistical significance, a considerable number of sample differences must be considered as the products of something other than chance. On two
of the illusions, the Müller-Lyer and Sander parallelogram, the
most clearly demonstrated differences result from the significantly
high illusion susceptibility manifested by the Evanstonians and the
Northwestern University students. On the two versions of the horizontal-vertical illusion, significant differences stem, for the most
part, from the relatively high illusion susceptibility indicated in
the performances of several African samples, specifically the
Ankole, Toro, Suku, mineboys, and Fang. The results of *t*-tests of
children's sample means on these four illusions are less clear since
in each case fewer differences appear significant.

On the fifth set of stimuli, the perspective drawing illusion, there were, not surprisingly, very few significant differences. This undoubtedly reflects the small range of scores obtained on this illusion. It should also be recalled that the scores on this illusion were all small; for no sample was there an illusion of any important magnitude (the highest PSE was 8 per cent).

For the four sets of stimuli on which any appreciable illusion effects occurred, it is clear from the *t*-tests that significantly different degrees of illusion susceptibility are found cross-culturally.

7 Several topics remain
to be discussed: first,
A Critical the possibility of alternative interpretations of the
Review of the findings, interpretations that
deny—or do not necessitate
Findings —that the differences in scores
across samples represent real
and Some differences in perception. These
possible alternatives include (1)
Additional differential failure to communicate
the task; (2) systematic differences in
Data test-administration; and (3) behavioral
or physiological differences of a nonper-
ceptual nature. We must then take into account some apparently
incompatible results of others and some inconsistencies in our own
data, as well as the complicating effects of age trends on the results.

Following this consideration of various challenges to our preferred interpretation are (1) a report on some additional data that
support it, and (2) a review of the kinds of future research to which
our mode of interpreting the present findings commits us.

ALTERNATIVE INTERPRETATIONS

FAILURE TO COMMUNICATE THE TASK

How can one be assured that the differences in
the mean number of illusion-supported responses shown to exist across cultures in the
present research are "real" differences,
potentially demonstrable by a variety
of methods? In general, how can one
discriminate between misunderstanding and genuine disagreement? How can one tell

when one is communicating well enough to know that people
see things differently and are not merely reporting identical visual
experiences in different fashions?

Campbell (1964) notes that differential responding often means
lack of communication. Consider an extreme form of the technique employed cross-culturally in the present research: Suppose
that an anthropologist armed with a set of our materials was
parachuted into a totally isolated village in New Guinea, and that
the anthropologist had first to learn the language without help of
an interpreter. From what is known of the process of language-
learning, which indicates that no person ever learns another's
language perfectly, it becomes obvious that here is a problematic
situation in which the cues and presumptions of communication
need to be specified. It would very likely turn out that the anthropologist's main cue for achieved communication is the degree
of similarity between his own response to a stimulus and the
response that the other would make. Disagreement would be
interpreted as a sign of communication failure. How, then, can
disagreement in response to the stimuli in the present research
be taken instead as a difference in perception?

It was concern for this sticky methodological problem that
prompted the many precautions built into the materials and into
the techniques for collecting and analyzing responses to them.
The complexity of the problem perhaps justifies the somewhat
tedious presentation of methodological details in Chapter 5. A
brief reference to some of them should now suffice.

The first four items shown to each respondent were comprehension checks (see Figures 6, 7, 8, and 9, pp. 107–110). On these
items, if the respondent did not respond as the anthropologist
would have, it was assumed that translation or comprehension or
cooperation had failed; in other words, a cross-cultural difference
in response was attributed to some technical failure. Yet on the
subsequent items, we were prepared to accept such differences in
response as signs of differences in perception. But how do we
know that the "wrong" responses to these so-called comprehen-

sion-check items did not result from illusions produced by them?

The fourth item is particularly relevant, for it is an approxima-tion of the Müller-Lyer figure. The point is that on this item, were an illusion to occur, it would be on the order of a 500 per cent illusion. It seems incredible, on epistemological grounds, that a person exists in any culture for whom the illusion is that strong. We prefer to say that persons making the illusion-supported re-sponse on items so far beyond the established range of illusion strength did so as the result of a systematic misinterpretation. On the other hand, when a respondent made the appropriate responses to the comprehension-check items and *then* deviated from Western norms in his responses to the test items, these devi-ations were accepted as evidence of a difference in perception, provided the deviations occurred *in an orderly fashion* and *not on items of extreme per cent discrepancy.*

This last point introduces an apparent paradox. Had any of our samples *responded* in a radically different way from ourselves (e.g., by making the illusion-supported response to *every* item in a set), we could not have distinguished between total failure of communication and total difference in perception. In fact, had any of our samples *perceived* every item in a radically different way from ourselves, we could not have determined that fact. In essence, we could only observe differences in perception because these differences were small enough to be enclosed in similarities. Because the stimuli employed in this research covered a range so broad that all samples responded alike in some instances, we were able to note the differences. Thus, a total context of agree-ment provided the base for noting particular, localized response discrepancies.

This argument illustrates a general epistemological principle: Discrepancy can be noted and interpreted only against a back-ground of nondiscrepant fit, or pattern repetition. Consider the reidentification of a single planet on successive nights, plus the inference that the planet migrates in an eccentric backtracking manner. Had Venus, say, been the only star in the sky, this might never have been documented. More important, had all the fixed stars been planets, the migrations of Venus might have gone unascertained; had the oscillations in the locations of the fixed stars been so great as to subtend several degrees of visual angle, the backtracking would not have been observed. It was the recurrent fixedness of an almost infinitely large number of stars that made the wanderings of the few planets interpretable as such.

A methodological point follows from this principle: When investigating the possibility of systematic differences in response patterns across groups, one must include some stimuli for which identical responses may confidently be expected to occur except when a communication breakdown occurs. Having employed this methodological caution in our research, we can conclude that since the reported differences are imbedded in similarities, they are based on data collected from respondents all of whom *interpreted the task* identically. Thus, it is concluded that the reported differences are not the result of faulty communication.

This conclusion, of course, refers primarily to the "pure" cases obtained after the cases of obvious communication failure were eliminated (pp. 116–121). Indeed, a rough index of communication difficulty may be found in the proportion of cases lost from each sample on each of the illusions. That there is no systematic relationship between the proportion of cases lost and the strength of the illusion (Table 29) adds further support to the contention that the cultural differences are not artifactual.

Table **29** *Rank-order Correlation Between Proportion of Cases Lost and Mean Illusion Score*

Illusion	R
Müller-Lyer	−.039
Sander parallelogram	.329
Horizontal-vertical (⊥)	.042
Horizontal-vertical (⌐)	−.078
Perspective drawing	.184

SYSTEMATIC DIFFERENCES IN TEST-ADMINISTRATION

One great bane of anthropological data when used for comparative purposes is the recurrent question: Do these two reports differ because of the cultures or because of the ethnographers? The discouraging outcome of attempts to replicate anthropological observations (see Campbell, 1961, for citations) indicates that this is a very real problem indeed. The difficulty is, of course, maximized where problem, perspective, and strategy of questioning differ. It is presumably minimized in the present setting, where physically identical stimuli have been used under specified conditions of administration. But systematic differences no doubt remain, including deviations from the specified instructions and differences on unspecified conditions. Respondent-to-respondent variations within a given culture are not the problem; rather, we are presently concerned with sample-to-sample variations resulting from idiosyncracies of administration. We questioned our colleagues about this after they completed their field work, and some examples of amended procedure were reported.

For example, Alan Merriam reported that his Songe interpreter presented the Sander parallelograms as "houses with red lines in them," hitting upon this after a trial-and-error process in which communication seemed difficult. We would have vetoed this translation had we been asked, for it seems to involve the very kind of reification of the drawing to which we attribute the strength of this illusion in the Western world. It is perhaps comforting to note that the Songe ranked even further away from carpentered-world samples than they did on the Müller-Lyer, which presumably was presented without introducing such third-dimensional connotations. Merriam also reports that his respondents consistently tilted their heads to see better, looking over their shoulders and sideward. Idiosyncracies of these kinds no doubt occurred in a number of other groups.

Most of our colleagues who described their procedures to us in detail seem to have followed instructions exactly. But when questioned further, even these colleagues expressed some concern that their use of interpreters meant they were not completely sure of exactly what was communicated to respondents at all times. On the other hand, some, at least, seemed to have considerable confidence in their communication of the task to the respondents. Igor Kopytoff, for example, reported that with the Suku we "had no trouble explaining what they were to judge. No reinterpretation of lines in some other terms, or via a metaphor, was necessary. The respondents were asked to judge *lines* and their *bigness/length,* and they did." It must, nonetheless, be acknowledged that differences of administrative idiosyncracies across samples could constitute a source of noise in the data. On the other hand, we doubt that such differences relate systematically to our major findings.

Outright administrative error is also a possibility. One administrator reports that after testing 10 or 20 respondents, he developed very strong expectations of what answer the respondents should give to a given item, and that if a respondent gave the *other* answer, there was the impulse to correct the respondent or to ask him to reconsider. Such a tendency, had it been acted upon, might account for the very low rate of inconsistency in some sets of data. Others report a tendency toward recording errors due to our unfortunate confounding of the symbols R (right) and L (left) with the spatial left and right positions on the answer sheet. Such errors, however, would only lead to greater apparent inconsistency in the data.

The Viewing Distance and the Angle of Regard. The administrative factors we initially thought the most likely source of bias were the requirements that the stimuli be held four feet from the respondent and in a position perpendicular to his line of regard. These stipulations proved to be difficult to achieve in the field, where they almost required two administrators, one to hold the booklet and turn the pages, the other to record responses. Lacking two administrators, the booklet had to be propped up some way.

To estimate the likelihood that variations in these factors could account for differences, we have tried deliberately to determine

Table **30**   *Comparison of Four Feet–Vertical vs. One and One-Half Feet–Horizontal Presentations (Evanston Sample)*

	4 feet vertical $\overline{X}_1$	1½ feet horizontal $\overline{X}_2$	N_1, N_2	t
Müller-Lyer				
Adults	5.38	5.04	(55,56)	1.47
Children	5.81	5.35	(37,40)	1.65
Horizontal-vertical (⌐)				
Adults	4.93	4.91	(59,59)	0.09
Children	5.17	4.58	(40,45)	2.53
Horizontal-vertical (⊥)				
Adults	5.54	6.32	(57,57)	3.75
Children	5.66	5.63	(41,43)	0.12
Sander parallelogram				
Adults	3.45	3.00	(58,57)	2.08
Children	3.40	3.28	(38,43)	0.53
Perspective drawing				
Adults	4.71	4.49	(56,57)	1.06
Children	5.20	4.88	(40,42)	1.15

their effects. In an experiment[1] with 30 Northwestern University students, three different booklet positions were used: 4 feet, vertical (correct); $1\frac{1}{2}$ feet, vertical; and $1\frac{1}{2}$ feet, horizontal. All 30 students responded to the Müller-Lyer task under all three conditions, but in three different orders. The three means were 4.93 (this corresponds to the 5.00 reported for 27 of the 30 Northwestern respondents in Tables 4 [p. 122] and 19 [p. 156]), 4.76, and 4.31. While the most casual condition produced the least illusion, even this 4.31 exceeds all non-Western groups in our cross-cultural data, the nearest being the Senegalese with 3.88.

Because of the differences found in this pilot study, it was decided to repeat the experiment with the larger Evanston sample, using only the two extreme positions.[2] With half of these cases the

---

[1]The initial experiment was carried out by Barbara LeVine.
[2]Donald Bender conducted the second version of the experiment.

task was presented correctly (4 feet, vertical), and with the other
half the casual extreme was used (1½ feet, horizontal). For the
adults, on the Müller-Lyer, the two means were 5.38 and 5.04, not
significantly different from each other ($t = 1.47$). These data have
been pooled for purposes of cross-cultural comparisons, to yield the
mean of 5.21 reported in Tables 4 and 19. For the Evanston children the two means were 5.81 and 5.35 ($t = 1.65$), corresponding
to the 5.57 reported in Tables 4 and 20 (p. 157). Table 30 presents
the details for all of the illusions. It seems probable that the Evanston 1½ feet, horizontal condition represents a more extreme deviation than any actual systematic deviation in any of the other samples. Yet, only in one instance (adults in the horizontal-vertical
[⊥], $t = 3.75$) does this gross modification in administration
result in a difference big enough to be possibly confused with the
intersample differences reported in Chapter 6. Clearly, casual
deviations in position cannot explain away these differences. However indirectly, we feel that this factor has been "controlled," and
that our results cannot be accounted for in terms of it.

Inspection Time. Although earlier studies had shown that repeated trials on the Müller-Lyer illusion reduced its effect, this had
been shown to occur only when the two figures were always in
the same position, not when the positions were reversed (Köhler
and Fishback, 1950). We therefore thought to control this reduction by reversing the positions of the figures from page to page.
However, after we had prepared our materials on this basis and
distributed them, several more recent studies (e.g., Moed, 1959)
provided data showing that exposure *per se* produces a diminution
in illusion.

These studies also yielded results that bear on the whole theory
of visual illusions. In 1950 Köhler and Fishback had noted that
were a progressive decline in the illusion to result from practice,
"neural satiation" could account for such response changes, and,
presumably, the same postulated mechanism could play some role
in the establishment of the illusion itself. In a later experiment,

Eysenck and Slater (1958) presented data that indicate striking individual differences in the nature of changes in illusion strength with practice, a finding that these authors argue is embarrassing to satiation theory. A study by Moed (1959) tested a prediction from satiation theory that illusion decrement in the Müller-Lyer would be more marked when one always presented it in the same orientation than when one presented it with 180-degree reversals occurring from trial to trial; this prediction was not borne out by the data. Day (1962) also provided data challenging the neural satiation theory. Rudel and Teuber (1963) reported an experiment that provides further evidence of a decrement in strength of the Müller-Lyer illusion over repeated trials, but exposure time per trial was not varied. Other findings from this study of relevance here include the facts that the Müller-Lyer illusion can be obtained tactually, that decrements with practice occur for both tactual and visual forms of the illusion, and that cross-modal transfer occurs. One of the implications of these findings is that, once again, neural satiation cannot explain them.

While it would be interesting to consider further the status of neural satiation theory, we must turn to the finding in Moed's study that exposure time (both frequency and duration of exposure) leads to a consistent decrement in illusion strength. Several others [e.g., Selkin and Wertheimer, 1957; Eysenck and Slater, 1958; Mountjoy, 1958; Day, 1962] also showed that as inspection time for a single figure was increased, this reduced the illusion.) This fact has obvious methodological implications for our own study, for in the initial instructions no limits had been placed upon time for fear of impeding rapport. Thus, if there were culture-to-culture differences in the duration of attention given to each page, this difference in attention might account for the differences in strength obtained.

To study the effect of differing inspection times upon our own materials, an experiment[3] was conducted in which 40 Northwestern

[3]The experiment was administered by Jill Budzien, under the supervision of Barbara LeVine.

University students responded to the Müller-Lyer and horizontal-vertical illusions under two sets of conditions: after a 30-second exposure to each item and (in counterbalanced order) with as rapid a response as possible. For the Müller-Lyer, the means for these conditions were respectively 3.95 and 4.63 ($t = 3.69$). For the horizontal-vertical, the means were 4.81 and 6.05 ($t = 5.75$). Thus, we confirm the previous findings for the Müller-Lyer and provide a new, similar finding for the horizontal-vertical.

While these are serious and dependable differences, how likely are they to account for our apparent cultural differences? It is our considered opinion that they do not. The 30-second exposure time was extremely tedious to our subjects. From conversing with our anthropologist-administrators and getting them to simulate administration times as they remembered them, it seems unlikely that any group was that slow—or, in fact, slow enough to average 5 seconds per page. In one of our samples—Segall's Ankole data— time records *were* obtained for 164 respondents. Ninety per cent took less than 5 seconds per page, and the average total elapsed time per illusion (or the time it took to expose each item, record each response, turn to the next page, etc.) was 45 seconds for the Müller-Lyer items and between 25 and 37 seconds for the others; in each illusion, the mean elapsed time per page was approximately 3 seconds. Furthermore, Morgan (1959) reported that the Bushman and mineboy samples were quicker and more spontaneous than the Europeans she tested. The Northwestern 30-second inspection time thus seems certainly more extreme than that of any other administration.

Other considerations also rule out inspection time as a determining factor in our results: The Bushmen and mineboys, although responding faster than the Europeans, were at the very lowest extreme in our set of samples. Also, even the Northwestern 30-second value of 3.95 on the Müller-Lyer exceeds those for all non-Western samples, and significantly so for most, so that even with the inspection time thus controlled or bracketed, the cultural differences remain. Finally, for the 164 Ankole cases, correlations were computed between the total elapsed time and the number of illusion-supported responses. A significant correlation ($-.23$) was found for the $\perp$-shaped horizontal-vertical illusion, but all other correlations were effectively zero (.07 for the Müller-Lyer, .02 for the Sander parallelogram, $-.07$ for the $\sqcap$-shaped horizontal-vertical). Further note that longer inspection decreases *both* the Müller-Lyer *and* the horizontal-vertical. Since the Europeans, for example, are highest on one illusion and low on the other, inspection time cannot be used to explain both sets of cultural differences; and if it is used to explain one illusion, the implication is that the true cultural differences are still greater on the other.

We thus conclude that while exposure time is an important variable, to be better controlled (or recorded) in future studies, it cannot be used to explain the basic differences found.

NONPERCEPTUAL, BEHAVIORAL, OR PHYSIOLOGICAL DIFFERENCES

As we have just seen, systematic variations in test-administration could generate many explanations for a given difference across samples. The only two conditions we are aware of that might have generally affected non-Western samples (the physical arrangement of the stimuli and the inspection time) we have ruled out in the preceding section. We also are not overly concerned with genuine idiosyncracies in administration (conditions peculiar to a particular sample) because the data provide many independent replications of the major cross-cultural differences in illusion susceptibility.

However, we also recognize the possibility that psychological differences across groups in motivation, attitude, general approach to a task, etc., might underlie the response differences that we are interpreting as perceptual differences. For example, it is conceivable that fearful, or unwilling, or uncomprehending compliance occurred more frequently in certain non-Western samples (see Segall, 1963), with the result that respondents might have made random choices. This could lead to a high frequency of errorful (in the Guttman sense) response patterns, as among the Zulu.

Recall, however, that the data analysis takes this into account and that this factor cannot contribute to the score based on "purified" cases. It is important, however, to note the actual effect on *total* sample scores of a factor like this one: Note that for our highly errorful Zulu sample (all cases included) the score places the Zulus close to the Western samples in Müller-Lyer susceptibility. Thus, if random responses were added as the result of any such factor as we are here considering, their effect very likely was to increase the apparent number of illusion-supported responses. This kind of motivational factor, we therefore conclude, does not plausibly account for our results.

Nonetheless, we should remain on the lookout for cultural differences of other sorts that might plausibly explain our findings; anthropologists in particular can be helpful in this. At the same time, it must be remembered that for each such possibility, functional validity is required for a complete explanation. Thus it has been suggested (Rivers, 1905; Doob, 1964) that the differences are due to a more analytic attitude in non-Western groups, as opposed to a tendency to syncretic, holistic perception in European cultures. As we have already seen, Titchener (1916) questioned the significance of the findings of Rivers on similar grounds.

For explanations of this sort to be complete, we feel there must be some plausible ecological condition that would produce such differences in attitude. For groups like the Bushmen, it might well be that the major task requiring close visual inspection was the identification of animal tracks in hunting, and that this reiterated discipline taught attention to particulars and an inhibition of the distracting effects of surrounding stimuli. Such an explanation would have little applicability to the agriculturists making up the majority of our samples (and would imply superiority of the hunters on other tasks, such as imbedded figures), but it illustrates the kinds of functional hypotheses that are required before "differences in attitude" constitutes an explanation. With the addition of a functional hypothesis, the argument that our results reflect differences in attitude would demand serious attention. For the moment, however, there is none that goes far enough. Moreover, as we must once again reiterate, our findings include Western vs. non-Western differences in both directions. We find it impossible to apply this kind of explanation to these findings considered in toto.

Still another possibility is that group differences are due to some systematic differences in the anatomy or physiology of the visual apparatus, differences that are environmentally produced. Pollack (personal communication) has suggested such a rival interpretation. Recent work by Pollack (1963) shows the contour-detection threshold to be correlated with the strength of the Müller-Lyer illusion. Contour-detectability, in turn, Pollack relates to corneal density, which increases steadily with age throughout one's lifetime. Correspondingly, he demonstrates an increase in the contour-detection threshold and a decrease in illusion strength with age, over the range 8 to 12 years. Extending this to our cross-cultural study, he hypothesizes that corneal density increases more rapidly for persons exposed to greater amounts of sunlight. Our low-scoring groups on the Müller-Lyer would thus be expected to be those with maximum sunlight exposure. This explanation could be checked through cross-cultural studies of the effect of different climates on corneal density and on contour-detection thresholds, as well as on illusion scores. However, we do not find the explanation very plausible. Note that in one sense it is directly contrary to the "greater acuity and attention" line of argument in Rivers' and Titchener's comments. It depends on an unchecked hypothesis relating sunlight and corneal density, and it does nothing to explain the direction of our results with the horizontal-vertical illusions.

INCOMPATIBLE RESULTS OF OTHERS

Our belief that our results indicate perceptual differences produced ecologically is reinforced by their conformity with the findings of Rivers (1901, 1905), whose non-European samples included two widely differing ethnic groups, the jungle-dwelling New Guinea islanders and the Todas of India.

As Chapter 3 indicated, we also think that the study of Allport and Pettigrew (1957) on the rotating trapezoidal illusion supports our line of reasoning. It should be noted, however, that the emphasis in their interpretation of their data was less empiricist than ours. With commendable caution, Allport and Pettigrew emphasized that although they obtained the kinds of differences predicted by an empiricist theory when the stimulus was presented under marginal illusion-producing conditions (binocular viewing from a distance of 10 feet), under optimal conditions (monocular viewing from a distance of 20 feet) rural Zulus reported the illusion about as often as did urban Zulus or Europeans. While the latter finding would seem to demand restraint in interpretation, it dominated Allport's and Pettigrew's conclusions. "The perception of motion as represented in the rotating trapezoidal window is governed, under *optimal* conditions, by nativistic determinants or by the unconscious utilization of residual (but not immediately relevant) experience, or by both. (Our experiment does not enable us to decide this issue.)" (Allport and Pettigrew, 1957, p. 113).

From this conclusion, it would appear that the Allport and Pettigrew study presents results incompatible with ours. We, however, are more impressed by the results they obtained under marginal illusion-producing conditions. Rural Zulus from uncarpentered environments reported the illusion 14 per cent of the time, while urban Zulus reported it 64 per cent of the time and Europeans in South Africa did so 55 per cent of the time. These data seem to indicate clearly that when differences are to be found at all, environment rather than race is the major determinant. In a recent critique of the Allport and Pettigrew paper, Slack (1959) also sees that paper as a more clear-cut demonstration of environmentally determined perceptual differences than its authors considered it to be. "Allport and Pettigrew leave the reader feeling that their study, which has a direct bearing on the nativism-empiricism controversy, does not support one side or the other, when actually their findings are inconsistent with the nativist position" (Slack, 1959, p. 128). The only part of Allport's and Pettigrew's findings that demands equivocation is the negative result (no significant difference) for optimal viewing conditions. But negative results are always equivocal. As Slack insists, their positive results can only be viewed as supporting an empiricist theory of perception, so that there is, in fact, no incompatibility between their results and ours.

Doob (1964) reviews several studies (e.g., Heuse, 1957; Morgan, 1959; Bonté, 1960, 1962) that employed materials similar to those used in our own research. The one body of data in serious contradiction to our findings is that reported by Bonté (1960, 1962), where the discrepancy is such as to suggest the need to restudy the problem using multiple methods of administration. As Bonté emphasizes, the first attack on the problem must be the examination of methodological details. For that reason, and because of the challenging discrepancy in the findings, we will discuss her procedures in the same detail with which we have discussed our own.

She used two procedures. The first employed a preliminary form of our own materials, prepared by us, consisting of "ditto"-duplicated figures. It differed from our final set of materials in being restricted to Müller-Lyer figures; in presenting several on one page; in having less bright, less sharply defined lines and less contrast or vividness; and, most important, in having the first 11 items in ascending magnitude of discrepancy, from 0 per cent to 50 per cent in 5 per cent steps. The final four items were in reverse order, 30 per cent, 20 per cent, 10 per cent, 0 per cent. With this she tested 400 Bashi (a people of the Central Kivu district of Congo round-house-dwelling agriculturalists living on a lake shore) and 74 Europeans. The mean per cent illusion for the Bashi was 23.0 per cent, that for the Europeans 29.4 per cent. This difference was highly significant statistically ($t = 4.85$, $P < .01$).

However, the magnitude of the illusion was very great with both groups. The items were like those of the present study in size, in angle and length of obliques, in the separation at junctures, and in the use of two colors—though in Bonté's case, the horizontals were black (ditto-type black-purple) and the obliques red (ditto-type red-purple) and the colors were subject to fading during the inevitable exposure to sunlight. Thus one might have expected weaker illusions for both groups, not stronger. However, our Western groups ran 14 to 19 per cent illusion, and our comparable African groups (e.g., Ijaw, Fang, Songe) 7 or 8 per cent.

Bonté provides the probable explanation for her higher values by pointing out the strong set induced by the item order. On the early items (0 per cent, 5 per cent differences, etc.) the decisions were easy, and everyone picked the >————< segment. As the items approached threshold, the decision became more difficult and the tendency, well reinforced by the first few trials, was to perseverate on the >————< segment. She cites early studies by Binet demonstrating the strength of such tendencies and recommends revision of the test to avoid them. She also strongly recommends presenting only one item per page and using a duplication process unaffected by sunlight. Thus by both her judgment and ours, the form of the test as used in the present study is much to be preferred.

Bonté found it absolutely impossible (1960, p. 78) to apply this procedure among the Bambuti pygmies, the principle obstacle being noncomprehension of the task due both to its intellectual demands and to the lack of sufficient motivation to provide fixed attention. For her second study, she built a Müller-Lyer figure in which the <————> part was on one piece of wood, while the ————< part was on another, which slid under the first. Combining her description of the apparatus with the evidence from a photograph of it, we have diagramed it to scale (except for the hidden part of the second board) in Figure 16. From the photograph it is apparent that the oblique lines in her figure were exceptionally short, approximately as we have represented them. It is also apparent that in addition to the drawn lines, the grain of the wood was visible. More important, perhaps, was the presence of the very prominent vertical line where the boards met. This was a more dominant discontinuity than it appears in the illustration because of the inevitable, but unspecified (perhaps 3mm), thickness of the top layer of wood, which would be apparent from many of the viewing angles.

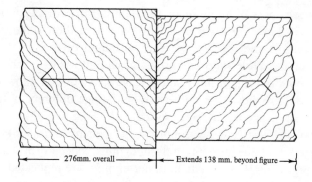

Figure **16**   *Diagram of Müller-Lyer apparatus employed by Bonté*

That any convenient position for manipulation was allowed is apparent from the photograph she provides of a Bambuti respondent manipulating the apparatus. She gives no details on the wording of the instructions or their translation equivalent, and it must have been hard to determine how the respondents understood the task and hard to keep them from matching the *total figure* on the left board with the *total figure* on the right board. Each respondent made five adjustments starting from a too-long setting, followed by five from a too-short setting. However, she had no method available to discard nonscale cases and no index of inconsistency.

On this instrument, her 20 Europeans showed an average of 22.5 per cent illusion (as computed by us in order to compare the performances of all groups); 100 Bambuti pygmies, 23.6 per cent; and 50 Bashi, 23.4 per cent. Not only were these differences not significant, they lay, in reference to our theorizing, in the wrong direction. While she had both children and adults in her sample, she does not report her results by age so we do not know whether her data replicate the universally found age differences. (See discussion of age trends, pp. 196–200.)

While we have no doubt of the general superiority of the methods of the present study and must conclude by tentatively disregarding Bonté's data until her findings are replicated by other methods, the issue remains a puzzling one. Of the many idiosyncracies in her technique, few specifically point in the direction of the results she obtained. However, the simple fact that under some conditions cross-cultural differences may not be found supports our belief that our many efforts to minimize artifactual differences were justified, and that the differences we discovered after employing these methodological safeguards are replicable provided similar safeguards are employed.

INCONSISTENCIES IN OUR OWN DATA

The strength of the ecological cue validity hypothesis is that it provides a plausible basis for predicting the general nature of the differences obtained. We know of no other hypothesis comparably plausible. Not only are the data reported in the present study compatible with the hypothesis, but so are the data of Rivers (1901, 1905), who similarly reported bidirectional differences. The finding that, under certain conditions, rural Zulus were less susceptible than Europeans to the rotating trapezoidal illusion (Allport and Pettigrew, 1957) is also compatible, since that illusion is a member of the class for which the carpentered-world hypothesis would predict maximum strength among Western peoples.

But while our data generally conform to the hypothesis, the fit is not so exact or so uniform as to rule out the possibility of other factors. To examine this more closely, a determination of the degree of fit of the findings for each illusion should be attempted. For the Müller-Lyer illusion, the fit could hardly be better, at least at a gross level. Among the adult samples, with only two exceptions, every non-Western sample was significantly less susceptible than all three Western adult samples. The PSE equivalents of the Western means ranged between 13 and 19 per cent, and of the non-Western means between 1 and 10 per cent, with more than half of them at 5 per cent or less. There seems little doubt that the Müller-Lyer illusion is considerably enhanced in Western urban environments.

Taking a closer look, there is some suggestion in the Müller-Lyer findings that three of the non-Western groups were somewhat more susceptible than the others: the Senegalese (whose mean was not significantly smaller than that of two Western groups, but was significantly larger than that of three non-Western groups), the Zulu (not significantly smaller than two Western groups), and the Ankole (significantly larger than two non-Western groups). The PSE's for these three groups were, respectively, 11, 8, and 6. From what is known to us about the environments of these three groups there seems to be no solid basis for predicting that they would obtain mean scores of intermediate magnitude; on the other hand, neither is there any solid basis for predicting that they would be among the least susceptible groups.

The three groups who had the lowest mean scores were the mineboys, the Bushmen, and the Bété. The Bushmen clearly "belong" near the bottom, since their environment is very likely the least carpentered of any. Although the Bété live in a moderately carpentered environment, they too ranked very low on the Müller-Lyer; but it should be noted that the Bété ranked at or near the bottom on *all five* illusions and this fact makes them somewhat of an enigma to begin with.

The performance of the mineboys on the Müller-Lyer illusion (and the Sander parallelogram) is also puzzling. As Doob commented after examining a preliminary report of these findings, ". . . it is strange to note that South African miners were less susceptible to the Müller-Lyer illusion. The guess can be uttered that the milieu of mines and mine 'reservations' in South Africa provides these men with a frequent opportunity to perceive the Western carpentered world and its rectangular forms" (Doob, 1964). It should be recalled, however, that the members of this sample were all relatively recent migrants to the mining regions of South Africa. The environments in which many of them spent the bulk of their lives, including in some instances much of their adult lives, were varied. Thus, it might be safe to state that there is no solid basis for predicting that this sample would have a relatively high mean score just because at the time of testing they were in a relatively carpentered environment. At the same time, it must be admitted that their apparently very low degree of susceptibility to the Müller-Lyer illusion is surprising.

In his examination of the unexpectedly low mineboy score, Doob asks, "Could this mean that cultural factors which influence perception must operate during childhood and that the adult experiences of these men, therefore, are less important?" (Doob, 1964). Indeed, the hypothesis put forth in Doob's question strikes us as highly plausible, and it would be applicable to the present problem. We shall discuss below (pp. 196–200) in greater detail our views concerning the development of relevant perceptual inference habits, in the context of a discussion of age trends in illusion susceptibility in our own and others' data.

Turning now to the Sander parallelogram data, the carpentered-world hypothesis seems to apply as well as it does with the Müller-Lyer data. Among adult samples, the three Western groups are most susceptible to the Sander parallelogram illusion. However, only two of them, the Northwestern University students and the Evanstonians, are significantly more susceptible than any non-Western samples; and six of the non-Western samples are not significantly less susceptible than any Western samples. Thus, while the rank-ordering of samples is in accord with the predictions based on the hypothesis, the magnitude of the cultural differences leaves something to be desired. Again, it is difficult to interpret the rank-ordering within the non-Western samples themselves, but, again, perhaps this is too much to ask of the hypothesis. Among the difficulties apparent in the Sander parallelogram data is the strikingly high illusion susceptibility of the Fang, as indicated by that sample's PSE of 17 per cent. Thus, for this illusion, as with the Müller-Lyer, the carpentered-world hypothesis is generally compatible with the data but falls somewhat short of being able to predict the precise position of a particular sample on the results continuum.

Since the foreshortening hypothesis leads to quite different predictions for the two horizontal-vertical illusions, it is most important to note how it holds up when the data are examined in detail. For both of these illusions, many non-Western samples were *more* susceptible than Western samples, but some of them were less susceptible. This is in accord with predictions, at least in a general way. When examined in closer detail, does the rank-ordering of samples appear as the hypothesis would have it? The three top-ranked adult samples on both illusions were the Ankole, Toro, and Suku, all of whom inhabit open savanna, the kind of terrain specified by the hypothesis as conducive to the illusion-generating inference habit. Unfortunately, other groups who live under similar conditions were not so highly ranked, e.g., the Songe and Zulu. The lowest ranking adult samples were the Bété (whose means, as we have already said, were consistently low over *all* illusions), the Zulu (who "belong" somewhat higher), and the Hanunóo. Of these, the Bété and the Hanunóo live in the kind of compressed environment in which we would predict the inhabitants to be minimally susceptible to the horizontal-vertical illusions. Also occupying such environments, but not low ranked, are the Fang and the Ijaw. The European samples occupy intermediate ranks, positions that seem appropriate in terms of the hypothesis.

On balance, then, the foreshortening hypothesis seems not drastically out of line with the data, although not every sample occupies the rank that the hypothesis, strictly interpreted, would seem to demand. Again, we plead, this might be asking too much, particularly since the ranks were based on mean estimates involving both variations in sample size and systematic error. Moreover, as was shown in Tables 23 and 25 (pp. 162 and 165), the greatest proportion of significant differences between means involves comparisons between samples with extreme means. We would thus conclude that within the limits of error of measurement, the relative standing of the samples on the horizontal-vertical illusions is quite in accord with predictions based on the foreshortening hypothesis.

No attempt will be made to apply this hypothesis to the perspective drawing since, as we argued above, the very small range of scores over all samples suggests that in the form employed here the perspective drawing produced only a very small illusion with any sample.

To recapitulate the discussion thus far, for four illusions—the Müller-Lyer, the Sander parallelogram, and two forms of the horizontal-vertical—cross-cultural differences were found that we consider to be reliable and not artifactual, probably best understood as the result of experience, and reasonably in line with the particular empiricist hypotheses offered in this report. But since the spec-

ific hypotheses offered here cannot account for the present findings in all particulars, it might be well to consider alternative, but
similarly empiricist hypotheses.

One possibility is that the *only* relevant factor is *specific experience with pictures* employing perspective cues. Hudson's findings
(1960)—that nonliterate mine workers in South Africa tend not to
perceive the third dimension in photographs and that among both
Bantu and European children the response to depth cues in drawings varies with the level of education—are consistent with the
hypothesis that specific experience with drawings is required
before depth is perceived in two-dimensional representations of a
three-dimensional world. However, it is not correct to conclude
from Hudson's study that such experience is the only relevant
factor. One sample that showed considerable difficulty in perceiving depth in pictures consisted of 60 white unskilled laborers,
most of whom had primary education. Hudson attributed *their*
failure to learn pictorial depth-perception to certain deprivations of
experience in the home (Hudson, 1960, p. 204). Hudson also found
pictorial depth-perception among white samples to be related to
measured intelligence. Thus, a single-factored explanation does not
account for all of Hudson's findings. He concluded that pictorial
depth-perception is learned through exposure to two-dimensional
materials, but that "the process can be retarded or prevented by
cultural environment and intellectual endowment" (Hudson, 1960,
p. 205).

Nonetheless, it could be argued that our findings with the
Müller-Lyer and Sander parallelogram illusions are consistent with
the hypothesis that the illusion-producing habits have to be acquired via experience with pictures. As in Hudson's study, workers
in the mines in South Africa responded to these materials in a
manner indicating a failure to interpret the third dimension in
photographs of outdoor scenes. The other sample in our study that
ranked very low were the Bushmen, who, it can safely be assumed,
have had a very limited experience with drawings and photo-

graphs. Since the top-ranked European samples have obviously had maximal experience with pictures and since within most of the non-Western samples it might be assumed that children, at least those in school, have had more experience of this nature than adults (recall that children tended to have higher scores in each sample than adults), it might even be argued that this hypothesis accounts for these data better than the carpentered-world hypothesis. Since the experience-with-pictures hypothesis, moreover, is simpler, it might be considered more attractive. However, it seems difficult, if not impossible, to apply this hypothesis to the findings with the horizontal-vertical illusions.

Still other versions of an empiricist hypothesis could be considered. However, given the complex nature of our results, it seems unlikely that any other would constitute a more satisfactory explanation than the hypotheses we are offering, despite the less-than-perfect fit of hypothesis to data. Even with its inadequacies, we believe our line of reasoning is not only valid for our data, but a useful guide for further thinking about cross-cultural differences in perception. Such differences seem to demand a theory that resembles ours, at least in general form.

AGE TRENDS

The interpretation that illusions result from learned habits of inference, varying in accord with ecological factors, is complicated by frequently confirmed age trends within European culture, particularly those pertaining to the Müller-Lyer illusion. A recent survey of developmental studies of perception by Wohlwill (1960) shows substantial agreement that this illusion decreases with age. In other words, children tend to be more susceptible than adults. In only two studies (Walters, 1942; Wapner and Werner, 1957) must this general statement be qualified. These studies showed a decrease in illusion strength from age 6 to age 10 and 12 respectively, followed by a rise from age 15 to 19. Similarly, using the same stimuli employed in the present study, Campbell and Wenar (1962) showed a continuous decrease in mean per cent illusion for age groups from 4 years to 9 years (ranging from 23 per cent down to 17 per cent) in a sample of Evanston children.

All the studies in which Western age-trend inferences have been made are limited, unfortunately, by obvious practical considerations. The youngest samples studied have been 4 years of age. We believe it is important to note this since European children, probably like children everywhere, have mastered visual-locomotor coordination by the age of 2 or 3, and certainly the inference habits useful in reaching for objects and moving toward or around them are well established by that age. Soon thereafter, European children have also mastered the cultural inference conventions of interpreting two-dimensional pictures in terms of three-dimensional solids and displays. At this stage they might be described, in epistemological terms, as naïve realists, or phenomenal absolutists, unaware of the sensory data from which their object inferences have been constructed. Thus, children, at least European children, should be maximally susceptible to illusions like the Müller-Lyer by 4 years of age. The implication that children under age 4 would be less susceptible remains to be tested.

It is interesting here to note the age trends for the Müller-Lyer illusion in the present study. Of 11 possible comparisons between children and adults, 9 showed greater susceptibility among children. The confirmation by non-Western data of the trends found among Western groups indicates the cross-cultural validity of those trends; it appears that the children (at least beyond six years of age) were more susceptible to the Müller-Lyer illusion than the adults in their societies. Further, the results indicated that the relative magnitudes of the illusion among children paralleled the relative magnitudes among adults. That is to say, in societies in which adults were minimally susceptible to the Müller-Lyer illusion, children also showed a relatively small illusion susceptibility. Indeed, only one of the non-Western samples of children had a mean illusion score as high as the score of any Western adult sample.

Now these results *per se* are not incompatible with the carpentered-world hypothesis, nor are they strikingly in accord with it. For the hypothesis to accommodate these data, it would now have to be argued that if the Müller-Lyer illusion is produced in part by learning, that learning occurs before the age of 4. We would thus have to hypothesize that maturation sometime after the age of 4 makes children more analytic, with greater access to the sensorial given and more ability to hold the inferential processes in abeyance so as to report on the specific stimulus components. Learning the transmitter's role in the communication of three-dimensional content in two-dimensional drawings would also support this development of analytic skills. For example, in order to construct perspective drawings one must inhibit perspective-related illusions, reduce object-constancy, etc. Thouless (1932) has demonstrated that artists are more able to free themselves from object-constancies. (The implication that trained artists should be less susceptible to illusions like the Müller-Lyer also remains undemonstrated.) Thus, from a learned peak magnitude of illusion, European and possibly all children gradually and partially unlearn it, or learn to inhibit it.

A recent experiment by Wohlwill (1962) bears out this line of argument. In it children and adults made erroneous size and distance judgments of stimuli imbedded in a two-dimensional perspective context that creates an illusion of depth. The results indicated that the illusion-producing habits are learned before a child is of school age. While Wohlwill found no clear age differences in illusion-reduction among primary school children, he did find significant reductions among college students, reductions that plausibly are attributed to learned tendencies to counteract the illusion. The results of this experiment are compatible with the view that the inference habits contributing to illusions of the class exemplified by drawings containing perspective cues are acquired during the preschool years and can be counteracted by compensatory habits based upon sophisticated cognitions.

The conditions for acquiring these inference habits are more common in the Western world—hence, we would presume, their greater strength among Western than among non-Western children. Similarly, the greater Western reinforcement of the originally learned habits may account for a finding not yet mentioned, that their decline by adulthood is relatively smaller among Western than among non-Western peoples. However, the conditions for acquiring these inference habits are not altogether lacking in non-Western societies; and in *all* societies, whatever the initial strength of the relevant habits, some decline occurs by adulthood. Why the illusion-producing habits should be acquired at all in noncarpentered worlds and why they should subsequently decline are questions for which an answer at the present time would be premature.

This examination of Müller-Lyer age-trend data indicates that the carpentered-world hypothesis in its original form is far from perfectly adequate. It should be restated that data collected from children under age 4 are required before the hypothetical details concerning the acquisition of the inference habits postulated above can be put to test.

Age trends on the Sander parallelogram in our data are not quite as clear cut, nor are the age differences as marked, as those on the Müller-Lyer illusion; but, in general, the pattern is the same. In 8 of 11 possible comparisons, children are more susceptible than adults. The problem this creates for our hypotheses, and its likely resolution, are also the same.

Age trends on the two horizontal-vertical illusions are not very clear. For the ⊥-shaped illusion, among six non-Western samples and the Evanstonians, adults had *higher* illusion scores than children, a fact that supports the belief that the processes underlying this class of illusion are different from those that underlie the Müller-Lyer and Sander illusions. However, this trend is not replicated in the data for the ⌐-shaped form of the horizontal-vertical illusion. Moreover, in the Campbell and Wenar (1962) study referred to above (p. 197), there were no age trends in susceptibility to the horizontal-vertical illusion.

ADDITIONAL SUPPORTING DATA

After obtaining the data presented in Chapter 6, we ceased to solicit additional responses to our sets of materials. However, we continued to acknowledge requests for them, and some who used them voluntarily reported their data to us. In addition, we had available in Evanston a set of 166 response protocols from young children ranging in age from 4 through 9 years, collected by Wenar and referred to above (Campbell and Wenar, 1962) for the age trends they revealed. These data were analyzed subsequent to the analyses reported in Chapter 6, and it is instructive to examine them in some detail at this time. In certain respects at least, it may be appropriate to consider these additional sets of data as tests of the replicability of the findings reported in Chapter 6.

From Africa we received data collected by Jacques Gomila, of the Musée de l'Homme in Paris, among the Bassari, an eastern Senegalese tribe. The Bassari are primarily agriculturalists, but they also hunt with bows and arrows and gather food. Their savanna landscape is hilly and grassy. For the most part, they live in round, straw-roofed cabins, with walls made of laterite blocks; furnishings and some of their implements are rectangular. Except for the fact that they live in round houses, the Bassari are very similar to our Senegalese sample. Accordingly, we should predict that the Bassari would be only slightly less susceptible than the Senegalese to the Müller-Lyer and Sander illusions and about equally susceptible to the two horizontal-verticals. Gomila provided us with a sample of 50 Bassari adults and one of 50 Bassari children. They will be treated separately here, as was our practice in Chapter 6.

James Gimigliano, of the University of Hawaii, provided us with data from two adult samples of Australian aborigines. One of these, called Hermannsburg Bushmen, are considered by Gimigliano to be considerably acculturated with respect to contemporary Australian society. They are monogamous and Christian and inhabit European-style shacks made of corrugated metal sheets. Most of the 50 respondents in this sample had had a minimum of eight years of schooling in a mission, and many were employed as tanners, mechanics, and vehicle drivers. The second sample, called Yuendumu Bushmen (N = 52) were described as "primitive, polygamous, and tribal." They inhabit native wurleys in remote sections of Central Australia. Both samples should therefore resemble our relatively noncarpentered samples in their performance on the Müller-Lyer and Sander illusions; at the same time, because of the differences in acculturation between the two groups, we should predict larger scores on these illusions for the Hermannsburg sample. On the horizontal-vertical illusions, we should predict very high scores for both groups because their environments provide extended vistas.

The "new" Evanston children's sample, very simply, should provide scores very similar to those of the original sample of Evanston children.

Table 31 contains the PSE scores obtained by these additional samples and the PSE's obtained by the samples in our original set that are the most interesting for purposes of comparison.

On the Müller-Lyer illusion, it is clear that Wenar's Evanston children behaved like the original sample of Evanston children. The Bassari samples resembled the Senegalese samples in earning PSE scores near the median for all groups. The two Australian samples displayed fairly low susceptibility to this illusion, although not as low as our South African Bushmen sample. Finally, it is encouraging to note that the five new samples occupy positions relative to each other that are completely consistent with the carpentered-world hypothesis.

Table **31** *Mean Number of Illusion Responses and PSE's of New and Selected Original Samples*

ORIGINAL SAMPLES	$\overline{X}$	PSE	NEW SAMPLES	$\overline{X}$	PSE
Müller-Lyer					
Evan. children	5.57	21	Evan. children	5.70	21
Sene. children	4.61	14	Bassari children	4.00	11
Sene. adults	3.88	11	Bassari adults	3.32	9
S. A. Bushmen	2.28	1	Hermannsburg Bushmen	3.34	7
			Yuendumu Bushmen	3.31	6
Sander parallelogram					
Evan. children	3.33	20	Evan. children	3.83	25
Sene. children	3.29	18	Bassari children	2.36	16
Sene. adults	2.59	12	Bassari adults	2.09	10
S. A. Bushmen (no data)			Hermannsburg Bushmen	3.00	18
			Yuendumu Bushmen	2.86	15
Horizontal-vertical (⊥)					
Sene. children	5.55	17	Bassari children	5.94	19
Sene. adults	6.48	24	Bassari adults	5.84	18
Evan. children	5.64	18	Evan. children	5.46	17
S. A. Bushmen	5.93	20	Hermannsburg Bushmen	7.02	26
			Yuendumu Bushmen	6.80	24
Horizontal-vertical (⌐)					
Sene. children	4.42	6	Bassari children	6.52	22
Sene. adults	4.46	7	Bassari adults	5.47	8
Evan. children	4.86	8	Evan. children	4.82	7
S. A. Bushmen	5.15	9	Hermannsburg Bushmen	6.78	21
			Yuendumu Bushmen	6.55	22

On the Sander parallelogram illusion the new Evanston sample was maximally susceptible, and the four non-Western samples all fluctuated about the median PSE found for non-Western samples in the original set of data. Here, the Hermannsburg group appears to have been somewhat more susceptible than the Yuendumu group, as we predicted. Another aspect of the data that conforms to expectations was the correspondence of the Bassari scores to those of the Senegalese.

Thus, for the two illusions to which the carpentered-world hypothesis is relevant, these additional data support the hypothesis and more or less replicate the original findings.

The reordering of tribes found in the original data as we moved from the Müller-Lyer and Sander to the two horizontal-vertical illusions is seen clearly in the new data. The two Australian sam-

Table **32**   *Tests of Significance of Differences Among New Samples and Some Original Samples*[a]

	Müller-Lyer		Sander parallelogram		Horizontal-vertical (⊥)		Horizontal-vertical (⌐)	
	t	*df*	*t*	*df*	*t*	*df*	*t*	*df*
ADULTS								
Bassari *vs.*								
Senegal	2.60	113	2.35	152	2.22	121	3.68	139
Hermannsburg Bushmen	0.82	82	6.41	94	4.84	91	5.80	78
Yuendumu Bushmen	0.63	68	3.28	88	3.34	82	3.45	79
Hermannsburg *vs.*								
Yuendumu	0.12	70	0.56	92	0.87	85	0.80	84
CHILDREN								
Bassari *vs.*								
Senegal	1.60	84	3.44	129	1.06	86	6.68	113
New Evanston	5.78	148	6.05	172	1.98	164	7.13	183
New Evanston *vs.*								
Old Evanston	0.65	189	2.65	211	1.01	211	0.20	212

[a]Applying the logic of the Scheffé test, no *t*-value in this table below 4.00 should be considered significant.

ples earned very high PSE's on both versions of the horizontal-vertical illusion, in contrast to their moderately low scores on the other illusions. Indeed, the two Australian groups earned the highest PSE's on the horizontal-verticals yet reported. The Evanston children here occupy a lower position, having earned PSE's on both these figures that are nearly identical to the comparable PSE's for the original Evanston sample. The Bassari samples' performances also appear similar to the performances of the Senegalese, with the exception of the curiously high PSE earned by the Bassari children on the ⌐-shaped horizontal-vertical.

This examination of the PSE's of the new samples in comparison with the PSE's of selected samples from the original data has revealed an encouraging degree of fit. Before leaving these additional samples, however, we should note some tests of significance of differences among them, as well as some tests of differences between their performances and those of some of the original samples. These are summarized in Table 32. It is apparent from the material in this table and from the examination of PSE's just completed that these additional data support our hypotheses to roughly the same extent as the data from the original study.

SUGGESTIONS FOR FUTURE RESEARCH

In spite of some troublesome details in the data, we maintain our theoretical orientation, stressing the acquisition of visual inference habits as relevant to illusion susceptibility. But because some features of the performances of our cultural groups on the five visual illusions remain as yet unexplained, a further reason for maintaining our hypotheses is the hope that they will stimulate and guide future research, for which we now offer some suggestions.

As is typical in science, in the effort to interpret plausibly one puzzling set of data, we have employed hypotheses that commit us to as yet unobserved data series. We have, for example, discussed certain theoretically relevant ecological differences that have not been adequately investigated. Starting from the carpentered-ecology hypothesis, we need now to develop methods of quantitatively scoring visual ecologies on the percentage of retinal obtuse and acute angles presented by rectangular objects. We need to select areas for their ecological extremity on these scores and study illusion-response in them. Our theory commits us to predicting both rural-urban and warm-climate–cold-climate differences within our own culture. These can and must be checked. (It should be reported here that in our Evanston sample, we asked people to indicate whether as children they had lived in a city or in the country. On the Müller-Lyer this produced a highly significant difference [rural mean, 4.45; urban, 5.57; $t = 4.93$; N's 33 and 152]. On the other illusions the differences were trivial but in the correct direction, the rural group showing less illusion on the Sander parallelogram and more illusion on the two horizontal-verticals. These two groups, now living in the same highly carpentered ecology, certainly represent smaller ecological contrasts than would be available if one collected data in rural American areas.)

The foreshortening hypothesis commits us to seeking out still different ecological extremes. We want to seek out deep-canyon and rain-forest dwellers (e.g., the Havasupi Indians in Arizona and the Bambuti pygmies in the Ituri Forest of the Congo) and, at the other extreme, some northern-plains dwellers, such as certain Eskimo groups.

We also must administer our materials to children younger than age 4, first solving the obvious technical problems involved. One such study was begun in 1964 by Julia Carlson at the University of Iowa.

Special groups in the population that may have interesting countertendencies with respect to the foreshortening of the frontal horizontal, e.g., artists and pilots, should also be studied. James Walker at Colorado University has done a preliminary study (1964) showing art majors to be less susceptible than psychology majors to the Müller-Lyer illusion; the difference was not significant, however. Alan Gross, at Stanford University, in 1964 also began research comparing illusion scores of architects and educators; as of this writing, the study has failed to uncover predicted differences, with the possible exception of a lesser susceptibility of architects to the ⌐-shaped horizontal-vertical illusion.

The size- and form-constancy problem should be explored further, with particular attention to the different results likely under different conditions and instructions (e.g., retinal size match *vs.* "real thing" match).

Other experiments are possible that might serve as a check on various implications of our hypotheses. For example, our analysis of the Müller-Lyer illusion contained the suggestion that the horizontal line with the obliques extending outward (>————<) is seen as farther from the viewer than the horizontal line with the obliques extending inward (<————>). When the two critical lines—the horizontals enclosed in obliques—are in fact equal in length, the differential distance inference forces the viewer to conclude that the "farther away" line is "really" longer. To check on this notion, a laboratory study employing Müller-Lyer-like figures as stimuli, in which distance judgments are required, seems essential.

Another area for experiment involves varying the orientation of figures like the Müller-Lyer and horizontal-vertical illusions. Clive Davis began in 1964, at the University of Iowa, to test the prediction that when the two Müller-Lyer segments are presented one above the other, the illusion will be more marked with the >————< segment on top, because of the useful inference habit of concluding that objects high in the visual field are farther away than objects low in the field. Davis reasons that there should be a greater tendency to exaggerate the length of an object assumed to be farther away than one assumed to be close. A similar line of reasoning has led Wayne Linder, also at the University of Iowa, to investigate the effect of figure orientation on the horizontal-vertical illusions.

An implication of our theoretical approach to illusions, and to visual perception in general, is that the mechanisms underlying the geometric illusions are the same as those underlying the phenomena of size- and shape-constancy. As was noted above (p. 76), in some recent papers (Tausch, 1954; Holst, 1957; Gregory, 1962, 1963; and Green and Hoyle, 1963) the idea has been developed that illusions may be explained as the result of learned tendencies to misapply constancy inferences. In a related effort in the University of Iowa laboratory, a study is being undertaken to determine correlations among various illusions and various constancy tasks and to determine the effects of different instruction-induced sets on both classes of tasks.[4]

It is hoped that additional research suggestions will be forthcoming from the readers of this report. If the cultural differences reported here are, as we believe them to be, indications of genuine differences in perceptual tendencies, produced by different learned inference habits possessing ecological validity, the differences constitute a provocative and puzzling challenge to all students of perception.

[4]This study is being conducted by Julia Carlson.

8   That human perception is culturally influenced has long been a proposition entertained by many social scientists. The plausibility of this proposition is high, based as it is upon certain contemporary philosophical and social scientific concepts, such as that of cultural relativism. Moreover, many facts gathered in psychological laboratories by students of perception, facts that delineate the important role of an individual's experiences in his subsequent perceptions, enhance the plausibility of this proposition. The present study began with a discussion of the proposition and the reasons for its widespread acceptance among social scientists.

Summary and Conclusion

But however plausible and however widespread its acceptance, the proposition cannot be considered to be unequivocally demonstrated by very many empirical data. In part because of the largely anecdotal character of the cross-cultural evidence available in the literature and in part because of certain methodological difficulties inherent in any research on perceptual differences, a review of the literature forced us to conclude that considerably more effort to amass systematic evidence of cultural differences in perception was called for.

We considered the theoretical and empirical materials that made cross-cultural research on perception appear to be a potentially fruitful enterprise, and the result of these considerations was a cooperative data-collection effort in some 15 societies. The stimulus materials employed were based upon five geometric illusions. These materials were chosen primarily because of their relation to a theoretical approach that appears both plausible and testable. Briefly, that approach is empiricist, in that it places emphasis upon the role of learning in visual perception. More specifically, it is based on the Brunswikian notions of ecological cue validity and probabilistic functionalism.

Proceeding within this framework, we predicted that people in different cultures would be differentially susceptible to geometric illusions because they have learned different, but always ecologically valid, visual inference habits. Depending upon the degree of ecological unrepresentativeness of the illusion-inducing figure, these habits may or may not result in illusion susceptibility. Then, applying this general hypothesis to the five illusions, we generated a number of specific, different hypotheses.

The illusions employed in this study were the Müller-Lyer and the Sander parallelogram illusions, two versions of the horizontal-vertical illusion, and an illusion we have termed "perspective drawing." (An attempt was also made to collect data with the Poggendorf illusion, but procedural difficulties hampered these efforts.) Each of these five illusions was represented by several items in the stimulus materials; and for each illusion, the discrepancy in the length of the segments to be compared varied from item to item. As each item was displayed, the respondent's task was simply to indicate the longer of two segments. Complete response protocols were collected from 1,878 persons in 14 non-European locations and in the United States. These were collected over a six-year period by a team of fieldworkers in anthropology, psychology, and, in one instance, psychiatry.

To minimize difficulties in communication between fieldworkers and respondents, the stimulus materials were designed so that the linear segments to be compared were not connected to each other or to any context segments, and different colors were employed. Respondents could indicate choice either by selecting one of two colors (on the horizontal-vertical items) or by indicating a position, e.g., right or left (on the other illusions). Other steps taken to enhance the validity of the response protocols included the administration of a short comprehension test requiring judgments similar to, but more obvious than, those demanded by the stimulus items. Moreover, an internal-consistency check was later made on each protocol, and wherever irrelevant response sets were detected, those protocols were withheld from one analysis. A comparable analysis was performed with *all* 1,878 protocols, and the results of both kinds of analysis were substantially identical. After the completion of these analyses, additional data, including three sets from societies not sampled in our original study, were analyzed, and the results of this analysis substantiated the previous findings.

It was found that on both the Müller-Lyer and the Sander parallelogram illusions the European and American samples made significantly more illusion-supported responses than did the non-Western samples. On the two horizontal-vertical illusions, the European and American samples had relatively low scores, with many, although not all, of the non-Western samples scoring significantly higher. All samples appeared to be minimally susceptible to the perspective drawing—this suggests that it was a weak illusion generally—and no significant intersample differences occurred.

The finding on which we place greatest stress is the bidirectionality of the differences found for the Müller-Lyer and the Sander on the one hand, and the two horizontal-verticals on the other. Cross-cultural comparisons made by Rivers over a half-century ago also indicated that non-Western peoples might be less susceptible than Europeans to illusions like the Müller-Lyer and, simultaneously, more susceptible to the horizontal-vertical illusions. Rivers' findings, like those of the present study, thus appear to be in accord with an empiricist, functionalist interpretation that relates visual response habits to cultural and ecological factors in the visual environments.

REPRISE OF THE HYPOTHESES

After presenting the data in full, we took a critical look at our hypotheses and considered various alternative hypotheses that seem partially to fit the data. We also reviewed some apparently incompatible results of others, called attention to certain inconsistencies in our own data, and discussed some disturbing age trends. We will now restate our hypotheses and assess their tenability in the light of what we have learned from all the data we have considered.

For the Müller-Lyer and Sander parallelogram illusions we put forth the "carpentered-world" hypothesis and an "experience with two-dimensional representation of reality" hypothesis; both of these hypotheses led to the prediction that Western peoples would prove more susceptible to these illusions than non-Western peoples. We found considerable support for both hypotheses in our own and others' (e.g., Rivers, Allport and Pettigrew) data. The data on age trends did not support these hypotheses, but we argue that a real test requires data collected from children younger than those thus far studied. We must also acknowledge that in terms of these hypotheses we are unable to explain the precise position occupied by each of our samples along the dimension of illusion susceptibility; but we claim that no other hypothesis we have considered provides a better over-all prediction of these positions. In sum, then, we find the "carpentered-world" and "experience with pictures" hypotheses both tenable and promising with respect to future research in perception.

We offered quite another hypothesis as a source for predicting different cultural susceptibilities to the horizontal-vertical illusions. This hypothesis argues that another aspect of the physical environment of peoples—specifically, the presence or absence of broad, horizontal vistas—is crucial in shaping the visual inference habit that leads to horizontal-vertical illusion susceptibility. If one lives in an environment that provides many opportunities for looking at horizontal expanses, one should become subject to the tendency to infer long, frontal-plane, horizontal distances from short, vertical retinal images. This inference habit, we argued, should contribute to the horizontal-vertical illusion. Accordingly, we predicted that plains dwellers would prove maximally susceptible, urban dwellers moderately susceptible, and groups that live in restricted environments (e.g., equatorial forests) minimally susceptible to the horizontal-vertical illusion. Again, with just a few qualifications, we found a good fit of our data to this hypothesis.

What is perhaps most encouraging about our findings is the clear-cut demonstration that the cross-cultural differences in our data were not the same for all illusions, and that for each illusion the differences were in accord with our predictions. Accordingly, in spite of certain inadequacies of detail, we feel confident in offering our hypotheses for further consideration. Our data lead us to expect that the findings likely to be uncovered by additional research will prove similar in kind to those reported here and will constitute important amendments to our hypotheses rather than contradictions of them, and that the hypotheses will continue to stand, at least in their general form.

CONCLUSION

Perception is an aspect of human behavior, and as such it is subject to many of the same influences that shape other aspects of behavior. In particular, each individual's experiences combine in a complex fashion to determine his reaction to a given stimulus situation. To the extent that certain classes of experiences are more likely to occur in some cultures than in others, differences in behavior across cultures, including differences in perceptual tendencies, can be great enough even to surpass the ever-present individual differences within cultural groupings.

We have reported here a study that revealed significant differences across cultures in susceptibility to several geometric, or optical, illusions. It should be stressed that these differences are not "racial" differences. They are differences produced by the same kinds of factors that are responsible for individual differences in illusion susceptibility, namely, differences in experience. The findings we have reported, and the findings of others we have reviewed, point to the conclusion that to a substantial extent we learn to perceive; that in spite of the phenomenally absolute character of our perceptions, they are determined by perceptual inference habits; and that various inference habits are differentially likely in different societies. For all mankind, the basic process of perception is the same; only the contents differ and these differ only because they reflect different perceptual inference habits.

The Environmental Inventory Questionnaire and Sample Descriptions

I. INVENTORY OF THE VISUAL ENVIRONMENT

This form permits various details of the visual environment to be recorded. These details will be examined carefully as an essential part of efforts to interpret the findings regarding extent of illusion. The topics included on this form were selected for their relevance to several major viewpoints in current theories of perception, some of which suggest that obtained differences in illusion-extent might correlate with differences in visual environment (see discussion in *Materials* booklet).

(1) Experimenter..................... (2) Group ....
(3) Location .... (4) Major occupations..............
(5) Degree of acculturation to EuroAmerican ways. Judged to be:

....

   none   slight   moderate   considerable   complete

The Natural Visual Environment

A. Land vistas (Indicate degree to which the categories below are adequate descriptions. Attempt to estimate the proportions of typical visual experiences during childhood.)

(6)   a. Dense jungle, no horizon..
     b. Horizon sometimes ....
     c. Flat land, frequent horizon ....
     d. Horizon always ....
     e. Horizon, if visible: straight .... hilly ....
     f. Indicate maximum distance usually visible ....
     g. Comments ....

B. Vistas over water

(7) a. Near open sea, lake .... Navigable? ....
     b. Near river......................... Navigable?.........................
     c. No water ....

The Artifactual Environment

(8) Containers (pots, vases, boxes, etc.)
     a. What approximate percentage of tops are in horizontal plane? ....
     b. Are there deliberate departures from horizontal tops? .... Estimate the percentage ....
     c. Estimate percentage which possess *angularity* in cross-section ....
        Precise rectangularity ...., rough rectangularity ...., deliberate nonrectangular angularity ....
     d. Estimate percentage which are *non-angular* in cross-section
        ....
        Precisely circular ...., roughly circular ....,
        deliberately elliptical ....
     e. Describe other containers if above categories not exhaustive ....
(9) Tools
     a. Estimate percentage having right-angle junctions ...., imperfect right angles ...., deliberate non-right angles ....
     b. Comments ....
(10) Dwellings and other buildings
     a. Estimate percentage that are perfectly rectangular ...., imperfectly rectangular ...., deliberately nonrectangular, but possess angularity ....
     b. Estimate percentage that are perfectly circular ....,
        roughly circular ...., deliberately elliptical ....
     c. Describe roof styles ....
     d. Comments ....

(11) Furnishings

    a. Describe, noting particularly angular characteristics (perfect right angles or departures therefrom) and whether furnishings tend toward rectangularity or circularity in cross-section.

    ....

    ....

    ....

(12) Graphic and plastic arts

    a. What are the approximate percentages of occurrence of the following representational art forms? Murals .... Sculpture .... Bas relief .... Paintings .... Drawings .... Others ....

    b. In what approximate percentage of two-dimensional works is three-dimensional space represented? .... How?

    ....

    ....

    c. Comments ....

(13) Contours and edges

    a. Are edges of objects sharp .... or rounded .... at points of junction.

    To what extent? ....

    Describe ....

    b. Comments ....

(14) Homogeneity of color

    a. Estimate percentage of objects of one color ....,
multicolored ...., any single surface in one color, but several colors on whole object ....

    Describe ....

    b. Comments ....

(15) Do games or serious occupations involve the use of spears ...., arrows ...., similar weapons or tools ....?

    Describe, noting manner used ....

    Comments ....

(16) Additional description

The inventory check-list above emphasizes geometric factors. The visual environment may here, and on the next page, be described in greater detail, with emphasis on similar factors. Additional information and comments will be most helpful. Additional sheets may be inserted in this inventory if necessary. Photographs, drawings, and other materials which will aid in describing the typical visual environment would also be welcome additions to this inventory.

II. SAMPLE DESCRIPTIONS

1. *Ankole*
   Group designation: Banyankole
   Location: Ankole District, Uganda
   Data collected by: Marshall H. Segall
   N = 344 (180 adults, 164 children)

The Ankole, numbering 500,000 people, are at the margin of the East African cattle area; more specifically, they belong to the interlacustrine group of Bantu peoples. Although they include a small percentage of Bahima (cattle herdsmen who live in round kraals), most Ankole are agriculturalists, today living primarily in mud and wattle rectangular houses. Homesites are widely scattered; compact villages are exceedingly rare. Several roads (one of them hard-topped) traverse the district, and it is becoming common for people to build homes near these roads although many Ankole still live in small clusters of houses, surrounded by plantain groves, built on the slopes of rolling hills. These hills are the most notable feature of the landscape, which is also dotted with papyrus swamps and occasional flat, grassy plains. Vistas may extend for many miles. Horizons are usually hilly.

Small general stores dot the district and make possible a very wide distribution of factory-made textiles, cooking implements, camp stoves, bottled soft-drinks, etc. Elementary schools, housed in mud and wattle rectangular buildings, are numerous.

The administrative center of the district is a small town containing many well-built structures, some multiple-storied. A typical house in this town is very nearly perfectly rectangular. If its owner is affluent enough, the house will have professionally carpentered window frames and doors and a corrugated tin roof. Furnishings are likely to be of European style. Wooden folding chairs are very common; rectangular tables are the rule. Even minimally educated Ankole are likely to decorate the interior walls of their houses with family photographs or pictures taken from magazines. These pictures are often enclosed in rectangular frames. Spears and walking sticks are common, but arrows are not used. The most widely used type of container is the calabash, but rectangular kerosene "debbies" are commonly employed. Clothing is simple, but usually in the European style. Women's fabrics are often multicolored, and geometric patterns are popular.

Although one would estimate the Ankole to be only "moderately" Europeanized and to be living in a moderately carpentered environment, considerable rectangularity exists.

2. *Toro*

    Group designation: Batoro
    Location: Toro District, Uganda
    Data collected by: Eva Perlman
    N = 109 (56 adults, 53 children)

The Toro live in an area immediately to the northwest of the Ankole. They, too, are an interlacustrine Bantu group. The physical environment is similar to that of the Ankole District. In Toro, there are broad, hilly, grassy areas, some extended plains, and many papyrus swamps. The Ruwenzori Mountains constitute a notable feature of the Toro landscape.

The Toro are primarily agriculturalists living in rectangular houses partially hidden in dense plantain groves. However, many Toro live in or near small urban centers, and nearly everyone in the district has spent some time in a town criss-crossed with blacktop streets along which are well constructed commercial buildings.

The Toro are known throughout Uganda for their woven furniture, grass tables and chairs that are roughly rectangular. These days, however, most Toro furnish their houses with European-style tables and chairs. Graphic art of indigenous origin is exceedingly rare, but pictures torn from calendars and magazines and advertisement posters adorn interior walls.

The Toro are estimated by the ethnographer to be "moderately" Europeanized; like the Ankole, they are regularly exposed to rectangular objects.

It should be noted that this sample may be considered a virtual replication of the Ankole sample. It was drawn from a different tribe, and data were collected by a different ethnographer, but the visual environments of the two samples, both natural and man-made, could hardly be more similar.

3. *Suku*

    Group designation: Basuku-Basonde

    Location: Kwango District, Congo Republic (formerly Belgian Congo)

    Data collected by: Igor Kopytoff

    N = 76 (53 adults, 23 children)

The Suku, numbering about 80,000, are in the southern subarea of the Congo culture area. The Sonde, some 30,000 strong, are their immediate eastern neighbors, occupying the same habitat as the Suku in the sample and scarcely distinguishable from them in ecology, language, technology, and most of the other aspects of culture. The distinction between the two groups is essentially of traditional political interest only. Both belong to what is generally called the "Central Bantu" group, whose location corresponds roughly to the northern portion of the Central African savanna belt. The Suku and Sonde live in the central portion of the Kwango-Kwilu basin. The subsistence economy is primarily agriculture, with farming the responsibility of women. Women also make pottery. Suku men hunt, fish, and engage in crafts such as weaving and basketry. Hunting is done with bow and arrow; no spears are used.

The characteristic countryside is open savanna, rather hilly, with only occasional strips of forest visible on the crest of hills or along riverbanks. Rivers, however, are not an important feature of the landscape; they are almost all small, winding, and nonnavigable and are usually hidden by growth along the banks. Horizons are always visible, but are hilly, and the typical vista extends to approximately five miles. It may be noted that there is rather heavier forestation, a more irregular topography, and somewhat more variable vistas in the western and northern portions of the Suku area; these regions, however, did not contribute to the sample.

The ethnographer estimates the Suku and Sonde to be "moderately" Europeanized insofar as material aspects of their culture are concerned, for imported goods, sold through country stores, are widely used. He also estimates that about half the villages follow the traditional layout of haphazardly grouped compounds, each surrounded by a roughly rectangular or circular hedge. The other half follow the administration-encouraged pattern of a central wide path, which may not be straight, with rectangular compounds ranged on both sides. All dwellings are rectangular and virtually perfectly so. Nowadays, a four-slope design in roofs is found, though not predominantly; the traditional style, adhered to in most cases, is the two-slope roof. Houses are thatched with straw, mounted vertically on wooden house beams set in a horizontal-vertical matrix. This rectangular emphasis is also found in household furnishings such as beds, stools, and storage platforms. Containers are either precisely rectangular in cross-section (20 per cent of them, as estimated by the ethnographer) or precisely circular. Axes and hoes typically have blades deliberately set at slightly less than a 90-degree angle.

Two-dimensional art work is lacking, but sculptured objects are found. Color is used to a very limited extent, although occasionally masks, baskets, and statues will be decorated, e.g., white and red, white and black, or natural wood contrasted with areas blackened by burning.

The ethnographer sums up the Suku and Sonde man-made environment as "rather colorless" and "geometric."

4. *Songe*
   Group designation: Bala-Basongye
   Location: Sentery, Congo (formerly Belgian Congo)
   Data collected by: Alan P. Merriam
   N = 98 (47 adults, 51 children)

The ethnographer estimates that the Songe display the effects of Europeanization to a "moderate" degree. The Songe live in the Sentery territory of the Congo. Though adjacent to the equatorial forest, the area is characterized primarily as flat, open savanna. The Songe are on the northern periphery of the Central Bantu group and, certain institutional differences aside, may be classified in that group (to which the Suku and Sonde also belong). Farming is the major occupation of the Songe. Swidden agriculture is a feature of life that is characteristic of most groups in this area. Raffia work is another important activity carried on in this region.

The landscape is much like that described for the Suku, with a generally hilly horizon visible, typically to the extent of a few miles. In this instance, however, dense tropical rain forest is present in some parts of the area. There are some minor, nonnavigable rivers, but no other bodies of water.

Again like the Suku, the Songe live in houses that are nearly perfectly rectangular, topped by center-peaked, four-sided roofs. Furnishings are mostly European-like in form. Almost all containers used by the Songe possess rectangularity in cross-section. Tools, on the other hand, almost always contain nonrectangular junctions; these departures from precise rectangularity are deliberate. Homesites are arranged in villages, typically consisting of two rows of houses placed along a single street.

Almost all artwork consists of sculpture. Probably as a result of European influence, drawings may occasionally be found. Geometric designs in several colors are common on raffia baskets and platters. Carved statues are not colored, but wooden masks typically contain two or three colors.

Both arrows and spears are employed, although hunting is of negligible importance. Many native objects have rounded edges, but European-made objects abound.

In many aspects of culture, the Songe sample may be considered very similar to the Suku sample.

5. *Fang*

Group designation: Fang (Pahouin)
Location: Gabon Republic
Data collected by: James W. Fernandez
N = 110 (49 adults, 61 children)

The Bantu-speaking Fang are in the northern subarea of the Congo culture area. They live in dense equatorial rain forest, within the forest belt dominating the north of Central Africa. In such a setting it is uncommon for vistas to extend more than a few hundred yards. The group studied by the ethnographer was judged by him to be "considerably" Europeanized. While most of the Fang in this sample live in the forest, about 10 per cent reside in villages located on hilltops. These villages typically consist of two rows of houses along the riverbank. The ethnographer reports that all houses are at least roughly rectangular, with approximately 20 per cent of them perfectly so. Roofs are gabled, with two sides slanting downward from a center beam. During his stay in the region (northern and central Gabon) the ethnographer encountered only one nonrectangular building, that one being circular.

In commenting on furnishings, the ethnographer states: "Practically all furnishings, e.g., beds, benches, etc., tend toward angularity. The greatest percentage are felt to be well built only when they possess perfect right angles. The 'rightness' of angles is, in fact, of first importance in Fang judgment when examining buildings or furnishings. It must be kept in mind that they build with long, straight strips of raffia, which makes right angles easier to achieve."

Rectangularity predominates also in traditional artifacts, though roundness appears in those used by women and is symbolically associated with femininity. The ethnographer points out that the men's artifactual world "is much more rectangular than the women's." Many round European-made containers are now widely used. Artwork includes sculpture, bas-relief, and wall painting. In two-dimensional works of art, three-dimensional space is represented by varying the size of figures. A small proportion of manmade objects are multicolored, with drums, masks, and murals usually containing three colors: black, red, and white.

Spears and arrows are used for hunting, and young boys use spears in a game in which the object is to hit a rolling disk.

The ethnographer concludes: "In sum, rectangularity is dominant. The natural visual environment is the compressed one of dense rain forest. But the Fang clear for themselves space for a rectangular village. Life is lived out of this general compressed, rectangular frame."

6. *Bété*
   Group designation: Ivory Coast Bété
   Location: Daloa, Ivory Coast
   Data collected by: Remi Clignet
   N = 95 (52 adults, 43 children)

The Bété, numbering approximately 100,000, fall in the western subarea of the Guinea Coast culture area. They are Kwa-speaking and represent one of the Kru tribes of the tropical forest zone of the Ivory Coast. They subsist primarily by agriculture; they also hunt, with guns if they can afford them and with spears or arrows. This is an area of interpenetration of house-styles, some related Kru groups having round huts with conical thatched roofs; the characteristic Bété house is, however, rectangular.

The sample studied by Clignet live only in rectangular houses of mud and wattle, the framework of which consists of horizontal and vertical rods tied together in right angles with raffia. These houses are roughly rectangular and are probably influenced by colonial architecture. Some houses have overhanging roofs that shelter a verandah. Doors and windows are rectangular and often are covered with shutters. Thatched roofs predominate, but corrugated tin roofs may be found. Villages typically are located in large clearings in the center of coffee or cocoa plantations. In this hilly, forested landscape, vistas beyond half a mile are very rare.

In the villages, one may find European-made containers such as biscuit tins and wooden crates. Furniture is locally made, but is fashioned after European models. There is almost no two-dimensional art, but an occasional charcoal mural, representing a hunting scene, may be found on a house façade. Masks are carved and may be colored either white or red. Gaily colored imported cloth is commonly used, as are enamel dish pans of colorful design.

The ethnographer judged this group to be "moderately" Europeanized.

7, 8. *Ijaw* and *Ijaw School Children*
   Group designation: Ijaw
   Location: Korokorosei and Patani, Niger Delta, Nigeria
   Data collected by: Philip Leis and Nancy Leis
   $N_7 = 101$ (51 adults, 50 children); $N_8 = 61$ (all children)

The Ijaw belong to the eastern subarea of the Guinea Coast culture area. They represent a separate linguistic branch of the Niger-Congo family, a fact suggesting a relatively long period of existence as a separate group. Numbering approximately 350,000, they inhabit a dense tropical forest area in the Niger Delta, an often swampy region interlaced with narrow winding rivers. Villages are usually built along riverbanks; only occasionally are clearings made in the bush.

Sample 7 was drawn from Korokorosei, a community of about

700, which the ethnographers describe as "unacculturated." Sample 8 is from Patani, a more acculturated community of over 2,000 persons. The visual environment of the two communities is sufficiently different to warrant comment in the following description.

In Korokorosei, vistas seldom extend beyond a half-mile along the river, and only those few inhabitants who have traveled to the seacoast are likely to have viewed a horizon in the usual sense of the term. In Patani, by contrast, the vistas are very extensive; Patani is located in an area where riverbanks are some 40 feet high in the dry season, and the river, about half a mile wide, provides wide horizons.

In both communities, the houses are nearly perfectly rectangular. In Korokorosei, the basic material is wattle and mud, and the roofs are made of thatch, gabled, and steeply slanted. In Patani, many houses are built of cement blocks with zinc roofs, though wattle and mud predominate; there are a couple of two-story dwellings.

Spears are used in fishing and in games. Fishing is done from canoes or, in the swamps, while standing in the mud; spears are mounted with a single- or three-pronged iron head on a shaft ten feet long. Round casting nets are also used.

European-style furniture predominates in both communities; rectangular benches, manufactured locally, are also in constant use. Although some table tops are round, most of the tables are rectangular.

Among the tools used by the Ijaw are axes, the blades of which are set on the handles at a 90-degree angle. Hoes and adzes typically have nonrectangular junctions, these departures from rectangularity being deliberate.

Wooden carvings constitute the bulk of works of art produced by the Ijaw. No paintings or murals were seen by the ethnographers. However, they do report seeing some raffia mats woven by women, especially in Patani; these mats contain colored designs composed primarily of rectangular blocks and parallel lines. They note, "The sign of a good weaver is that the lines are straight and truly parallel."

The other multicolored objects noted are clothes. These are usually made from imported fabrics and typically contain many colors in bright geometric patterns.

In Korokorosei, the men engage in palm-wine tapping and gin-distilling, palm-oil manufacture, canoe-carving, hunting, and fishing. In Patani, most of the men migrate periodically to the coast and to urban centers, to work as clerks and houseboys. Upon "retirement" back in Patani, only a few of them engage in such traditional pursuits as fishing. As for the women, in both communities they farm, fish, weave mats, and trade.

It is estimated by the ethnographers that the Korokorosei Ijaw are only "slightly" Europeanized insofar as their social and political organization is concerned, but that their material culture shows greater acculturative effects. The Patani Ijaw show greater acculturation in both respects.

9. *Zulu*

   Group designation: Zulu
   Location: Natal, South Africa
   Data collected by: Norman Scotch
   N = 100 (51 adults, 49 children)

The Zulu, a Bantu people, represent an amalgamation of many tribes that have occupied Natal for many centuries. Culturally, they are representative of the southern variant of the East African cattle area. Numbering over 2,000,000, they engage in peasant agriculture and animal husbandry. Cattle are extremely important, for milk as well as for purposes of prestige and bride-wealth. As a result of European contact, house styles have changed considerably in recent years. The predominant type of house is the cone-cylinder hut, roughly circular and topped with a thatched, conical roof. Formerly, beehive-shaped huts, made from bent saplings and arranged in a rough circle to form a kraal, were very common. Today, according to the ethnographer, perhaps as many as 25 per cent of the houses in the region are roughly rectangular.

Since a number of Zulu have worked for a time in South African urban centers, considerably acculturated persons may be found in the area. However, the ethnographer estimates the majority of Zulu in his sample to be "moderately" Europeanized.

The region is characterized by open savanna, with many hills and extended valleys. Since this sample inhabits an area in the foothills of the Drakensberg Mountains, vistas extending as far as 50 miles may be possible. The horizon is, of course, usually hilly. There are no vistas over open water.

Furnishings are virtually lacking, the ethnographer reports. Most huts contain only tree stumps and mats. Few indigenous tools or containers were noted; however, the ethnographer reports seeing tools, bottles, boxes, tins, trunks, etc., of European origin in widespread use.

The production of works of art is limited to carvings, which the ethnographer describes as "inferior." However, many utilitarian objects are decorated with color. Shields, for example, are usually multicolored, and there is much beadwork in evidence. Spears and shields are often used in fencing games.

10. *Bushmen*
   Group designation: Kalahari Bushmen
   Location: Ghanzi District of the Kalahari
   Data collected by: H. Ruening
   N = 46 (adults only)

This sample of Bushmen inhabits an area that is part of the Kalahari Desert. They are seminomadic hunters and herdboys. The ethnographer states that these people display virtually no evidence of Europeanization.

The countryside they inhabit is quite flat, but horizons, often seen at a distance of five or more miles, are hilly. In the sandy soil of this desert, few trees or bushes are visible. A few dry river beds and some boreholes are found, but, in general, no significant bodies of water can be seen by these Bushmen.

They are sheltered in simple windbreaks, consisting of semicircular or parabolic arrangements of saplings set into the ground. These shelters contain no furnishings other than blankets. Containers in general use are limited to ostrich eggs and tortoise shells, although an occasional tin of European manufacture may be found.

No rectangular tools are reported, but spears and arrows are in use. The ethnographer also reports some European-like pocket-knives. In general, however, the man-made environment is sparse. No works of art are reported, except for etchings or engravings on bows, sticks, and eggshells. Beadwork is used to decorate clothes (animal skins) and female coiffures. This beadwork constitutes the only use of color reported by the ethnographer.

With the exception of an occasional European farm building, rectangular objects are not a part of the visual world of the Bushmen.

11. *South African Europeans*
    Group designation: South Africans of European descent
    Location: Johannesburg, South Africa
    Data collected by: Phyllis Morgan
    N = 44 (adults only)

This is a sample of adults resident in or near Johannesburg, a large, modern, urban center. It may be assumed that this sample has been thoroughly exposed to a visual environment comparable to that of any group living in a contemporary urban Western community. Precise, highly "carpentered" rectangularity pervades such environments. However, the moderate climate may lead to less carpenteredness in the net visual environment of children than is the case for the Evanston sample, for example.

12. *Mineboys*
    Group designation: Baluvale, M'lozi, Machusa, Bechuana, Pondo, and Chimbundu
    Location: Data collected at a gold mine near Johannesburg among laborers from diverse locations, including Tanganyika, Mozambique, and various provinces in South Africa
    Data collected by: Phyllis Morgan
    N = 72 (adults only)

Considering the diverse origins of this sample, it is impossible to characterize in a general way the environment in which these persons live. It should be noted that a wide range of natural environmental features—desert, savanna, flat vistas, hilly vistas, wooded vistas, sparse vistas, vistas over large bodies of water, etc. —is reported as characteristic of the home territories of these mineworkers. Some members of the sample come from areas in which rectangular dwellings are the rule; others have lived in round huts. The ethnographer's estimate of the degree of acculturation ranges from "slight" to "moderate" for various groups within the sample. Since the subgroups included are not large enough to justify separate treatment, they have been pooled. Perhaps the most important fact to note about this sample is that while its members are of diverse origin, they have all spent some time in an environment that contains much of European origin.

13. *Senegalese*
    Group designation: Ouolof, Bambara, Serer, and Peuhl
    Location: Several villages in Senegal
    Data collected by: M. Boye
    N = 262 (137 adults, 125 children)

With the exception of one small subsample (Peuhl, N = 7) of nomadic herdsmen inhabiting round houses, this sample consists of agriculturalists inhabiting rectangular houses. For most subgroups in the sample, the ethnographer comments on the virtual lack of works of art. Color is noted only in clothing, and then not universally. Few other generalizations are possible, since few data are provided. The entire sample, however, has been judged by the ethnographer to be "slightly" Europeanized.

14. *Dahomean Children*
    Group designation: Central Dahomean tribes
    Location: Abomey, Dahomey
    Data collected by: Jules S. Golden
    N = 65 (children only)

This sample from the Guinea Coast culture area consists of children attending school in Abomey, the inland ancient capital of Dahomey. They are members of a group that has been judged by the observer (a psychiatrist) to be "moderately" Europeanized. The natural environment is described as rather flat savanna, with moderately heavy vegetation. Horizons, only sometimes visible, tend to be flat. The maximum distance usually visible is reported to be only 200 yards, but there is not a feeling of a dense, enclosed environment. There are no lakes or waterways nearby.

Houses are usually roughly rectangular, although as many as 20 per cent of the structures in the area are circular. Many religious edifices, usually small, are roughly circular. Some reasonably well-carpentered houses, with metal roofs, can be found, but rougher structures with thatched roofs are predominant. Most artifacts are nonangular in cross-section, with 65 per cent of them circular; about 10 per cent are reported to possess right angles. Most furniture is rectangular, however.

The most prevalent art form is appliqué cloth; other art works consist of bronze statuettes and some sculpture, but esthetic productions are the work of a very small segment of the population. (The general esthetic expression of the populace is in the dance.) No paintings, murals, or drawings are found. Native implements tend to be blunt or rounded, but knives of European manufacture are used. No spears or arrows have been used in recent years. Color is widely used, mostly on clothing and religious ornaments.

15. *Hanunóo*

    Group designation: Hanunóo
    Location: Yagaw, Mansalay, Mindoro (Philippines)
    Data collected by: Harold C. Conklin
    N = 57 (43 adults, 14 children)

The Hanunóo are an agricultural people living in the Philippines. The whole group numbers approximately 8,000 people; however, the particular group sampled by this ethnographer numbers less than 200. They live in about ten hamlet-like clusters in a single drainage system covering a total area of about six square miles. Their environment may best be described as mountainous terrain, covered with mixed rain and second-growth forest. The Hanunóo in this sample live within a day's walking distance of open sea, but there are no navigable bodies of water in their immediate vicinity. Thus, although from some mountain hamlet sites the distant shore and sea can be seen, in their day-to-day activities they lack extensive vistas over broad expanses of land or water. The natural environment of these people is a very irregular and somewhat compressed one.

Hanunóo houses are all roughly rectangular, with the frameworks constructed of unhewn wooden poles with many natural crooks and the walls woven from long strips of bamboo. These houses are usually raised on stilts, and bamboo floors are a universal feature. Roofs are gabled and made of thatch. Inside, the furnishings are sparse. No chairs or tables exist. There are, however, roughly rectangular benches, and shelves made of bamboo strips. Other furnishings include mats, baskets, and pitch candleholders, which are either flexible or irregular in shape. Tools rarely include rectangular objects; the most commonly used tool is a curved steel blade. Containers used by the Hanunóo are pliable woven baskets, open clay pots, circular wooden pans, bamboo tubes, and circular woven trays. The ethnographer reports that it is only by chance that a container will have a flat, horizontal top opening.

He also states that there are no murals, paintings, or drawings made by the Hanunóo. However, decorative incisions are made on tabular containers, relief carvings are made on bolo handles and sheaths, and some wooden toys are carved. In addition, geometric designs, often involving small angles, perpendicular intersections, and other intricate details, are commonly woven on baskets and embroidered on shirts. While most artifacts are monochrome, clothing is usually multicolored. Spears, javelins, and arrows are used for hunting. Other fairly straight objects in daily use include digging and planting sticks, dibbles, and fence posts.

The ethnographer estimates this group to be almost "not at all" Europeanized. He reports that only one person included in the sample has had any contact with missionaries.

16. *Evanstonians*
    Group designation: Residents of Evanston, Illinois
    Location: House-to-house in Evanston
    Data collected by: Donald Bender, with sample construction
        and interview design by Barbara LeVine
    N = 208 (119 adults, 89 children)

A total of 208 persons, children and adults, was administered the materials by a research associate on a house-to-house basis. Evanston is a surburban community located immediately to the north of Chicago. There is no reason to doubt that this environment is representative of the highly carpentered sort of environment that is assumed to be most characteristic of the Western world. The relatively long, cold winters no doubt enhance this. Some residents of Evanston, however, are migrants from more rural environments; whenever this applied to a member of the sample, a note was made of the fact in order that any difference in perception that might relate to it might be detected. Half of the data were collected under strict adherence to spacing instructions, half under simulated sloppy presentation. The minimal results of this administrative difference are reported in the discussion; all cases are pooled in the main report.

17. *Northwestern University Students*
    Group designation: Undergraduate students at Northwestern
        University
    Location: Evanston, Illinois
    Data collected by: Barbara LeVine
    N = 30 (all adults)

A total of 30 students was administered the materials in a laboratory setting at the university. In addition to the standard administrative procedures, two additional procedures were used; they constitute departures from standard technique that might inadvertantly occur under field conditions. The results of this methodological study are reported in the discussion. The only data from this sample employed for cultural comparisons were those collected under the standard procedures. In terms of visual environment, this sample is comparable to the Evanstonian sample, although the higher degree of psychological sophistication likely to be possessed by this sample might make it unique.

The Poggendorf Illusion

The materials prepared for this study included six examples of the Poggendorf illusion, described in our materials booklet as the "arrow behind a tree" figures. The instructions on the administration of these six items indicated our anticipation of administrative difficulty:

> The final set of drawings (pages 55 through 60) will probably prove the most difficult to handle, and some ingenuity may be necessary to obtain adequate data. The object of questioning should be to determine whether or not the respondent sees the two red segments as parts of a single straight line, partially hidden by the central part of the figure. The question might be phrased: *Could the two red lines be part of one straight arrow which is partially hidden by this tree?* Record *Yes* or *No*. The question should be phrased to suit local conditions. The appropriate question may be determined by pre-testing a few individuals before beginning the experiment proper. The question finally used should be reported [Herskovits, Campbell, and Segall, 1956].

Although most of our collaborators did report difficulties in administering the Poggendorf items, response protocols were made available for every one of the 28 samples, with the sole exception of the Bushmen. A total of 1,668 protocols were collected. Approximately 500 of these protocols, however, consisted of either all *Yes* or all *No* responses. From such protocols it is difficult, if not impossible, to draw inferences regarding illusion strength. A protocol consisting of all *Yes* responses can only be interpreted as the result of some irrelevant source of variance, e.g., failure to comprehend the task, acquiescent response-set, etc. An all-*No* protocol can be interpreted similarly as the result of an irrelevant source of variance, or alternatively as an indication that the range of the stimuli employed stopped short of the PSE. Although the interpretation of such a protocol is ambiguous, support for the latter interpretation is contained in the data reported below. In any event, in an effort to discern whatever orderly phenomena might exist in the Poggendorf illusion data, all protocols containing only *Yes* or *No* responses were set aside, and the remaining 1,166 protocols were subjected to a psychophysical analysis similar to that performed on the five illusions discussed in the text.

The six items were arranged in ascending order of size of discrepancy (− 4, − 2, 0, 2, 3, and 4 millimeters), with the discrepancy here being simply the distance of the right-hand segment above the straight-line extrapolation of the left-hand segment. Negative values indicate that the right-hand segment was actually placed below the left-segment extrapolation. The following diagram may help to clarify this point. The dotted line in the diagram indicates

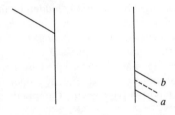

the left-segment extrapolation. One of the six items contained a right segment in precisely that position; hence, the discrepancy value for that item was 0. In two items, the right segment was located below the left-segment extrapolation; see, for example, the line designated *a* in the diagram. In these two cases, therefore, the discrepancy values bear a minus sign. In the remaining three items, the right segment was located as is the line designated *b* in the diagram; in one, that line was 2 millimeters above the extrapolation, in another, the discrepancy was 3 millimeters, and in the third, the discrepancy was 4 millimeters.

With the six items so designated and arranged, proportions of *Yes* responses to each item were computed for each sample. These proportions are shown in the accompanying table.

| Item number | | 57 | 59 | 60 | 56 | 58 | 55 |
| Discrepancy (mm.) | | −4 | −2 | 0 | 2 | 3 | 4 |
SAMPLE	N						
Ankole adults	75	.15	.24	.61	.52	.65	.87
Ankole children	84	.25	.37	.49	.49	.71	.81
Toro adults	22	.18	.14	.45	.82	.82	.77
Toro children	10	.30	.30	.50	.80	.40	.90
Suku adults	5	.00	.00	.40	.60	.60	1.00
Suku children	18	.06	.06	.44	.44	.61	.94
Songe adults	35	.09	.14	.57	.29	.46	.54
Songe children	33	.15	.09	.61	.52	.79	.64
Fang adults	29	.14	.21	.45	.69	.69	.86
Fang children	46	.22	.22	.52	.59	.74	.74
Bété adults	38	.16	.18	.53	.74	.66	.76
Bété children	36	.08	.36	.56	.72	.58	.83
Ijaw adults	39	.08	.15	.51	.51	.69	.77
Ijaw children	42	.36	.43	.55	.40	.57	.71
Ijaw school children	52	.13	.35	.46	.44	.69	.71
Zulu adults	30	.37	.37	.37	.43	.30	.53
Zulu children	23	.30	.52	.43	.61	.43	.52
S. A. European adults	42	.05	.05	.36	.55	.74	.74
Mineboy adults	48	.04	.08	.42	.48	.67	.79
Senegal adults	93	.16	.14	.45	.38	.69	.89
Senegal children	68	.18	.13	.47	.51	.57	.71
Dahomey children	47	.34	.34	.66	.62	.81	.79
Hanunóo adults	26	.15	.15	.62	.81	.85	.77
Hanunóo children	10	.10	.20	.80	.90	1.00	1.00
Evanston adults	112	.00	.03	.35	.59	.76	.77
Evanston children	75	.03	.07	.39	.45	.75	.68
Northwestern adults	28	.00	.00	.14	.39	.79	.89

If the illusion were operative, and if the discrepancy range covered by the six items were adequate to bracket the PSE, what would the data displayed in this table look like? Since the illusion effect is that the right segment appears lower than its actual position, the proportion of *Yes* responses should increase with increasing discrepancy to the point where the right-hand segment is so high that it is beyond the PSE. (The reader should note that in contrast with the procedure used for the other illusions studied, we are here focusing on proportions of *Yes* responses and not on what have been termed "illusion-supported responses." Given the nature of this particular illusion and the method of administration employed, there is no alternative.) This being granted, it should be clear that the 27 rows of proportions displayed in the table would have to be nonmonotonic in order for PSE estimates to be made. In other words, in this illusion the PSE for a given sample would be indicated by the discrepancy value of the item for which the proportion of *Yes* responses is a maximum, whatever its magnitude. It is apparent that the series of proportions obtained have not reached their maxima; they are not nonmonotonic. The prevailing pattern is a continuous increase in the proportion of *Yes* responses.

The orderly increase in the proportion of *Yes* responses is, in one respect, encouraging. It indicates that the procedure used to study this illusion was appropriately conceived and that the task was interpretable and could be administered, although with difficulty, as the high respondent-discard rate shows. More importantly, however, the fact that the pattern consists only of a steady increase in the proportion of *Yes* responses, with no indication of an inflection point, suggests that this stimulus series was not extended far enough in the positive discrepancy direction to encompass the point of subjective equality for any of the samples. Since PSE's could not be estimated and since the discard rate for many samples was so high, it was decided to proceed no further with efforts to compare illusion susceptibility across samples. In future research, the Poggendorf illusion will again be employed, but the stimulus series will have to include items more discrepant than any in the present study.

APPENDIX C
The Effect of the Use of Colors on Illusion Strength

In order to minimize communication difficulties in the field, the five sets of illusion stimuli employed in this study were printed in contrasting colors, red and black (see p. 117 for a discussion of other approaches to this problem). Before trying the stimuli in the field, a preliminary experiment was performed in order to determine the effect on illusion strength of the use of contrasting colors.

The items in this experiment were similar to those that appear in the materials booklet (Herskovits, Campbell, and Segall, 1956); they included several examples each of the Müller-Lyer, the Sander parallelogram, the two versions of the horizontal-vertical, and the perspective drawing. For each illusion, both a red and black and a black-only set of stimuli were used; in all other respects the items were identical. All stimuli were drawn on 5″ × 7″ white index cards.

Subjects participating in this experiment were recruited from undergraduate summer-session psychology courses at Northwestern University. Twenty subjects were employed.

Each subject was randomly assigned to one of two groups, so that for half the subjects the two-color stimuli preceded the black-only stimuli, while for the other half the reverse order obtained. Order of stimuli within each set was randomly determined, as in the cross-cultural study reported in the text. Other potential variables (position of standard and variable, etc.) were also randomized as in the cross-cultural study. Also, all the items were administered in the manner described in the text.

No order effects were found in this experiment. It was thus possible simply to compare each subject's two sets of protocols, ignoring the order in which they were obtained. This was done separately for each of the five illusions.

The data indicated that the use of colors had a statistically significant effect on illusion strength *only* in the case of the Müller-Lyer illusion. In that one case, illusion strength was considerably diminished in the two-color version. The accompanying table contains the PSE values determined in this experiment. They were determined according to the procedure used in the cross-cultural study.

Illusion	Two-color	Black only
Müller-Lyer	13%	22%
Sander parallelogram	21	22
Horizontal-vertical (⊥)	13	16
Horizontal-vertical (⌐)	4	3
Perspective drawing	8	6

That the PSE values in this table vary somewhat from the Northwestern University PSE's determined in the cross-cultural study reflects the administrative conditions peculiar to this control experiment. These variations are of no importance. What is of interest is the fact that the use of colors appears to affect only the Müller-Lyer illusion. In the cross-cultural study, however, all comparisons of Müller-Lyer responses—like those on the other four illusions—were made on data collected with identical stimulus materials; this experimental finding therefore has no practical significance here.

This control experiment is reported here for its intrinsic interest to psychologists. That the use of contrasting colors seems to lessen the impact of the Müller-Lyer illusion but not of several other illusions constitutes an empirical finding that should provoke additional research.

Sample Scores: Means and PSE's, with Standard Deviations and Sample Sizes

	All cases				*Consistent cases*			
	MEAN	*SD*	*N*	*PSE*	*MEAN*	*SD*	*N*	*PSE*
				ANKOLE ADULTS				
M-L	3.54	1.54	180	7	3.34	1.22	131	8
Sander	2.52	1.16	180	14	2.63	1.10	132	17
H-V ($\perp$)	6.48	1.55	180	22	6.56	1.47	144	21
H-V ($\neg$)	5.94	1.47	180	18	6.16	1.33	158	17
Persp.	4.81	1.35	180	4	4.78	1.21	125	5
				ANKOLE CHILDREN				
M-L	4.35	1.71	164	10	3.61	1.34	93	10
Sander	2.71	1.02	164	17	2.75	1.04	130	17
H-V ($\perp$)	6.40	1.46	164	23	6.53	1.44	117	23
H-V ($\neg$)	5.95	1.36	164	14	6.15	1.29	133	16
Persp.	5.24	1.43	164	7	5.22	1.26	105	8
				TORO ADULTS				
M-L	3.16	1.15	56	6	3.02	1.12	49	6
Sander	2.32	0.93	56	12	2.31	0.93	55	12
H-V ($\perp$)	6.50	1.28	56	20	6.56	1.27	54	20
H-V ($\neg$)	6.30	1.15	56	19	6.38	1.15	52	19
Persp.	4.75	1.34	56	6	4.74	1.18	50	6
				TORO CHILDREN				
M-L	4.40	1.34	53	14	4.27	1.27	37	15
Sander	2.64	1.12	53	17	2.68	1.09	50	17
H-V ($\perp$)	6.30	1.62	53	19	6.31	1.65	51	19
H-V ($\neg$)	6.13	1.44	53	18	6.37	1.29	46	21
Persp.	4.28	1.53	53	5	4.40	1.38	42	5

APPENDIX D (cont.)

	All cases				Consistent cases			
	MEAN	SD	N	PSE	MEAN	SD	N	PSE
				SUKU ADULTS				
M-L	2.96	1.43	53	4	3.03	1.39	40	6
Sander	2.19	0.91	53	10	2.28	0.83	50	11
H-V ($\perp$)	6.38	1.80	53	21	6.65	1.33	48	22
H-V ($\neg$)	5.38	1.66	53	9	5.67	1.30	48	9
Persp.	4.70	1.62	53	6	4.72	1.61	50	7
				SUKU CHILDREN				
M-L	2.04	1.04	23	0	2.05	0.90	21	0
Sander	1.83	0.64	23	5	1.81	0.59	21	6
H-V ($\perp$)	6.35	1.13	23	20	6.33	1.17	21	20
H-V ($\neg$)	5.01	0.78	23	12	5.90	0.75	21	12
Persp.	4.87	1.45	23	6	4.90	1.31	21	6
				SONGE ADULTS				
M-L	2.91	1.15	47	5	2.98	1.09	45	5
Sander	2.21	0.92	47	11	2.22	0.93	46	11
H-V ($\perp$)	5.47	1.13	47	16	5.46	1.14	46	16
H-V ($\neg$)	5.53	0.79	47	10	5.54	0.80	46	10
Persp.	4.26	0.93	47	4	4.26	0.93	47	4
				SONGE CHILDREN				
M-L	3.31	1.02	51	7	3.16	0.88	44	7
Sander	2.59	0.82	51	17	2.59	0.82	51	17
H-V ($\perp$)	5.92	1.54	51	20	6.16	1.28	45	20
H-V ($\neg$)	5.67	1.00	51	9	5.65	1.02	49	9
Persp.	4.27	1.21	51	4	4.23	1.23	48	4
				FANG ADULTS				
M-L	3.41	1.70	49	5	2.98	1.30	42	5
Sander	2.78	1.11	49	17	2.72	1.02	43	17
H-V ($\perp$)	6.31	1.33	49	21	6.31	1.30	45	21
H-V ($\neg$)	5.43	1.11	49	8	5.45	1.13	47	8
Persp.	4.82	1.85	49	5	4.83	1.69	42	5

APPENDIX D (cont.)

	All cases				Consistent cases			
	MEAN	*SD*	*N*	*PSE*	*MEAN*	*SD*	*N*	*PSE*
				FANG CHILDREN				
M-L	3.84	1.38	61	7	3.58	1.40	43	9
Sander	2.95	1.18	61	18	2.98	1.14	53	19
H-V ($\perp$)	6.08	1.18	61	18	6.08	1.24	53	19
H-V ($\lnot$)	5.52	1.08	61	11	5.52	1.09	58	11
Persp.	4.85	1.72	61	6	4.95	1.63	43	6
				BÉTÉ ADULTS				
M-L	3.19	1.79	52	4	2.74	1.04	38	4
Sander	2.19	1.19	52	9	2.24	1.16	46	10
H-V ($\perp$)	4.44	1.50	52	8	4.37	1.40	43	9
H-V ($\lnot$)	3.75	1.04	52	2	3.71	1.04	48	2
Persp.	3.25	1.73	52	-2	3.22	1.66	49	-2
				BÉTÉ CHILDREN				
M-L	2.74	1.56	43	3	2.70	1.23	37	3
Sander	2.53	1.00	43	16	2.53	1.00	40	16
H-V ($\perp$)	5.05	1.28	43	11	4.92	1.23	36	11
H-V ($\lnot$)	4.05	1.41	43	2	3.93	1.35	40	1
Persp.	4.14	1.64	43	5	4.36	1.47	36	6
				IJAW ADULTS				
M-L	2.78	1.19	51	3	2.89	1.10	47	4
Sander	2.94	0.85	51	18	2.94	0.85	51	18
H-V ($\perp$)	6.08	1.08	51	20	6.08	1.08	51	20
H-V ($\lnot$)	5.24	0.96	51	8	5.24	0.96	51	8
Persp.	3.98	1.16	51	2	4.00	1.18	49	2
				IJAW CHILDREN				
M-L	3.84	1.54	50	10	3.49	1.03	37	10
Sander	2.52	1.04	50	13	2.53	1.07	47	13
H-V ($\perp$)	6.12	1.49	50	19	6.03	1.58	35	18
H-V ($\lnot$)	5.80	1.52	50	14	5.89	1.55	46	14
Persp.	4.24	1.19	50	4	4.20	1.27	40	5

APPENDIX D (cont.)

	All cases				Consistent cases			
	MEAN	SD	N	PSE	MEAN	SD	N	PSE
IJAW SCHOOL CHILDREN								
M-L	4.10	1.62	61	11	3.74	1.28	54	11
Sander	3.20	1.21	61	19	3.15	1.23	53	19
H-V ($\perp$)	6.33	1.17	61	20	6.28	1.21	46	20
H-V ($\neg$)	5.85	1.45	61	18	6.02	1.29	57	18
Persp.	5.15	1.32	61	7	5.28	1.28	53	7
ZULU ADULTS								
M-L	4.63	1.90	51	5	3.33	1.39	21	5
Sander	2.71	1.39	51	16	2.70	1.49	33	18
H-V ($\perp$)	4.88	1.38	51	8	4.67	1.60	18	8
H-V ($\neg$)	4.69	1.13	51	7	4.77	1.12	39	7
Persp.	4.43	1.03	51	4	4.56	0.91	34	4
ZULU CHILDREN								
M-L	4.57	1.62	49	10	4.14	1.51	14	11
Sander	3.04	1.31	49	20	3.24	1.33	34	22
H-V ($\perp$)	5.65	1.73	49	10	4.94	1.83	17	12
H-V ($\neg$)	5.24	1.57	49	8	5.31	1.72	35	8
Persp.	4.78	1.47	49	5	4.75	1.58	40	6
BUSHMAN ADULTS (only)								
M-L	2.37	1.24	46	1	2.28	0.93	36	1
Sander	—	—	—	—	—	—	—	—
H-V ($\perp$)	5.76	1.37	46	20	5.93	1.24	41	20
H-V ($\neg$)	5.11	1.03	46	9	5.15	0.92	39	9
Persp.	4.46	1.72	46	5	4.39	1.71	44	4
S. A. EUROPEAN ADULTS (only)								
M-L	4.48	1.20	44	13	4.33	1.00	36	13
Sander	2.95	1.36	44	17	2.98	1.39	42	17
H-V ($\perp$)	5.30	1.25	44	14	5.33	1.23	42	15
H-V ($\neg$)	4.68	1.16	44	5	4.67	1.19	42	5
Persp.	4.02	1.32	44	3	3.98	1.34	42	3

APPENDIX D (*cont.*)

	All cases				Consistent cases			
	MEAN	*SD*	*N*	*PSE*	*MEAN*	*SD*	*N*	*PSE*
MINEBOY ADULTS (*only*)								
M-L	2.19	1.25	72	1	2.23	0.84	60	1
Sander	2.03	0.85	72	9	2.06	0.82	71	9
H-V ($\perp$)	6.32	1.41	72	19	6.28	1.42	69	19
H-V ($\neg$)	5.72	1.22	72	12	5.71	1.24	69	12
Persp.	4.18	1.17	72	3	4.20	1.19	69	3
SENEGAL ADULTS								
M-L	4.42	1.75	137	10	3.88	1.64	74	11
Sander	2.58	1.42	137	11	2.59	1.34	109	12
H-V ($\perp$)	6.03	1.80	137	24	6.48	1.63	79	24
H-V ($\neg$)	4.39	1.65	137	6	4.46	1.61	99	7
Persp.	4.05	2.03	137	1	4.04	1.68	89	2
SENEGAL CHILDREN								
M-L	5.36	1.85	125	17	4.61	1.75	51	14
Sander	2.85	1.85	125	15	3.29	1.64	89	18
H-V ($\perp$)	5.23	2.01	125	15	5.55	1.93	51	17
H-V ($\neg$)	4.04	1.90	125	5	4.42	1.88	69	6
Persp.	3.75	2.09	125	1	3.99	2.05	69	3
DAHOMEY CHILDREN (*only*)								
M-L	4.55	1.30	65	12	4.22	1.33	40	12
Sander	2.45	1.15	65	14	2.55	1.04	58	16
H-V ($\perp$)	6.42	1.49	65	22	6.49	1.51	57	22
H-V ($\neg$)	6.51	1.10	65	19	6.52	1.10	63	19
Persp.	3.83	1.99	65	3	4.36	1.49	39	5
HANUNÓO ADULTS								
M-L	3.12	1.08	43	8	2.97	1.08	37	8
Sander	2.47	0.76	43	13	2.41	0.71	39	13
H-V ($\perp$)	5.23	0.98	43	15	5.26	1.01	39	15
H-V ($\neg$)	4.40	1.20	43	5	4.44	1.17	41	5
Persp.	5.07	1.23	43	7	5.03	1.27	38	7

APPENDIX D (cont.)

	All cases				Consistent cases			
	MEAN	SD	N	PSE	MEAN	SD	N	PSE
HANUNÓO CHILDREN								
M-L	3.43	1.29	14	8	3.08	1.04	12	7
Sander	2.93	0.96	14	16	2.85	0.95	13	15
H-V (⊥)	6.00	1.77	14	19	6.08	1.82	13	19
H-V (⌐)	5.64	1.11	14	13	5.58	1.11	12	13
Persp.	5.57	1.24	14	8	5.50	1.32	12	8
EVANSTON ADULTS								
M-L	5.19	1.54	119	19	5.21	1.53	111	19
Sander	3.25	1.33	119	19	3.23	1.35	115	19
H-V (⊥)	5.94	1.27	119	20	5.93	1.26	114	20
H-V (⌐)	4.92	1.01	119	7	4.92	1.02	118	7
Persp.	5.59	1.25	119	5	4.60	1.26	113	6
EVANSTON CHILDREN								
M-L	5.64	1.60	89	22	5.57	1.50	77	21
Sander	3.38	0.97	89	20	3.33	0.97	81	20
H-V (⊥)	5.61	1.34	89	18	5.64	1.33	84	18
H-V (⌐)	4.81	1.27	89	7	4.86	1.25	85	8
Persp.	5.02	1.45	89	7	5.00	1.47	82	7
NORTHWESTERN ADULTS (only)								
M-L	4.93	1.24	30	16	5.00	1.25	27	16
Sander	3.57	1.02	30	20	3.54	1.05	28	20
H-V (⊥)	5.70	1.32	30	19	5.72	1.34	29	19
H-V (⌐)	4.83	1.04	30	7	4.83	1.04	30	7
Persp.	4.90	1.33	30	7	4.90	1.35	29	7

References

(Numbers in brackets represent the pages of this book
on which the works listed below are cited.)

Allen, G., 1879. *The colour-sense: its origin and development.* London: Trübner, and Boston: Houghton. Also reprinted as "second edition," London: Kegan, Paul, Trench, and Trübner, 1892 [39–41].

Allport, F. H., 1955. *Theories of perception and the concept of structure.* New York: Wiley [72, 73–74, 75].

Allport, G. W., and Pettigrew, T. F., 1957. Cultural influence on the perception of movement: the trapezoidal illusion among Zulus. *J. abnorm. soc. Psychol., 55,* 104–113 [66–67, 70, 185–187, 191].

Ames, A., Jr., 1949. *Nature and origin of perception.* Hanover, N.H.: The Hanover Institute [73].

———, 1951. Visual perception and the rotating trapezoidal window. *Psychol. Monogr., 65,* Whole No. 324, p. 14 [89].

———, 1961. The rotating trapezoid: description of phenomena. In Kilpatrick, F. P. (ed.), *Explorations in transactional psychology.* New York: New York University Press, pp. 222–256 [73].

Asch, S. E., 1952. *Social psychology.* Englewood Cliffs, N.J.: Prentice-Hall [5, 6, 20].

———, and Witkin, H. A., 1948. Studies in space orientation. II. Perception of the upright with displaced visual fields and with the body tilted. *J. exp. Psychol., 38,* 455–477 [5].

Bagby, J., 1957. A cross-cultural study of perceptual predominance in binocular rivalry. *J. abnorm. soc. Psychol., 54,* 331–338 [50–51].

Berkeley, G., 1713. *Three dialogues between Hylas and Philonous.* London: Henry Clements. Reprint edition, Chicago: Open Court, 1927, p. 18 [8–9].

Beveridge, W. M., 1935. Racial differences in phenomenal regression. *Brit. J. Psychol., 26,* 59–62 [57, 58].

———, 1939. Some racial differences in perception. *Brit. J. Psychol., 30,* 57–64 [57–58].

Boas, F., 1904(a). Introduction. In Krauss, F. S., Sudslavishe Volksüberlieferungen. *Anthropophyteia,* 1. v–vi (Cited on p. 4 in A. L. Kroeber *et al., Franz Boas 1858–1942,* Memoir 61, *Amer. Anthropologist,* 1943, *45,* No. 3, Pt. 2) [16].

———, 1904(b). Some traits of primitive culture. *J. Amer. Folklore, 17,* 243–254 [9, 14, 16].

———, 1911. *The mind of primitive man.* New York: Macmillan [15].

Bohannan, P., 1953. Concepts of time among the Tiv of Nigeria. *South-western J. Anthropol., 9,* 251–262 [68].

Bonté, M. L., 1960. *Contribution a l'étude des illusions optico-géométri-ques: Essais de measure de l'Illusion de Müller-Lyer chez les Bashi et les Bambuti (Pygmées) de Congo Belge.* Unpublished thesis, Univer-sité Catholique de Louvain [187–190].

———, 1962. The reaction of two African societies to the Müller-Lyer illusion. Unpublished manuscript [67, 187–190].

Boring, E. G., 1942. *Sensation and perception in the history of experi-mental psychology.* New York: Appleton-Century [71, 75–76].

Brandt, R. B., 1954. *Hopi ethics: a theoretical analysis.* Chicago: Uni-versity of Chicago Press [13].

Brentano, F., 1892, 1893. Über ein optisches Paradoxen. *Z. Psychol. Physiol. Sinnesorgane, 3,* 349–358; *5,* 61–82 [75, 86].

Brown, R. W., 1956. Language and categories. Appendix to Bruner, J. S., Goodnow, J. J., and Austin, G. A., *A study of thinking.* New York: Wiley, pp. 247–312 [35].

———, 1958. *Words and things.* Glencoe, Ill.: The Free Press [36].

———, and Lenneberg, E. H., 1954. A study in language and cognition. *J. abnorm. soc. Psychol., 59,* 454–462 [36–37].

Brunswik, E., 1956. *Perception and the representative design of psychologi-cal experiments.* Berkeley: University of California Press [74].

———, and Kamiya, J., 1953. Ecological cue validity of proximity and other Gestalt factors. *Amer. J. Psychol., 66,* 20–32 [74, 77].

Campbell, D. T., 1961. The mutual methodological relevance of anthro-pology and psychology. In Hsu, F. L. K. (ed.), *Psychological anthro-pology.* Homewood, Ill.: The Dorsey Press, pp. 333–352 [177].

———, 1963. Social attitudes and other acquired behavioral dispositions. In Koch, S. (ed.), *Psychology: a study of a science, Vol. 6. Investi-gations of man as socius.* New York: McGraw-Hill, 94–172 [4, 21, 45].

———, 1964. Distinguishing differences of perception from failures of communication in cross-cultural studies. In Northrop, F. S. C., and Livingston, H. H. (eds.), *Cross-cultural understanding: epistemology in anthropology.* New York: Harper & Row, pp. 308–336 [117, 174].

———, and Wenar, S. C., 1962. *Perceptual and cognitive bias in children.* Unpublished manuscript, Northwestern University [197, 200–204].

Cantril, H., 1950. *The "why" of man's experience.* New York: Macmillan [73].

Child, A., 1950. The sociology of perception. *J. genet. Psychol.*, 77, 293–303 [25, 27, 68].

Conklin, H. C., 1955. Hanunóo color categories. *Southwestern J. Anthropol.*, 11, 339–344 [47].

———, 1960. Lexicographical treatment of folk taxonomies. In *Conference on lexicography, Indiana University.* Bloomington, Ind., mimeographed [47].

Day, R. H., 1962. The effects of repeated trials and prolonged fixation on error in the Müller-Lyer figure. *Psychol. Monogr.*, 76, Whole No. 533 [181].

Dennis, W., 1951. Cultural and developmental factors in perception. In Blake, R. R., and Ramsey, G. V. (eds.), *Perception: an approach to personality.* New York: Ronald Press, pp. 148–169 [24, 25].

———, 1960. The human figure drawings of Bedouins. *J. soc. Psychol.*, 52, 209–219 [58–59].

Doob, L., 1964. Psychology. In Lystad, A. (ed.), *Social research in Africa.* New York: Praeger [184, 187, 192].

Duncker, K., 1929. Über induzierte Bewegung. Ein Beitrag zur Theorie optisch wahrgenommener Bewegung. *Psychol. Forsch.*, 12, 180–259 [6].

Eggan, D., 1956. Instruction and affect in Hopi cultural continuity. *Southwestern J. Anthropol.*, 12, 347–370 [13].

Ewert, P. H., 1930. A study of the effect of inverted retinal stimulation upon spatially coordinated behavior. *Genet. Psychol. Monogr.*, 7, 177–363 [82].

Eysenck, H. J., and Slater, P., 1958. Effects of practice and rest of fluctuations in the Müller-Lyer illusion. *Brit. J. Psychol.*, 49, 246–256 [180–181].

Foley, J. P. Jr., 1938. Observation on the effect of prolonged inverted retinal stimulation upon spatially coordinated behavior in the rhesus monkey (Macaca mulatta). *Psychol. Bull.*, 35, 701–702 [82].

French, D., 1963. The relationship of anthropology to studies in perception and cognition. In Koch, S. (ed.), *Psychology: a study of a science. Vol. 6. Investigations of man as socius.* New York: McGraw-Hill, pp. 388–428 [18, 25, 36].

Geiger, L., 1871. *Zur Entwickelungsgeschichte der Menschheit.* Stuttgart. Translated by D. Ascher, *Contributions to the history and development of the human race.* London, 1880 [38].

Gibson, E. J., Walk, R. D., Pick, H. L., and Tighe, T. J., 1959. The effect of prolonged exposure to visual patterns on learning to discriminate similar and different patterns. *J. comp. physiol. Psychol.*, 51, 584–587 [79].

Gibson, J. J., 1933. Adaptation, after effect, and contrast in the perception of curved lines. *J. exp. Psychol., 16,* 1–31 [82].
———, 1950. *The perception of the visual world.* Boston: Houghton
Mifflin [72, 73].
———, 1952. The visual field and the visual world: a reply to Professor
Boring. *Psychol. Rev., 59,* 149–151 [94–95].
———, 1960. Pictures, perspective, and perception. *Daedalus, 89,* 216–
227 [5, 73, 94].
Gladstone, W. E., 1858. *Studies on Homer and the homeric age.* Vol. III.
Oxford: Oxford University Press, pp. 457–499 [38].
Glenn, E. S., 1957. On the developmental theory of languages. *Amer.
Anthropologist, 59,* 537–538 [18].
Goldiamond, I., 1958. Indicators of perception: I. Subliminal perception,
subception, unconscious perception: An analysis in terms of psychophysical indicator methodology. *Psychol. Bull., 55,* 373–411 [45].
———, and Hawkins, W. F., 1958. Vexierversuch: the log relationship
between word-frequency and recognition obtained in the absence of
stimulus words. *J. exp. Psychol., 56,* 457–463 [45].
Goodenough, W. H., 1956. Componential analysis and the study of
meaning. *Language, 32,* 195–216 [18].
Green, R. T. and Hoyle, E. M., 1963. The Poggendorff illusion as a constancy phenomenon. *Nature, 200,* 611–612 [76, 202].
Gregory, R. L., 1962. How the eyes deceive. *The Listener, 68,* 15–16
[76, 202].
———, 1963. Distortion of visual space as inappropriate constancy scaling.
Nature, 199, 678–680 [76, 202].
———, and Wallace, J. G., 1963. Recovery from early blindness. *Exp.
Psychol. Monogr.* (Cambridge, England), Whole No. 2 [79–81].
Guttman, L., 1947. The Cornell technique for scale and intensity analysis.
Educ. psychol. measmt., 7, 247–279 [119].
Hallowell, A. I., 1942. Some psychological aspects of measurement among
the Salteaux. *Amer. Anthropologist, 44,* 62–77 [68].
———, 1951. Cultural factors in the structuralization of perception. In
Rohrer, J. H., and Sherif, M. (eds.), *Social psychology at the crossroads.* New York: Harper, pp. 164–195 [28–29, 49].
———, 1955. *Culture and experience.* Philadelphia: University of Pennsylvania Press [30–32].
Hebb, D. O., 1949. *The organization of behavior.* New York: Wiley [79].
Held, R., and Bossom, J., 1961. Neonatal deprivation and adult rear-
rangement: complimentary techniques for analysing plastic sensory-
motor coordinations. *J. comp. physiol. Psychol., 54,* 33–37 [82].
———, and Schlank, M., 1959. Adaptation to disarranged eye-hand

coordination in the distance dimension. *Amer. J. Psychol., 72,* 603–605 [82].

Hering, E., 1861–64. *Beiträge zur Physiologie.* Vol. 5. Leipzig: W. Englemann, 355 [89].

Herodotus. *History,* translated by G. Rawlinson, *The history of Herodotus.* New York: Tudor, 1932 [12].

Herskovits, M. J., 1927. *The Negro and intelligence tests.* Hanover, N.H.: The Sociological Press [18].

———, 1948. *Man and his works.* New York: Knopf [9, 10, 12, 17, 32].

———, 1951. On cultural and psychological reality. In Rohrer, J. H., and Sherif, M. (eds.), *Social psychology at the crossroads.* New York: Harper, pp. 145–163 [11, 17].

———, 1958. Some further comments on cultural relativism. *Amer. Anthropologist, 60,* 266–273 [17].

———, 1959(a). Art and value. In Redfield, R., Herskovits, M. J. and Ekholm, G. F., *Aspects of primitive art.* New York: The Museum of Primitive Art, pp. 42–97 [18, 32].

———, 1959(b). A cross-cultural view of bias and values. Danforth lecture. 1958–59. Greenville, N.C.: East Carolina College [13].

———, 1963. Review of Schoeck, H. and Wiggins, J. M. (eds.), *Relativism and the study of man.* Princeton: Van Nostrand, 1961. In *Bijdragen: Tot de Taal-, Land-, en Volken Kunde, 118,* 469–473 [17, 18].

———, Campbell, D. T., and Segall, M. H., 1956. *Materials for a cross-cultural study of perception.* Evanston, Ill.: Program of African Studies, Northwestern University, Second edition, Indianapolis: Bobbs-Merrill Company, Inc., in preparation. [69–71, 102, 111–113, 235, 239].

Heuse, G. A., 1957. Études psychologiques surs les noirs Sudannais et Guinéens. *Revue de Psychologie des Peuples, 12,* 35–68 [67, 187].

Hilgard, E., 1951. The role of learning in perception. In Blake, R. R., and Ramsey, G. V. (eds.), *Perception: an approach to personality.* New York: Ronald Press [72, 73].

Hochberg, J. E., 1957. Effects of the Gestalt revolution: the Cornell symposium on perception. *Psychol. Rev., 64,* 73–84 [72, 82].

———, 1961. Visual world and visual field: perception, sensation and pictorial observation. Personal communication, mimeographed [95].

Hoijer, H., 1954. *Language in culture; proceedings of a conference on the inter-relations of language and other aspects of culture.* Memoir No. 79, *Amer. Anthropologist, 56,* No. 6, Pt. 2 [36].

Holst, Erich von, 1957. Aktive Leistungen der menschlichen Gesichtswahrnehmung. *Studium Generale, 10,* 231–243. Translated into English as "The active side of human visual perception," by Elisabeth

Braitenberg, rough draft, mimeographed. [76, 207].

Hudson, W., 1960. Pictorial depth perception in sub-cultural groups in Africa, *J. soc. Psychol., 52,* 183–208 [59–60, 94, 195].

Ittelson, W. H., 1960. *Visual space perception.* New York: Springer [51, 73].

———, and Cantril, H., 1954. *Perception; a transactional approach.* New York: Doubleday [51].

Kaplan, B., 1961(a). Cross-cultural use of projective techniques. In Hsu, F. L. K. (ed.), *Psychological anthropology.* Homewood, Ill.: The Dorsey Press [28].

———, 1961(b). *Studying personality cross-culturally.* Evanston, Ill.: Row-Peterson [28].

Kilpatrick, F. P. (ed.), 1952. *Human behavior from the transactional point of view.* Princeton: Institute for Associated Research [73].

———, (ed.), 1961. *Explorations in transactional psychology.* New York: New York University Press [9].

Klineberg, O., 1935. *Race differences.* New York: Harper [19, 24].

———, 1964. *The human dimension in international relations.* New York: Holt, Rinehart and Winston [9].

Kluckhohn, C., 1954. Culture and behavior. In Lindzey, G. (ed.), *Handbook of social psychology.* Vol. II. Cambridge, Mass.: Addison-Wesley, pp. 921–976 [25, 36, 47].

———, and Leighton, D., 1946. *The Navaho.* Cambridge, Mass.: Harvard University Press [13].

Köhler, W., 1938. *The place of value in a world of fact.* New York: Liveright [20].

———, and Fishback, J., 1950(a). The destruction of the Müller-Lyer illusion in repeated trials. I. An examination of two theories. *J. exp. Psychol., 40,* 267–281 [82, 180].

———, and Fishback, J., 1950(b). The destruction of the Müller-Lyer illusion in repeated trials. II. Satiation patterns and memory traces. *J. exp. Psychol., 40,* 398–410 [82, 180].

———, and Wallach, H., 1944. Figural after-effects: an investigation of visual processes. *Proc. Amer. Philos. Soc., 88,* 269–357 [82].

Kohler, I., 1951. Über Aufbau und Wandlugen der Wahrnehmungswelt, *Oesterr. Akad. Wiss. Philos.-Histor. Kl.; Sitz.-Ber., 227,* 1–118 [82].

Krech, D., and Crutchfield, R. S., 1948. *Theory and problems of social psychology.* New York: McGraw-Hill [20].

Kroeber, A. L., 1909. Classificatory systems of relationship. *J. Royal Anthropol. Inst., 39,* 77–85 [18].

Latta, R., 1904. Notes on a case of successful operation for congenital cataract in an adult. *Brit. J. Psychol., 1,* 135–150 [79].

Lindzey, G., 1961. *Projective techniques and cross-cultural research.* New York: Appleton-Century-Crofts [28].

Lipps, T., 1891. *Aesthetische Faktoren der Raumanschauung. Beiträge zur Psychologie und Physiologie der Sinnesorgane.* Hamburg und Leipzig, pp. 219–307 [89].

Locke, J., 1690. *An essay concerning human understanding.* London [8].

London, I. D., 1960. A Russian report on the postoperative newly seeing. *Amer. J. Psychol., 73,* 478–482 [79].

McHugh, R. B., and Ellis, D. S., 1955. The "postmortem" testing of experimental comparisons. *Psychol. Bull., 52,* 425–428 [153].

Magnus, H., 1877. *Die geschichtliche Entwicklung des Farbensinnes.* Leipzig [38].

————, 1880. *Untersuchungen über den Farbensinn der Naturvolker.* Jena [38].

————, 1883. *Über ethnologische Untersuchungen des Farbensinnes.* Breslau [38].

Malinowski, B., 1923–24. The psychology of sex and the foundations of kinship in primitive societies. *Psyche, 4,* 98–129 [26–27].

————, 1927. *The father in primitive psychology.* New York: Norton [26–27].

————, 1929. *The sexual life of savages.* London: Routledge & Kegan Paul [26–27].

Mead, M., 1930. Adolescence in primitive and modern society. In Calverton, V. F., and Schmalhausen, S. D. (eds.), *The new generation.* New York: Macauley. Reprinted in Newcomb, T. M., and Hartley, E. L. (eds.), *Readings in social psychology.* New York: Holt, 1947, pp. 6–14 [18].

Michael, D. N., 1953. A cross cultural investigation of closure. *J. abnorm. soc. Psychol., 48,* 255–230 [24, 61–62].

Moed, G., 1959. Satiation-theory and the Müller-Lyer illusion. *Amer. J. Psychol., 72,* 609–611 [180–181].

Montaigne, M., 1580. *Essais.* Translated by D. M. Frame, *The complete works of Montaigne.* Stanford, Calif.: Stanford University Press, 1948. Bk. I, Ch. 31, pp. 150–159 [12].

Morgan, P., 1959. A study in perceptual differences among cultural groups in Southern Africa, using tests of geometric illusion. *J. of the Nat. Instit. for Personnel Res.* (South Africa), *8,* 39–43 [67, 182, 187].

Mountjoy, P. T., 1958. Effects of exposure time and intertrial interval upon decrement to the Müller-Lyer illusion. *J. exp. Psychol., 56,* 97–102 [181].

Mueller, C. G., in press. *Sensory psychology.* Englewood Cliffs, New Jersey: Prentice-Hall [75].

Murphy, G., 1947. *Personality.* New York: Harper [21].

Osgood, C. E., 1953. *Method and theory in experimental psychology.* New York: Oxford University Press [75].

Pettigrew, T. F., Allport, G. W., and Barnett, E. D., 1958. Binocular resolution and perception of race in South Africa. *Brit. J. Psychol., 49,* 265–278 [51–52].

Pierce, J., 1963. Determinants of threshold for form. *Psychol. Bull., 60,* 391–407 [51].

Plato. *The republic.* Translated by W. H. F. Rouse, *The great dialogues of Plato.* New York: Mentor Books, The New American Library, 1956, pp. 312–315 [7–8].

Pollack, R. H., 1963. Contour detectability threshold as a function of chronological age. *Percept. mot. Skills, 17,* 411–417 [185].

Pratt, C. C., 1950. The role of past experience in visual perception. *J. Psychol., 30,* 85–107 [73].

Ray, V. F., 1952. Techniques and problems in the study of human color perception. *Southwestern J. Anthrop., 8,* 251–259 [24, 45].

———, 1953. Human color perception and behavioral response, *Trans. of N.Y. Acad. Sciences., 16,* 98–104 [45].

Riesen, A. H., 1947. The development of visual perception in man and chimpanzee. *Science. 106,* 107–108 [79].

———, 1958. Plasticity of behavior: psychological aspects. In Harlow, H. F., and Woolsey, C. N. (eds.), *Biological and biochemical bases of behavior.* Madison: University of Wisconsin Press, pp. 425–450 [79].

Rivers, W. H. R., 1901(a). Introduction and vision. In Haddon, A. C. (ed.), *Reports of the Cambridge anthropological expedition to the Torres Straits.* Vol. II, Pt. I. Cambridge, Eng.: The University Press, [19, 41, 62–65, 185, 191].

———, 1901(b). Primitive color vision. *Popular Science Monthly, 59,* 44–58 [41–43].

———, 1905. Observations on the senses of the Todas. *Brit. J. Psychol., 1,* 321–396 [19, 24, 62–65, 184, 185, 191].

Rudel, R. G., and Teuber, H. L., 1963. Decrement of visual and haptic Müller-Lyer illusion on repeated trials: a study of crossmodal transfer. Mimeographed manuscript [181].

Sanford, E. C., 1908. *A course in experimental psychology. Part I: Sensation and perception.* Boston: Heath [75, 83–84, 89].

Sapir, E., 1928. The unconscious patterning of behavior in society. In Dummer, E. S. (ed.), *The unconscious: a symposium.* New York: Knopf, pp. 114–142. Reprinted in Mandelbaum, D. G. (ed.), *Selected writings of Edward Sapir in language, culture, and personality.* Berkeley: University of California Press, 1958, pp. 544–559 [12, 36, 43].

Saporta, S. (ed.), 1961. *Psycho-linguistics: a book of readings.* New York: Holt, Rinehart & Winston [36].

Scheffé, H., 1953. A method for judging all contrasts in the analysis of variance. *Biometrika, 40,* 87–104 [153].

Schwitzgebel, R., 1962. The performance of Dutch and Zulu adults on selected perceptual tasks. *J. soc. Psychol., 57,* 73–77 [52–53].

Segall, M. H., 1963. Acquiescence and "identification with the aggressor" among acculturating Africans. *J. soc. Psychol., 61,* 247–262 [183].

———, Campbell, D. T., and Herskovits, M. J., 1963. Cultural differences in the perception of geometric illusions. *Science, 139,* 769–771.

Selkin, J., and Wertheimer, M., 1957. Disappearance of the Müller-Lyer illusion under prolonged inspection. *Percept. mot. skills, 7,* 265–266 [181].

Senden, M. von, 1932. *Raum und Gestaltauffassung bei operietăn Blindge-bornen vor und nach der Operation.* Leipzig: Barth. Translated by P. Heath, *Space and Sight.* London: Methuen, 1960, and Glencoe, Ill.: Free Press, 1960 [79, 80].

Shapiro, M. B., 1960. The rotation of drawings by illiterate Africans. *J. soc. Psychol., 52,* 17–30 [53–55].

Sherif, M., 1936. *The psychology of social norms.* New York: Harper [5, 9, 25].

———, and Sherif, C. W., 1948. *An outline of social psychology.* New York: Harper [20].

Slack, C. W., 1959. Critique on the interpretation of cultural differences in the perception of motion in the Ames trapezoidal window. *Amer. J. Psychol., 72,* 127–131 [186–187].

Snyder, F. W., and Pronko, N. H., 1952. *Vision with spatial inversion.* Wichita, Kan.: University of Wichita Press [82].

Spindler, G. D., 1955. *Sociocultural and psychological processes in Menomini acculturation.* Berkeley and Los Angeles: University of California Press [28].

Stanley, J. C., 1957. Additional "post-mortem" tests of experimental comparisons, *Psychol. Bull., 54,* 128–130 [153–154].

Stratton, G. M., 1896. Some preliminary experiments in vision without inversion of the retinal image. *Psychol. Rev., 3,* 611–617 [82].

Sumner, W. G., 1906. *Folkways.* Boston: Ginn [9, 10, 13].

Tausch, R., 1954. Optische Täuschungen als artifizielle Effekte der Gestaltungsprozesse von Grössen- und Formenkonstanz in der natürlichen Raumwahrnehmung. *Psychologische Forschung, 24,* 299–348 [76, 207].

Thiery, A., 1895, 1896. Über geometrische-optische Tauschungen. *Philos. Studien, 11,* 307–370; *12,* 67–126 [76, 86].

Thouless, R. H., 1932. Individual differences in phenomenal regression. *Brit. J. Psychol., 22,* 217 [96, 198].

———, 1933. A racial difference in perception. *J. soc. Psychol., 4,* 330–339 [55–57].

Titchener, E. B., 1916. On ethnological tests of sensation and perception with special reference to tests of color vision and tactile discrimination described in the reports of the Cambridge anthropological expedition to Torres Straits. *Proceedings of the American Philosophical Society, 55,* 204–236 [45–47, 65, 184].

Triandis, H. C., 1964. Cultural influences upon cognitive processes. In Berkowitz, L. (ed.), *Advances in experimental social psychology, Vol. I.* New York: Academic Press [25, 47].

Virchow, R., 1878, 1879. Über die Nubier. *Zeitschrift fur Ethnologie, 10,* 333–356; *11,* 449–456 [39].

Walters, Sister Annette, 1942. A genetic study of geometrical-optical illusions. *Genet. Psychol. monogr., 25,* 101–155 [196].

Wapner, S., and Werner, H., 1957. *Perceptual development: an investigation within the framework of sensory-tonic field theory.* Worcester, Mass.: Clark University Press [196].

Whorf, B. L., 1940. Science and linguistics. *Technology Review, 54,* 229–231, 247, 248. Reprinted in Maccoby, E. E., Newcomb, T. M., Hartley, E. L. (eds.), *Readings in social psychology.;* 3rd ed., New York: Holt, 1958, pp. 1–9 [36, 43].

Witkin, H. A., 1949. Perception of body position and the position of the visual field. *Psychol. Monogr., 63,* 1–46 [5].

Wohlwill, J. F., 1960. Developmental studies of perception. *Psychol. Bull., 57,* 249–288 [96, 196].

———, 1962. The perspective illusion: perceived size and distance in fields varying in suggested depth, in children and adults. *J. exp. Psychol., 64,* 300–310 [198–199].

Woodworth, R. S., 1905–06. Color sense in different races of mankind. *Proceedings of the Society for Experimental Biology and Medicine, 3,* 24–26 [43–45].

———, 1910(a). The puzzle of color vocabularies. *Psychol. Bull., 7,* 325–334. Reprinted in Woodworth, R. S., *Psychological issues: selected papers of Robert S. Woodworth . . . with a bibliography of his writings.* New York: Columbia University Press, 1939 [43, 45].

———, 1910(b). Racial differences in mental traits. *Science, 31,* 171–186. Reprinted in Woodworth, R. S., *Psychological issues: selected papers of Robert S. Woodworth . . . with a bibliography of his writings.* New York: Columbia University Press, 1939 [43].

———, 1938. *Experimental psychology.* New York: Holt [75, 89].

Index